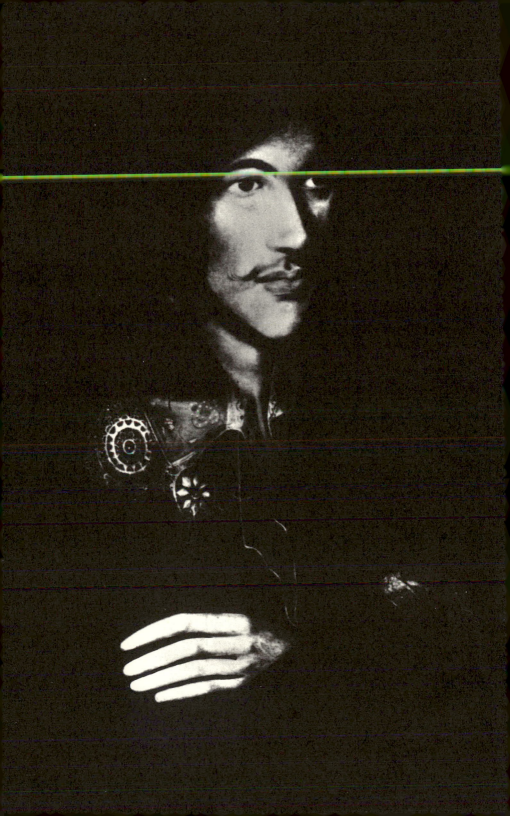

John Donne CONSERVATIVE REVOLUTIONARY

John Donne

CONSERVATIVE REVOLUTIONARY

BY N. J. C. ANDREASEN

PRINCETON UNIVERSITY PRESS

PRINCETON, NEW JERSEY

1967

Publication of this book has been aided by the
Whitney Darrow Publication Reserve Fund of
Princeton University Press

Printed in the United States of America
By Princeton University Press

To George and Susan

PREFACE

When I first began to write of Donne's love poetry, I wanted most of all to let the poems speak for themselves as individual creations, not to use them to support generalizations about Donne's philosophy of love: Donne's poetry, not Donne's background or his influence, was to be the thing. That objective accounts for my heavy emphasis on explication, and it is still the main one. But like all well-intentioned but infinitely fallible parents, I watched this child of my mind violate my predictions and assume its own tenuous independence—Donne's background and his philosophy of love gradually became more important than I ever intended them to be. For I myself grew to realize that the poems could not speak for themselves as they spoke to the audience for whom Donne intended them unless I tried to recapture something of the varied traditions which inspired their varied tones. Accordingly, a chapter had to be devoted to defining terms or traditions which are slippery and ambiguous, if only to let the reader know what I meant by such phrases as "Petrarchan love" or "Platonic love"; much that is said in that chapter will be familiar to many, and I can only ask that they either be patient or skim and skip impatiently. And I also found it necessary to consider what Donne himself thought about love—even to make this consideration another of the main objectives of the book, since what I thought Donne thought was not always what other scholars have thought.

I am not unaware that I am disagreeing with a considerable body of scholarship or that many will disagree with me; however, in the pages which follow I do not delineate specific areas of disagreement and offer a rebuttal, for contentiousness strikes me as ungracious to the many scholars who have enriched our understanding of Donne through presenting other interpretations; my disagreements with them will be obvious enough to all who are acquainted with Donne scholarship. And it is my hope that the historical evidence for the relatively conservative Donne whom I describe will be sufficient to support my point of view, or at any rate to make it worth reading and considering.

Like all scholars I feel a sense of debt to many for helping make this book possible—to Ross Garner of the University of Nebraska, who supervised it with intelligence and kindness when it was in its early stages as a doctoral dissertation; to Robert E. Knoll, Paul A. Olson, and Leslie Whipp, also of the University of Nebraska, for providing encouragement and friendship; to D. W. Robertson of Princeton University, for introducing me to the techniques of historical criticism; to my colleagues at the University of Iowa—specifically to Rosalie Colie and Curt Zimansky for reading the manuscript and offering valuable suggestions and to Frederick Will for advice about the Latin translations; to the editors and anonymous readers of Princeton University Press for offering further helpful suggestions; to the Graduate College of the University of Iowa for providing funds to finance the typing of the manuscript; and to the Marquess of Lothian for permission to use his handsome portrait of Donne as a frontispiece.

I am also indebted to the Clarendon Press for permission to quote from H.J.C. Grierson's edition of *The Poems of John Donne* and from Helen Gardner's edition of *The Divine Poems*, as well as to the Oxford University Press for permission to quote from W. H. Gardner's edition of *The Poems of Gerard Manley Hopkins*, to Harvard University Press and the Loeb Classical Library for permission to quote from the Grant Showerman and J. H. Mozley translations of Ovid's *Heroides and Amores* and *The Art of Love and Other Poems*, and to Random House for permission to use Anna Marie Armi's translation of Petrarch's *Songs and Sonnets*. I regret that Miss Gardner's edition of the love poetry was available too late for me to take advantage of it in this work.

But of all these debts, my greatest is to my husband, who did nothing but be himself.

CONTENTS

John Donne CONSERVATIVE REVOLUTIONARY

I · PARADOXES AND PROBLEMS

That wit, borne apt high good to doe,
By dwelling lazily
On Natures nothing, be not nothing too. . . .

The young Donne who appears on the frontispiece—so sensitive, sensuous, and self-conscious—looks to us more like a nineteenth-century romantic masquerading in Elizabethan costume than a hard-headed intellectual surviving fitly by his wits in the cutthroat and competitive world of the sixteenth-century court and Inns of Court. He looks, it is true, as if he could write *The Canonization* and elope with Anne More. And at times, perhaps, the full passionate mouth, the soulful eyes, and the slender hands seem to be those of the real John Donne, who has been captured in paint through the sympathetic realism of some lesser Titian. But then we recall the other John Donne, who wrote law briefs and religious tracts, comic love poems and crude satires, whose mouth could smile and his eyes twinkle, whose hand could hold a sword as well as a pen, whose intensity found expression in gaiety and religiosity as well as in love. And we are reminded by the elongated face and hands that the painter has distorted and interpreted, not captured, the real John Donne. The real John Donne is not a nineteenth- or, for that matter, a twentieth-century romantic in Elizabethan garb, but a complicated and paradoxical Renaissance man who synthesizes many attitudes and strikes many poses. The romantic pose of the portrait is only one of them.

The quest for the historical Donne is, however, a biographical problem. This book concentrates on the poetry rather than on the man who wrote it. But in analyzing the poetry, we are faced with a similar multiplicity of attitude and a similar temptation to capsulize and oversimplify. Just as the man fascinates us by his quicksilver elusiveness, so too a single poem teasingly scoots away just when we think we can reach out and grab it. If we put the quicksilver

3

in a bottle, we have only deprived it of its essential nature by imprisoning it; in trying to capture it, we only reveal our own defeat. We are wiser if we simply read the poems, enjoying their shimmer of wit and paradox, than if we write books or articles which attempt to "explain" them.

Why then another book on Donne's poetry? And especially why, if every book is at best a limited interpretation and at worst a deceptive distortion? Although no book is a substitute for the poetry (God forbid) and no book can capture the whole of even a single poem (thank God), it can show that a poem is more complicated than has been suspected or call attention to an aspect which has been neglected. I, for one, am grateful to the artist who painted the romantic young Donne of the frontispiece, even if his Donne is not the only Donne. Even if a total vision of the tiniest corner of reality is impossible, something is accomplished in trying to achieve it. Donne's poetry is admittedly an especially paradoxical and problematic corner, for each poem (and sometimes even each line in each poem) presents a variant and partial view of human love, and each crowds forward, eloquently arguing that it is the only view. But if we are to see Donne's love poetry in the round, we must not listen to any single poem or to any single line; instead we must note the contradictions and paradoxes, ponder their implications and purposes, and wonder if any governing principle lies behind them.

i   Donne's Wit and Its Difficulties

Most of the paradoxes and problems in Donne's poetry can be traced in one way or another to Donne's most characteristic feature, to his "metaphysical wit." Of this Dr. Johnson's oft-quoted definition and criticism in the *Life of Cowley* is still the best.

> But wit, abstracted from its effects upon the hearer, may be more rigorously and philosophically considered as a kind of *discordia concors*; a combination of dissimilar images or the discovery of occult resem-

4

blances in things apparently unlike. Of wit, thus defined, they [the metaphysical poets] have more than
enough. The most heterogeneous ideas are yoked by
violence together; nature and art are ransacked for illustrations, comparisons, and allusions; their learning
instructs, and their subtlety surprises; but the reader
commonly thinks his improvement dearly bought, and,
though he sometimes admires, is seldom pleased.[1]

For Aristotle, of course, "an intuitive perception of the
similarity in dissimilars" was both the essence of metaphor
and a "sign of genius," requiring a penetrating intelligence
which is born rather than acquired.[2] But for Dr. Johnson
the yoking of dissimilars has been carried too far by the
metaphysical poets, and so he suggests that their poetry is
too often a mere exhibition of cleverness and learning.
What should seem easy and obvious seems hard and obscure instead. The surprises and subtleties of metaphysical
poetry seem decorative rather than functional, and, what is
worse, they draw the reader's attention to the poet's skill
rather than to the subject of the poem. Thus the reader may
react to the poet's "admire me" with some annoyance.

Since Dr. Johnson's time, we have perhaps recovered the
seventeenth century's facility for being pleased by metaphysical poetry, for we have been nourished on the dialectical thought of Blake, Coleridge, Hegel, and Yeats and
have become more accustomed to seeing homogeneity and
clarity emerge from apparent heterogeneity and obscurity.
But the subtlety of the wit and the occult nature of the resemblances remain, and although we may understand the
principle, we do not always understand the practice. Like
Dr. Johnson, we sometimes wonder if Donne's wit is anything more than an exhibition of learning and cleverness,
or if, on the other hand, it does serve some functional purpose. And if Donne's wit is functional as well as decorative,
we are often confused and unsure about what its function is.

Dr. Johnson seems to have viewed metaphysical wit as

[1] *Lives of the Poets*, Everyman's edition (London, 1925), I, 11-12.
[2] *Poetics*, Section 22.

primarily a matter of imagery. But in the broadest sense the yoking of heterogeneous elements is characteristic of Donne's poetry, appearing in many aspects besides imagery. In the organization of individual poems, for example, Donne has a habit of providing a surprise reversal at the end. The reader, having followed a tricky labyrinth of imagery, argumentation, and word-play, is suddenly faced at the conclusion with a statement or attitude which seems opposed to all that has preceded it. *Loves Deitie*, for example, begins with a truculent announcement of rebellion against the god of Love and his laws:

> I long to talke with some old lovers ghost,
>   Who dyed before the god of Love was borne:
> I cannot thinke that hee, who then lov'd most,
>   Sunke so low, as to love one which did scorne.

This mood of revolt continues throughout three stanzas, as the lover presents his argument that love is only love when it is reciprocated and that unrequited affairs are the unnatural and irrational result of the tyranny of Cupid and custom. But suddenly his mood shifts in the final stanza, and he wonders why he has been rebelling against his present condition, since there are certainly worse possibilities:

> Love might make me leave loving, or might trie
>   A deeper plague, to make her love mee too.
> Which, since she loves before, I'am loth to see;
> Falshood is worse then hate; and that must bee,
>   If shee whom I love, should love mee.

In view of all the arguments in favor of reciprocity and against amatory custom which have gone before, these final lines seem an emotional and logical *volte face*. Faced with this yoking of apparently incompatible attitudes, one presented at length but contradicted by another briefly asserted in a surprise conclusion, the reader is apt to react with bewildered confusion. What are these intellectual fireworks all about? Or are they about anything? Is the poem simply a trick played on the reader? A trick played by a clever lover

6

on his mistress in order to gain her sympathy and admiration? The monologue of a lover who himself reacts to his love affair with bewildered confusion? Or the monologue of a lover who is at first confused by repeated rejections but who finally reaches something like Truth at the end of the poem?

In short, this poem and others like it may be word-and-idea games, lightly intended, a form of clever diversion designed simply to make the reader jump with surprise and then smile because he has jumped at a shadow. If that is so, their concern is not with reality, but with creating an illusion of reality and then destroying it; the poet delights in manipulating and tricking a reader, and the reader delights in the skill of the manipulation, but neither takes the game seriously. Or, a second possibility, poems like *Loves Deitie* may be attempts to create an illusion of reality which does reflect reality; they may be dramatizations of the way lovers react and behave in the situations presupposed by the poems. If so, their paradoxes and contradictions suggest that the nature of man and the nature of Truth are fairly complicated: men may strike poses to gain some end or they may see both sides of a question at the same time, and Truth may be relative or double. The difference between the first and the second possibility is the difference between playing football (which everyone knows is a game, even if it does have undertones of civilized warfare) and writing a play (which, the word reminds us, is still a form of play, but a serious form that transcends game-playing through its obvious attempt to reflect the way things are). Or, thirdly, the *volte face* in *Loves Deitie* and other similar poems may result from an intellectual and moral progression experienced by the speaker in the poem; they may be not just dramatizations of reality, but dramas with a beginning, a middle, and an end. And, if that is so, then these poems do not juxtapose two apparently inconsistent points of view in order to show that both may be held simultaneously, but in order to show that one eventually emerges as more desirable or more true than the other—to show in *Loves Deitie*, for example, that conformity to moral conventions is better than rebellion against them. If the difference between the first and second possibility is the difference between playing football and writing a play, the difference between the second and the third is that between writing a play about "is" and writing one about "ought." Or, to borrow a metaphor from M. H. Abrams, it is the difference between using a mirror to reflect the chaos of reality and using a lamp to illuminate the order of Reality. Which kind of game, we wonder after reading a poem like *Loves Deitie*, is Donne playing? Is he writing to amuse, to represent, or to judge?

If the contradictions in *Loves Deitie* raise questions about Donne's aesthetic purpose, other poems contain a somewhat different kind of contradiction which lead us to wonder about the extent of his aesthetic distance. In *The Extasie*, for example, imagery and subject seem strangely, even ludicrously, at odds with one another. For the main subject of the poem, the spiritual union of two lovers, is introduced by a rather peculiar description of the setting and their physical contiguity. The lovers sit on a pregnant bank begetting pictures on one another's eyes while their hands are cemented together with perspiration:

> Where, like a pillow on a bed,
>   A Pregnant banke swel'd up, to rest
> The violets reclining head,
>   Sat we two, one anothers best.
> Our hands were firmly cimented
>   With a fast balme, which thence did spring,
> Our eye-beames twisted, and did thred
>   Our eyes upon one double string;
> So to'entergraft our hands, as yet
>   Was all the meanes to make us one,
> And pictures in our eyes to get
>   Was all our propagation.

There is no denying the sexual connotations of the imagery used in this introduction; pillows, pregnant banks, perspiration, and propagation all suggest that the subject of the

8

poem is lust rather than Platonic love, and the speak
subsequent assertion that he and his beloved have experienced an intermingling of souls which is the amatory equivalent of religious ecstasy does not seem quite believable
after this beginning. Donne's witty yoking of heterogeneous
ideas, of sexual love in the initial imagery with Platonic
love in the remainder of the poem, seems so violent as to be
ridiculous, and we cannot help suspecting that he is being
ironic and satiric. That is, the incongruity between the love
which the speaker describes and the imagery he uses to describe it may be a device used by the poet to suggest that
the lovers' motives are more complicated than they themselves may realize: the lovers see their relationship as spiritual, but the sexual imagery betrays their self-deception,
and the poet who has created them may be asking his readers to step back and to see the lovers more clearly than they
see themselves. In this case, the incongruities would be used
to add another dimension to the poem, to increase the objectivity and aesthetic distance from which the subject is
viewed.

Examples of the different ways in which Donne yokes
heterogeneous elements together, violently or not, might be
multiplied at length. But the net result is the same. A reader
is often unsure about the spirit in which the poem is written
and the mood with which he should approach it. The juxtaposition of incongruities often seems ridiculous, implying
irony or satire; yet a plausible literal and straightforward
meaning is nearly always possible. Yet we also need to
know the rules of the word-game being played if we are to
play it ourselves as we read the poem.

As a way of accounting for a second kind of problem in
the poetry of Donne, the biographical method of interpretation was developed; for the entire corpus of Donne's love
poetry contains many poems which express apparently
mutually exclusive attitudes toward love. We find, for example, a poem like *Communitie*, which seems to argue that
only sex is important, and a poem like *The undertaking*,
which is idealistic and Platonic. How could any one man

9

manage to hold such different attitudes toward love? The answer seemed to be that the sensual or cynical poems were the work of the young Donne, the joyous the work of the happily married man, and the conventionally Platonic or Petrarchan a variety of courtly compliment designed for the eyes of aristocratic patrons and friends.

The biographical method is suspiciously circular: the poetry is evidence for Donne's biography, and the biography reconstructed from the poetry is used to interpret the poetry. But, in addition, it produces at least as many problems as it solves. In the first place, the comparatively idealistic (certainly moral and highly serious) *Satyre III* seems to have been written at about the same time as much of the cynical and apparently amoral love poetry. *The Progresse of the Soule*, as cynical in its attitude toward women as any of the "early" poems, dates from 1601, the year of Donne's marriage to Anne More and three years later than the probable date of his first acquaintance with her. So inconsistency within a single "period" of Donne's life still remains unaccounted for. Secondly, the biographical reading of Donne has encouraged the assumption that *Twicknam Garden* and *A nocturnall upon S. Lucies day* are addressed to the Countess of Bedford—in spite of the fact that Grierson admits in his editorial notes that the latter "speaks a stronger language than that of Petrarchian adoration" (II.10), that both poems contain much that the Countess could not find particularly complimentary, and that both are totally unlike the verse epistles which we *know* to be addressed to her. Again, reference to biography seems to complicate and confuse rather than clarify.

Instead of reading poems as landmarks in Donne's private life, it seems wiser to employ the elementary critical principles already hinted at. That is, we cannot necessarily identify the speaking voice of a poem with the poet himself. The "chameleon poet" of Keats and the "masks" of Yeats tell us emphatically what common sense tells us anyway: poetry is more often the result of self-effacement and imaginative projection than of simple self-expression, and although a poet may be recreating some aspect of his personality or experience when he writes a poem, he may also be imagining an experience he has never had or the kind of man he is not. The lover who speaks in a Donne poem is best seen, therefore, as a more or less fictional mouthpiece of Donne's mind and imagination; we must pause hesitantly before taking the lover to be Donne himself. And especially we must because Donne so often uses the techniques of the dramatic monologue, a highly objective poetic mode. In the *Satyres* we even find dialogue, and the love poetry almost always presupposes a situation, a speaker, often a listener, and sometimes a setting. Browning, the modern master of the dramatic monologue, was a close student of Donne and admitted that he learned much from him. Although the distinction between Browning and his characters is obviously much sharper, we cannot ignore the probability that Donne too is distinct and perhaps distant from the characters he has created.[3]

But if we eliminate the biographical explanation for the variety of attitudes toward love which Donne's poetry expresses, the inconsistencies between one poem and another still remain and with them the problem of accounting for them. If the difference between *Communitie* and *The undertaking* is not the difference between the young Donne and the happily married Donne or between the advice of his worse angel and his better, why has he written poems whose speakers, apparently quite seriously, advocate such antithetical and incompatible kinds of love? Like a ventriloquist, Donne has created a number of men (and even a woman, in *Breake of day*) who discuss love in different voices, in different tones, and from different points of view. Of course, each poem may be an individual entity, complete in itself, and totally unrelated to any other poem. If so then inconsistency ceases to be a problem, except within individual poems: Donne is simply imagining and dramatizing different attitudes toward human love without passing judg-

---

[3] For a further discussion of Donne's use of the dramatic monologue, see my "Theme and Structure in Donne's *Satyres*," *SEL*, III (1963), 59-75.

11

ment on their validity. But it is also possible that Donne may be doing something more than painting speaking portraits. His very concern with different and opposing attitudes toward love suggests that he may be exploring them not only in order to dramatize them, but also in order to understand and evaluate them. People who bother to immerse themselves in both sides of a question are usually interested in answering it. Behind the surface anatomy of contradictions may lie a single animating attitude which synthesizes them.

A third difficulty, at least if we accept the latter possibility, is Donne's attitude toward the role of the body and soul in love. That is perhaps the key area in which the apparent inconsistencies and contradictions between one poem and another are most perplexing and confusing. A lyric poem and a philosophical treatise are, of course, two different things, and defining Donne's "philosophy of love" would not be necessary if individual poems were simpler and clearer. But since determining whether Donne is being satiric or serious is so often a problem, knowing what he thought about the goodness or badness of sex or of spiritual love would be helpful. Yet Donne can seem both to embrace physical love joyfully and reject it with repulsion. He can make a lover in *Loves growth* say mockingly:

> Love's not so pure, and abstract, as they use
> To say, which have no Mistresse but their Muse. . . .

He can write in *Elegie XIX*:

> Full nakedness! All joyes are due to thee,
> As souls unbodied, bodies uncloth'd must be,
> To taste whole joyes.

And yet in *Elegie XVIII* he can describe intercourse with scientific coldness and graphic ugliness:

> Rich Nature hath in women wisely made
> Two purses, and their mouths aversely laid:
> They then, which to the lower tribute owe,
> That way which that Exchequer looks, must go:

12

He which doth not, his error is as great,
As who by Clyster gave the Stomack meat.

Or he can make the lover of *Loves Alchymie* compare love of women, even at their best sweetness and wit, to the possession of "mummy," or dead flesh. Faced with this blend of monkish revulsion and Whitmanical delight, we find it hard indeed to generalize about what Donne himself thought.

Thus Donne's poetry contains an abundance of paradoxes and problems. There is, first of all, the problem of wit within individual poems: the dichotomies between argument and conclusion, between idealism and cynicism, between imagery and theme, which enjoy an often incongruous coexistence within a single poem and which make us wonder whether Donne is playing or being serious and whether he is being ironic or straightforward. There is, in the second place, the problem of determining why such a variety of attitudes toward the one subject of love is yoked together within the corpus of Donne's poetry. And, finally, there is the problem of defining what "philosophy of love" informs Donne's poetry. The crux upon which these difficulties converge might be called the central problem in Donne's love poetry: the nature of the love dramatized in each poem and the attitude expressed by the poem toward that kind of love and toward the nature and purpose of love in general. Ultimately, that is the crux which this book tries to uncross.

ii Donne and Tradition

Literature is not written in a vacuum. When we are faced with difficulties in a poem or a group of poems, we can sometimes resolve them by observing the aesthetic assumptions and literary or intellectual traditions with which the poet is working. Customarily we do not, of course, think of Donne as a traditional poet. More than enough has been said in the past about his innovations in imagery. Few precedents exist for his stanza forms and rhyme schemes. And many poems seem to protest against old-fashioned beliefs about the purpose of love. But we still cannot lift Donne out of his Renaissance context. If he avoided the mythological allusions so popular among his contemporaries, he nevertheless forged his imagery from Renaissance materials, the less obviously "poetic" ones of contemporary alchemy, medicine, or astronomy. If he wrote "strong lines" and unusual stanzas, he still stuck to conventional genres—elegies, satires, sonnets, and songs. And some critics have suggested that he mocked the Petrarchan tradition by drawing instead on the Ovidian tradition. No one can invent everything anew. Beneath Donne's surface innovations a firm bedrock of tradition—aesthetic, literary, and intellectual—necessarily remains. And the nature and structure of that bedrock helped dictate the form which Donne's poetry took, for it was the foundation upon which he built.

But before examining that bedrock and the way it influenced Donne's craftsmanship, a word of warning and qualification. A critic's appeal to historical traditions to explain a poem or group of poems may often produce a line of argument as circular as that of the biographical method. Fortunately or unfortunately, literature is evasive before the inquisition of pure reason. At best, if we wish to avoid the relativity of pure subjectivity, we can attempt to use the more fallible methods of induction as rigorously as possible. Faced with problems in a poem, we can try to account for them by forming an hypothesis, and the test of the hypothesis is the extent to which it explains all the facts and details at hand. That, for better or worse, is the method of this book. Given the problems in Donne's poetry outlined above, the hypothesis that Donne writes from Renaissance attitudes about literature and love is used to account for them, and that hypothesis seems to account for more facts than any other. The flaw in the biographical hypothesis is not so much its circularity as that it does not account for enough details.

When Donne wrote his love lyrics, a didactic aesthetic was overwhelmingly pervasive among his English contem-

14

poraries. Though they may disagree about which literary works are valuable and how literature should teach, men so diverse as Gosson and Lodge and Sidney are all agreed that it should provide moral instruction. Borrowing from the Horatian dictum that literature should be *dulcis et utilis,* Sidney, for example, asserts that it should delight and teach; that it should provide delight alone never seems to have entered his mind, and his discussion of these dual objectives of the poet indicates that sweetness is for him but a means to the more important end of didacticism. Of the poets he says: ". . . these indeede doo meerely make to imitate, and imitate both to delight and teach, and delight to moue men to take that goodnes in hande, which without delight they would flye as from a stranger; and teach, to make them know that goodnes whereunto they are mooued. . . ."[4] Sidney even makes such high claims for poetry that in his view the poet surpasses the philosopher and the historian in ability to inspire moral improvement.

If we postulate that Donne shared this didactic aesthetic, then the problem of his wit can be partially resolved, for it must be functional rather than frivolous. His yoking of incongruities is not meant merely to trick or amuse, but to serve some useful purpose. Although he is certainly playing a word-and-idea game on the surface, he is also fulfilling his later plea in *A Litanie*:

> That wit, borne apt high good to doe,
> By dwelling lazily
> On Natures nothing, be not nothing too. . . .

And if at the time he wrote his love poetry he shared the beliefs of his era, implicit in this plea, then he not only wrote "apt high good to doe" but he also believed that art should not merely hold a mirror up to "Natures nothing." For according to Sidney, poetry teaches by dramatizing positive and negative moral *exempla*, and the poet is superior to the historian because he can improve upon reality by creating

---

[4] *An Apologie for Poetrie, Elizabethan Critical Essays*, ed. G. Gregory Smith (Oxford, 1904), I, 159.

"feigned examples" which reflect a Reality above nature. And since Donne shared the Augustinian-Platonic metaphysic upon which Sidney's aesthetic is based, he probably shared the aesthetic as well.

That Donne lived in the Renaissance and that Renaissance aestheticians professed that literature served a moral purpose are fairly obvious propositions, but it is somewhat less obvious that a lyric poem, especially a lyric poem about erotic love, could be didactic. Neither Sidney nor Donne thinks a poem and a sermon are the same thing, however, and if didacticism is a heresy which overemphasizes moral teaching at the expense of narrowing the range of experience which poetry may express, then that is not what the didacticism of the Renaissance humanists means. Poe and Gosson both go to the extreme of assuming that to be moral one must be narrow-minded, though the former thinks narrowness is bad and the latter thinks it good. Men like Sidney and Donne would disagree with that assumption. Sidney can both mean what he says in his *Apologie* and write *Astrophil and Stella* because he does not believe with Mme de Staël that "Tout comprendre c'est tout pardonner." He can convey Astrophil's moods and acts convincingly without sympathizing with them, expecting his readers to see Astrophil as a perfect example of an imperfect lover. We have seen that several of Donne's poems contain incongruities which suggest that he is being ironic and satiric; others eloquently express a positive and happy love. If we remember that poets can be didactic without being heavy-handed or sanctimoniously solemn, then we can see the lovers who speak in Donne's poems from the same distance that he saw them from—some of them to be laughed at, some of them to be pitied, some to be admired.

As we read through the *Elegies* and *Songs and Sonets,* trying to sense what kind of love relationship each poem dramatizes, we find most of them falling rather naturally into three groups. Donne is, of course, a poet of splendid variety, and we could if we wished define as many groups as there are poems, so individualized are the speakers and their situations. But though such a refusal to classify would pay tribute to the complexity of Donne's achievement, it would hardly be useful; and it is nearly as accurate to over-simplify a bit in order to generalize, for a sizable number of Donne's poems can with some fairness be seen as sub-types within three general categories, each of which concentrates on a particular kind of love and draws to some extent on a particular literary tradition. One group, those poems which treat love cynically or see it as limited to sexual attraction, follows the Ovidian tradition. Although Donne is sometimes said to be anti-Petrarchan, mostly because of the anti-idealism which characterizes his Ovidian poems, there is another group of poems (sometimes called the "courtly compliments") which draw on Petrarchanism and portray a more impassioned and romantic love. And finally there is a group which reflects the doctrines of Christian Platonism, although in this case the tradition upon which Donne draws is perhaps more philosophical than literary. But whenever he writes, Donne assumes an audience which accepts Christian teachings about love, and consequently its ethic indirectly informs nearly all his love poems, even the pagan Ovidian ones, and gives them their unifying and governing principle.

J. B. Leishman has, in *The Monarch of Wit*, written a fine and suggestive treatment of Donne's Ovidian poetry.[5] There he stresses Donne's indebtedness to Ovid and makes some points that one wishes had been made sooner and more often: he argues that much of Donne's poetry is literary in inspiration rather than personal and that much of it is meant to be both fun and funny. He finds the wit which pervades the *Elegies* and the Ovidian poems within *Songs and Sonets* to be preposterous, impudent, ingenious, mockingly illogical and paradoxical, and intentionally shocking and outrageous. But because he does not read them within the context of the Renaissance Ovid, he also finds them totally playful. What one misses in Leishman's study is Ovid the moralist, the Ovid which Donne knew and used.

[5] (London, 1951), 52-106, 184-186, and *passim*.

As Chapter II shows more fully, Ovid's *Amores, Ars Amatoria,* and *Remedia Amoris* (the works which exercised the greatest influence on Donne) were often read in the Renaissance as didactic works, using techniques of comic irony and satire, and not as prurient lessons on the art of lust. Although an occasional Gosson might protest, Ovid was thought by most humanists to be presenting dramatic portraits of deviations from a moral ideal. And Donne seems to have written his Ovidian poems in a similar spirit. In those poems which seem to advocate a cheerful devotion to illicit lust, Donne is probably writing tongue in cheek and creating *personae* who are to be seen as deviations from a moral ideal, just as he does more obviously in his five formal verse satires, which were written about the same time. But in the *Elegies* and *Songs and Sonets* he follows Ovid rather than Horace and Juvenal, and he wields his irony more subtly. Admiration for the satiric qualities in this early poetry is probably behind the somewhat strange remark of Ben Jonson (no mean satirist himself) that he "esteemeth John Done the first poet jn the World jn some things . . ." and "affirmeth Done to have written all his best pieces err he was 25 years old."[6] If we ignore the moral satire behind the surface levity, we miss much of the humor which Donne's contemporaries probably enjoyed in these poems.

Nor is there any inconsistency between Donne's "Ovidian or naturalistic" poetry and his "Petrarchan or idealistic" poetry. In some of his poems, in fact, Donne seems to be using elements from both the Petrarchan tradition and the Ovidian tradition within the same poem. As we shall see in Chapter II, Petrarchan love was usually regarded in the Renaissance as profane and sinful, since the lover's emotions were excessively irrational and passionate. And Donne's Petrarchan poems usually reflect this moral judgment of his contemporaries. Neo-Petrarchan rather than anti-Petrarchan, Donne experiments with conventions in a

[6] *Ben Jonson*, ed. C. H. Herford and Percy Simpson (Oxford, 1925-52), I, 135.

number of ways, but always retains their essential spirit. Petrarchanism offered to the Renaissance poet a convenient vehicle for treating profane love; its set themes—the beloved's scorn, the lover's frustration, floods of tears and tempests of sighs—are used and reused by Donne's fellow poets and refreshed by Donne himself. And when we encounter these standard images in Donne's poetry, we can speculate that he may be drawing on literature rather than life, that he could be transforming literary conventions rather than revealing personal experience, that he is perhaps writing a poem rather than addressing the Countess of Bedford.

Donne's Ovidian and Petrarchan poems are dramatic monologues spoken by lovers who are in a sense meant to be seen as negative moral *exempla*. Since the Ovidian lovers err by placing excessive emphasis on physical love and the Petrarchan lovers by a misguided and excessive idealism, these two groups of poems complement one another. And they are further complemented by a third group, those poems which are at least partially inspired by Christian Platonism. The lovers who deliver these monologues are positive examples, men who experience a love which is joyous, satisfying, and righteous. Their love is the true ideal, from which the cynical Ovidian and the masochistic Petrarchan deviate.

Insofar as Donne has a "philosophy of love," it is to be found in this third group of poems. But for all his interest in intellectual matters, Donne is a great poet and psychologist rather than a great philosopher; and to say that the beliefs affirmed in these poems are essentially derivative hardly detracts from his originality. Donne did not need to invent a new philosophy of love, for he had an ample system of doctrines ready at hand in the Bible, the Church Fathers, and the works produced by the Florentine and French Academies. As Sidney says, however, the poet sur passes the philosopher in that the poet presents both precept and example, both doctrine and experience. And this is why Donne shines. Although he does not invent dogma, he so vivifies the old clichés about the nature of righteous human love, so brilliantly dramatizes the joy which it produces, so uncompromisingly refuses to soften or sentimentalize, that these poems emerge as his finest, strongest, and most admired.

When we thus look at Donne's poetry in the light of the traditions that it borrows from, the man who created it emerges as somewhat more conservative than he is sometimes considered to be. Of course he is also restless, skeptical, rebellious, and mercurial, but *Satyre III* reminds us that even the very young Donne saw his Protean intellectual metamorphoses as a way of climbing a cragged and steep hill toward a Truth he knew was at the top. Like Dante's souls in purgatory (with whom he was no doubt identifying himself as he wrote those lines), that faith gives a continuity to his transformation and development. And if we see the man who wrote the love poems as a poet whose wit is functional rather than simply decorative and whose ethic is intrinsically Christian rather than pagan, we can resolve some of the paradoxes and problems which pervade his work. Any attempt to clarify anything worth clarifying—a great era, a great poet, a great idea—must necessarily oversimplify, but I have tried in the pages which follow to chart what I think to be the mainstream of Donne's life and work, knowing nevertheless that no one can encompass the whole man in any single critical study. Since Donne's innovations have been sufficiently stressed and his iconoclasm overstressed, however, a reminder that he is a conservative revolutionary is perhaps in order.

II · VARIETIES OF AMATORY EXPERIENCE

From being anxious, or secure,
Dead clods of sadnesse, or light squibs of mirth,
From thinking, that great courts immure
All, or no happinesse, or that this earth
Is only for our prison framed,
Or that thou art covetous
To them whom thou lovest, or that they are maim'd
From reaching this worlds sweet, who seek thee thus,
With all their might, Good Lord deliver us.

Even if there is no such thing as "the unchanging human heart," varieties of love have probably not changed much over the past two or three thousand years. Sexual love is inevitably omnipresent, and idealized love, married love, and selfless religious love are probably present everywhere as well. But if all kinds of love and ways of expressing it probably occur in every society, the official view as to what love should do and be certainly seems to change from society to society and from one time to another. Freud is now the greatest authority on a subject about which St. Augustine was once thought to have said the final word. These shifts in attitude would be of only antiquarian interest, of course, if love were not so common a theme of literature and if literature did not usually reflect the mores of the society which nourishes it. But since attitudes do change, we can easily misunderstand or only partially understand literature based on a point of view different from our own. Passionate and experienced as he was, even St. Augustine might have some trouble seeing *Lady Chatterley's Lover* from Lawrence's perspective unless he learned something about the twentieth-century attitude toward sex.

Since moral issues are almost always controversial and since there is almost always a vast gap between ideals and practice, discovering the official view is not always easy.

But many books were written about love during the Renaissance, and they show a surprising unanimity. Available resources range from philosophical disquisitions to popularized handbooks on "How to Succeed at Love" and from literary works to commentaries on them. Yet because all the authors seem to agree about basics (for example, that reason should rule the passions) and because nearly all appeal to religious philosophy for these basics, they seem to say more or less the same thing in book after book. One wonders after a time why the market was not surfeited with these repetitive volumes, until one recalls the Elizabethan taste for being morally edified. No doubt the rules of the Renaissance love game were frequently broken, but there seems to have been no doubt about what the rules were, and consequently we can perhaps speak more precisely about what people believed 350 years ago than we can about what they believe today, when very few rules exist to be broken. But even granted a fairly precise set of rules, "love" is an elusive word, and we need to recover the Renaissance vocabulary as well as the Renaissance assumptions before we try to pursue other concepts as elusive as Ovidianism, Petrarchanism, and Platonism.

i Fundamental Assumptions

Renaissance love doctrines are oddly pragmatic. Their objective is to produce a maximum of happiness and pleasure, and yet that happiness is theologically defined. They assume, as Sidney says in his "Leave me o love," that "what ever fades, but fading pleasure brings." And so man, if he is to love happily, must base his love on something which is not transient and must recognize that the incidental joys of love are inevitably transient. Good or righteous love works that way, and bad or sinful love, on the other hand, produces sorrow and misery because it is directed solely toward things which are mutable and yet often refuses to admit their mutability. Arranged schematically, the possible types of love look something like this:

22

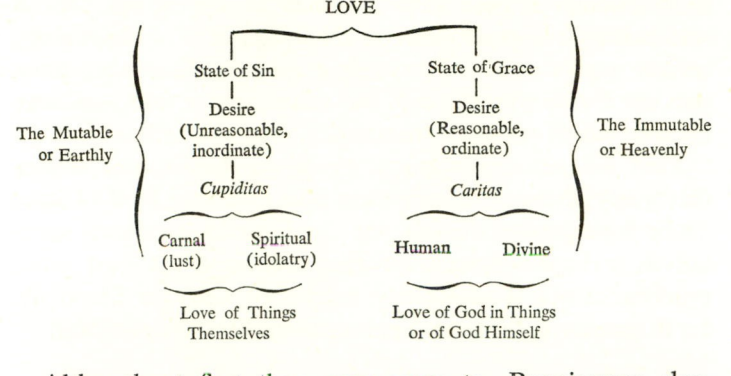

LOVE

	State of Sin	State of Grace	
	Desire	Desire	
The Mutable	(Unreasonable,	(Reasonable,	The Immutable
or Earthly	inordinate)	ordinate)	or Heavenly
	Cupiditas	*Caritas*	

| Carnal | Spiritual | Human | Divine |
| (lust) | (idolatry) | | |

Love of Things   Love of God in Things
Themselves   or of God Himself

Although at first they may seem to, Renaissance doctrines do not advocate asceticism. Rather, they affirm the beauty and goodness of the world which God has created and assert that it is natural and proper for man to love God's creation and God's creatures. The difference between good love and bad is not that bad love is directed toward things of the earth, but that the things of the earth are loved in the wrong way. The sin is not in the object, but in the mind of the beholder. *Cupiditas* is sinful because it is unreasonable and inordinate, and it is unreasonable and inordinate because it sees earthly goods as an end in themselves rather than a means by which God is glorified. When inordinate love is expressed physically, it is called lust by the Elizabethans. When love is spiritually inordinate, it is idolatry, or giving a mortal being the worship due only to God. On the other hand, *caritas*, the love which derives from and constitutes a state of grace, is reasonable and ordinate because it recognizes that earthly goods are good only within their given place on a hierarchy of values, that their fading pleasures are gifts of an eternal Being, and that they are to be enjoyed with the ultimate purpose of glorifying God.[1] In the human (or physical) sphere, *caritas* expresses

---

[1] The relevant Biblical text is I Corinthians 10:31, "Whether therefore ye eat or drink, or whatsoever ye do, do all to the glory of God." This distinction between *caritas* and *cupiditas* is, of course, fundamentally Augustinian; see *Of the City of God*, XII.8, XIV.7, XIV.28; *On Christian Doctrine*, I.3. But it is also current during the Renais-

itself through selfless love of other human beings, for it sees human beings as made in the image of God. Spiritually, *caritas* expresses itself through a man's selfless absorption into the divine will, through the attainment of that total love for God which enables a man to say "Thy will be done."

Lust seemed so obviously wrong to Renaissance writers that many of them did not even classify it as a kind of love. Their fundamental reason for condemning excessive sexuality is perhaps religious, but they also argue that lust is impractical, since it ultimately injures or destroys the body. La Primaudaye, for example, inveighs against it as follows:

> And truly there is nothing more certaine, than that immoderate use of the venereous act spoileth beautie, defileth the bodie, drieth it up, and causeth it to stinke, maketh the face pale, wan or yellow, weakeneth the members and joints, ingendreth Sciaticke goutes, collicke passions, griefes of the stomacke, giddines of the head, or dimnes of sight, the leprosie and pocks. It shorteneth life, taketh away the understanding, darkeneth the memorie, and as the prophet *Osey* saith, taketh away the heart [Osey.4.11]. Moreover, how odious all whoordome ought to be unto us, so that it be not so much as once named amongst us, the onely curse that is laid upon it of God, ought sufficiently to persuade us, seeing thereby he condemneth it both with temporall and eternall death.[2]

In *Farewell to love* Donne states even more explicitly the practical objections to lust which were an accepted part of sixteenth-century medical teaching:

> . . . each such Act, they say,
> Diminisheth the length of life a day. . . .

---

sance; see Pierre de la Primaudaye, *The French Academie* (London, 1589), 744; *The Sermons of John Donne*, ed. Evelyn M. Simpson and George R. Potter (Berkeley and Los Angeles, 1953-62), II, 132-133.
[2] *French Academie*, 225.

Thus lust was thought literally to destroy the body, as well as to destroy the soul because it was a mortal sin. In La Primaudaye's words, it produces "both temporall and eternall death." Renaissance writers were not blind, of course, to the fact that sex is enjoyable; but Renaissance prostitutes are said to have worn rings decorated with a skull and crossbones, and sexual pleasure seemed but a dangerously and deceptively gaudy mask covering over a reality of death, grief, and bestiality. One of the more eloquent expressions of lust's terrible blend of attractiveness and repulsiveness is Shakespeare's sonnet 129:

Th' expense of spirit in a waste of shame
Is lust in action; and till action, lust
Is perjur'd, murd'rous, bloody, full of blame,
Savage, extreme, rude, cruel, not to trust;
Enjoy'd no sooner but despised straight;
Past reason hunted, and no sooner had,
Past reason hated, as a swallowed bait
On purpose laid to make the taker mad;
Mad in pursuit, and in possession so;
Had, having, and in quest to have, extreme;
A bliss in proof—and prov'd, a very woe;
Before, a joy propos'd; behind, a dream.
    All this the world well knows; yet none knows well
    To shun the heaven that leads men to this hell.

Though these views sound puritanical (using the word in its modern sense), they are in fact founded on a reverence for the body rather than a scorn for it. Juxtaposed with these visions of sex as potential filth and poison are others of the holiness of the body. In his *Enchiridion*, for example, Erasmus condemns lust by reminding his readers

    . . . how noble a thyng the soul is, how worshypfull a thyng the body of a man is . . . what the deuyls peuyshnes is it than for so lytle, so vnclenly tickling of the momentany pleasures to defyle at one tyme both soule and body with vngoodly maners, to profane and

25

vnhalow that temple which Christ hath consecrate to himself with his blode.[3]

Other writers stress that sex can be used righteously and can even be called chaste. Discussing the role of sex within marriage, Donne says:

> The Roman Church injures us, when they say, that we prefer mariage before virginity: and they injure the whole state of Christianity, when they oppose *mariage* and *chastity*, as though they were incompatible, and might not consist together. They may; for *mariage is honourable, and the bed undefiled*; and therefore it may be so.[4]

Especially in Protestant England, where marriage of the clergy was of course permitted, sex was seen as a potential good, and a Manichaean equation of the physical world with sin and evil was considered heretical. But though sex could only be righteous within marriage, marriage alone could not make it righteous; if sexual intercourse were motivated solely by inordinate and selfish desire rather than a desire to glorify God (usually through having children), it could become the sin of lust even within marriage. As Donne says in the marriage sermon already quoted from:

> . . . the fitnesse that goes through all, is a *sober continency*; for without that, *Matrimonium jurata fornicatio*, Mariage is but a continuall fornication, sealed with an oath: And mariage was not instituted to prostitute the chastity of the woman to one man, but to preserve her chastity from the tentations of more men.[5]

Thus Renaissance men saw sex with a peculiar double vision: it could be the ugly and repulsive sin of lust, or it could be a chaste and pure physical expression of love. The former survives today in the notion of the "dirty joke," but

---

[3] *A booke called in latyn enchiridion militis christiani* . . . (London, 1512), S[4v]; see also *French Academie*, 18-36.
[4] *Sermons*, II, 349.
[5] *Sermons*, II, 346-347; see also III, 241-255.

the latter is relatively unfamiliar, since we (perhaps the greater puritans after all) tend to equate chastity with abstinence.

The Renaissance attitude toward idolatrous love is even more alien. This is the kind of love which literary critics identify as "courtly love" in its medieval form, as "Petrarchan love" in its Renaissance form; modern theologians have come to call it *eros* and other modern writers call it simply "romantic love."[6] We all know what its conventions are: the lover passionately adores or worships his beloved, thinks the world well lost for her, prostrates himself before her, performs heroic deeds to win her admiration, declares he loves her soul more than her body, refuses ever to consider loving another woman, and tenaciously continues to love her even if she rejects him. Because it is apparently unselfish and idealistic, most people today regard this form of love as admirable and assume that their historical predecessors agreed. But in earlier times such worship of another human being was usually considered to be sinful, forbidden by God's commandment that "Thou shalt have no other gods before me."[7] Phylopolo, a character in Etienne Pasquier's dialogue *Monophylo*, states this conventional view:

And I thinke singularitie is no lesse displeasing to God, than if a manne made diuision of his hart to many women, seeing amongst the rest, it bringeth this lothsome inconuenience, that the loue of men to women beeing extreeme, and a rage aboue all other passions,

[6] There are three significant modern studies which attempt to define abuses of love (*eros*) and righteous love (*agape*). The Roman Catholic point of view is represented by M. C. D'Arcy's *The Mind and Heart of Love* (London, 1954); the Lutheran position by Anders Nygren, *Agape and Eros*, trans. Philip S. Watson (London, 1953); the Anglican by C. S. Lewis, *The Four Loves* (New York, 1960). Although the least ambitious and scholarly, Lewis's book is perhaps the most useful for the student of Donne.

[7] For the traditional theological statement of this belief see, e.g., *Summa Theologica*, II.ii.Q.94.Art.3-4. In *A Preface to Chaucer* (Princeton, 1962), D. W. Robertson has dealt rather fully with "courtly love," demonstrating the medieval belief that idolatry is sinful; see 391-503.

makes vs oftentimes forsake the loue of God, and imagine our God to rest in them, as if we shoulde doe worship to Idols, whose nature is vnder vaine resemblances, to corrupt the deuotion of men. . . .[8]

Like lust, idolatrous love turns out to be wrong on pragmatic as well as theological grounds. Idolatry, usually defined as giving a creature the love due to the Creator, is seen as producing sorrow and satiety because an inferior being is unable to support such a heavy burden of devotion. Women, after all, are just women—a good enough thing to be, but hardly divine. They can be fickle, as Cressida is, or seem fickle as Desdemona does, or die as Juliet does. Troilus, Othello, and Romeo all love excessively and therefore unrealistically, and they reap only misery when they give up all for love of a woman.[9] But idolatrous love, because it produces a deceptively pure commitment and is such a close imitation of divine love, easily masquerades as admirable. For just this reason, idolatry is a graver and more dangerous sin than lust; unlike lust, it has a blasphemous sanctity about it.[10]

The grave weaknesses of idolatrous love appear most vividly when it is compared with righteous love of human beings or *caritas*. Just as there is nothing wrong with sex when it is enjoyed in the right spirit, so there is nothing wrong with love of creatures, if they are used as a means of ascent to the Creator. Thus Donne complains of idolatrous love: ". . . in this idolatrous love of the Creature, love hath wings, and flies not; it flies not upward, it never ascends to the contemplation of the Creator, in the Creature."[11] But there are two important assumptions about how and why the ascent occurs. One is that human beings become trans-

[8] (London, 1572), 9r. Phylopolo, like several other characters in this dialogue, is saying the right thing for the wrong reason; he attacks idolatry in order to defend promiscuity.

[9] Donne attacks idolatrous love of women in this vein at some length in one of his early sermons; see *Sermons*, I, 199-203.

[10] Idolatry is a sin of the spirit; lust, a sin of the flesh; moral theology always sees spiritual sins as graver. See, e.g., *Summa Theologica*, II.ii.Q.73.Art.5.

[11] *Sermons*, I, 200.

formed into that which they love; as Donne puts it: "Love is a Possessory Affection, it delivers over him that loves into the possession of that that he loves; it is a transmutatory Affection, it changes him that loves, into the very nature of that that he loves, and he is nothing else."[12] Hence it is important that man love the right object, for love is "due to very few things, and very few things worthy of it" (184). The other assumption is that God is immanent in His creation,[13] and more particularly that human beings reflect the image of God.

Oddly enough, these doctrines often provide liberal men of the Renaissance with a hedge against asceticism rather than a justification for it. For human beings can be loved for what they are, human beings who reflect the *imago Dei,* rather than idolatrously worshipped as supernatural or divine beings; and when loved in this way, they can never be loved too much, for *caritas* can do no wrong. Donne is often at his most eloquent in describing the joyous sense of liberation which righteous love produces:

> *O dementiam nescientem amare homines humaniter*! what a perverse madness is it, to love a creature and not as a creature, that is, with all the adjuncts, and circumstances, and qualities of a creature, of which the principal is that, that love raise us to the contemplation of the Creator; for if it do so, we may love our selves, as we are the Images of God; and so we may love other men, as they are the Images of us, and our nature; yea, as they are the members of the same body; for *omnes homines una humanitas*, all men make up but one mankind, and so we love other creatures, as we all meet in our Creator, in whom Princes and Subjects, angels and men, and wormes are fellow servants.[14]

[12] *Sermons*, I, 184-185.
[13] The relevant text is Romans 1:20: "For the invisible things of him from the creation of the world are clearly seen, being understood by the things that are made, *even* his eternal power and Godhead. . . ."
[14] *Sermons*, I, 243; a similar statement about the nature of righteous love also appears in the well-known Meditation XVII of the *Devotions*.

29

And as *caritas* is fundamentally selfless, so idolatry is a form of *cupiditas* which is only apparently selfless. Donne asks of it:

> . . . is this love which we bear to other creatures, within that definition of love, *velle bonum amato*, to wish that which we love happy? doth any ambitious man love honor or office therefore, because he thinks that title, or that place should receive a dignity by his having it, or an excellency by his executing it? . . . doth any licentious man covet or solicite a woman there-fore, because he thinks it a happiness to her, to have such a servant? No, it is only himself that is within the definition, *vult bonum sibi*, he wishes well (as he mis-takes it) to himself, and he is content, that the slavery, and dishonor, and ruin of others should contribute to make up his imaginary happiness.[15]

If an idolatrous lover becomes apparently better in behavior in order to win the admiration of his mistress, the change is only outward; but *caritas* produces genuine improvement by transforming and regenerating the lover from within; for men become what they love, and the charitable lover loves the image of God:

> . . . if a man addict himself only to feeding and nour-ishment, hee becommeth a Plante, if to things sensuall, he is a brute beast, if to things reasonable and ciuil, he groweth a celestial creature: but if he exalt the beauti-ful gift of his mind, to thinges inuisible and diuine, hee transformeth himselfe into an Angel; and to conclude, becommeth the sonne of God.[16]

Thus through Renaissance eyes love and desire were seen as neutral things, capable of becoming either positive or negative according to whether they were used in the spirit of charity or the spirit of concupiscence. Sex, of itself, was not

---

[15] *Sermons*, I, 242-243.

[16] Annibale Romei, *The courtiers academie* . . . (London, 1598), 47-48.

sinful; it was a positive good when used for the end of pro-creation, but when it was abused through intemperate self-indulgence, it became the sin of lust. Admiration of a woman was not sinful, when it recognized that the real object of admiration was the image of God in which she was made and which she revealed through her piety and good-ness; but the error of mistaking the vessel of the image for God Himself, the temple of the Holy Ghost for the Holy Ghost Itself, was idolatry. The one sin erred through mak-ing man sub-human and the other through making him seem super-human. Moral laws were not seen as preventing man from reaching this world's sweet, however, but as a preven-tion against turning sweetness into the gall of sin. Thus either marriage or friendship between men and women was seen as a part of this world's sweet which man was free to enjoy, made righteous through the rule of charity and re-maining righteous so long as he conformed to that rule.

ii   The Ovidian Strand

Ovid is a racy poet, and although he may occasionally portray a mood of romance, the witty dissection of that kind of love which Elizabethans called lust is more to his taste. Yet, like Aristophanes, he can hardly be considered pru-rient, for all his frank bawdry. Ovid simply cannot take sex seriously; he sees it from the emotional distance of the born ironist. As we read his roguish love books today, we cannot help but notice that he occasionally is mocking this lowest common denominator of all human beings. Many Eliza-bethans, reading with somewhat sterner presuppositions, probably went a step further and saw him as a satirist who humorously exposed the ridiculousness of lustful love.

None of the Renaissance editions of these love books contain the elaborate commentaries which characterize the editions of the *Metamorphoses*.[17] But the latter suggest that the Renaissance Ovid was a moral poet who mingled *laus*

[17] Bartolomeus Merula's *Ovidius De Arte Amandi & De Remedio Amoris Cum Commento* (Venetia, 1494) explains only the mytho-logical allusions.

et vituperatio, praise of virtue and condemnation of vice. As
Arthur Golding explains in the dedicatory verse epistle to
the Earl of Leicester with which he prefaced his translation
of the *Metamorphoses,* the reader must go to some small
pain in order to discern the difference between the letter and
the spirit, but the reader who does so will be rewarded with
an insight into Ovid's enunciation of ethical truths:

> If Poets then with leesings and with fables
> shadowed so
> The certeine truth, what letteth us too pluck
> those visers fro
> Their doings, and too bring ageine the darkened
> truth too lyght,
> That all men may behold thereof the cleerenesse
> shining bryght?
> The readers therefore earnestly admonisht are
> too bee
> Too seeke a further meaning than the letter
> gives too see.
> The travell tane in that behalf although it
> have sum payne
> Yit makes it double recompence with pleasure and
> with gayne. . . .
> For sure theis fables are not put in wryghting
> to thentent
> Too further or allure to vyce: but rather this
> is ment,
> That men beholding what they bee when vyce dooth
> reigne in stead
> Of vertue, should not let their lewd affections
> have the head,
> For as there is no creature more divine than man
> as long
> As reason hath the sovereintie and standeth firme
> and strong:

So is there none more beastly, vyle, and devilish,
   than is hee,
If reason giving over, by affection mated bee.[18]
(537-544, 561-568)

Nor was the didactic and allegorical reading of the *Meta-morphoses* typified by Golding an eccentric remnant of the medieval world-view which rapidly dissolved. Writing sixty years after Golding, Sandys has exactly the same view of Ovid's purpose. Sandys concludes the verse epistle which he places at the beginning of his edition with these lines:

   . . . in these antient Fables lie
The mysteries of all Philosophie.

Some Natures secrets shew; in some appeare
Distempers staines; some teach vs how to beare
Both Fortunes, bridling Ioy, Griefe, Hope, and Feare.

These Pietie, Deuotion those excite;
These prompt to Vertue, those from Vice affright;
All fitly mingling Profit with Delight.

   This course our Poet steeres: and these that faile,
   By wandring Stars, not by his Compasse, faile.[19]

Like Golding, Sandys believes that the *Metamorphoses*

[18] *Shakespeare's Ovid Being Arthur Golding's Translation of the Metamorphoses*, ed. W. H. D. Rouse (Carbondale, Ill., 1961), lines 537-544, 561-568.

[19] *Ovid's Metamorphosis Englished, Mythologiz'd And Represented in Figures* (Oxford, 1632). Both Golding and Sandys are following traditional medieval interpretations of the *Metamorphoses*, as does Lodovico Dolce in *Le Trasformationi di Lodovico Dolce tratte da Ovidio* . . . (Venetia, 1570); for examples of the medieval interpretation see *Ovide Moralisé En Prose (Text du Quinzième Siècle)*, ed. C. De Boer, *Verhandelingen der Koninklijke Nederlandse Akademie van Wetenschappen, Afdeeling Letterkunde*, Nieuwe Reeks, LXI, No. 2 (1954); *Ovide Moralisé, Poeme du Commencement du quatorzième siècle*, ed. C. De Boer, *Verhandelingen der Koninklijke Akademie van Wetenschappen, Afdeeling Letterkunde*, Nieuwe Reeks, XXI (1920), XV (1915). The continuity between medieval and Renaissance interpretations of the *Metamorphoses* suggests that we are warranted in seeing a similar continuity in the case of the love books.

33

produces profit and delight through the commendation of virtue and the condemnation of vice.

The didactic presuppositions with which Golding and Sandys approach the *Metamorphoses* seem to carry over to the interpretation of the love books as well. But evidence is scant, and the *Amores* and *Ars Amatoria* can, of course, lend themselves to the criticism that Ovid seems to recommend vice, not to condemn it. On the surface, these works seem to be straightforward accounts of the best way to make successful seductions and to hold a mistress once she has been won, and the literal-minded or puritanical of any era can easily find them shocking or even obscene. Renaissance humanists and intellectuals, however, generally tend to defend Ovid's love books as harmless and even as morally edifying.

In his treatise *Of English Poetry*, for example, William Webbe firmly asserts that he believes works ostensibly written to encourage lust were actually written to condemn it. Having just discussed the Horatian notion that literature should mingle profit and delight, he goes on to show how it applies even to works which seem merely light or trivial to the light-minded reader:

> For among all the auncient works of poetrie, though the most of them incline much to that part of delighting men with pleasant matters of small importaunce, yet euen in the vainest trifles among them there is not forgotten some profitable counsaile, which a man may learne, either by flatte precepts which therein are prescribed, or by loathing such vile vices, the enormities whereof they largelie discouer. For surelie I am of this opinion that the wantonest Poets of all, in their most liciuious workes wherein they busied themselves, sought rather by that meanes to withdraw mens mindes (especiallie the best natures) from such foule vices then to allure them to imbrace such beastly follies as they detected.[20]

[20] *Elizabethan Critical Essays*, ed. G. Gregory Smith (London, 1904), I, 251.

On the following page Webbe makes it clear that he has Ovid's love books and other similar works in mind, and he defends them more specifically against the charge that they may teach men vicious behavior rather than virtue:

> Nowe, if the ill and vndecent prouocations, whereof some vnbridled witts take occasion by the reading of laciuious Poemes, be obiected—such as are Ouids loue Bookes and *Elegies, Tibullus, Catullus,* and *Martials* workes, with the Comedies for the most part of *Plautus* and *Terence*—I thinke it easily aunswered. For though it may not iustlie be denied that these workes are in-deede very Poetrie, yet that Poetrie in them is not the essential or formall matter or cause of the hurt therein might be affirmed, and although that reason should come short, yet this might be sufficient, that the workes themselues doo not corrupt, but the abuse of the vsers, who, vndamaging their owne dispositions by reading the discoueries of vices, resemble foolish folke who, comming into a Garden without anie choise or circum-spection, tread downe the fairest flowers and wilfullie thrust their fingers among the nettles.
>
> And surelie to speake what I verelie thinke, this is mine opinion: that one hauing sufficient skyll to read and vnderstand those workes, and yet no staie of his selfe to auoyde inconueniences, which the remem-braunce of vnlawfull things may stirre vppe in his minde, he, in my iudgement, is wholy to be reputed a laciuious disposed personne, whom the recitall of Sins whether it be in a good worke or a badde, or vppon what occasion soeuer, wyll not staie him but to pro-uoke him further vnto them.

Webbe thus says in effect that whatever viciousness is to be found in the love books of Ovid is in the mind of the be-holder, not in the works themselves.[21]

---

[21] This is a very common notion, appearing also in Golding's Dedi-catory Epistle (lines 557-560) and Nashe's *A General Censure* (*Eliz-abethan Critical Essays,* I, 332-333). Golding says that those who

Unfortunately, Webbe does not support his defense of Ovid by discussing specific passages, since literary criticism is not his primary concern. But Coluccio Salutati, writing during the earlier Italian Renaissance, does. In dealing with the importance of *laus et vituperatio*, Salutati admits that some readers may wonder where the *vituperatio* is in some works. Conveniently enough, Salutati defends his case by referring to the love books:

> . . . habemus libros tres Ovidii qui inscribuntur Amorum vel, ut vulgo dicitur, Sine Titulo. In quibus licet a consueta dulcedine stilique elegantia non discedat, multas amoris turpitudines exprimit atque canit, pro pulcerrimo celebrans que turpia spurcissima cognoscuntur. Ad quod quidem facile responderim, admonens quod idem autor quodammodo obivienda refellens immediate post prohemium initiali capitulo nichil agit nisi quod se ligatum atque captivum ducit post triumphalem currum amoris, hoc commento designans amantium fedam et non occultam, sicut in plerisque, vitiorum sed apertam et manifestam in omnium oculis servitutem. Et cetera que volumine toto prosequitur, quanto turpiora sunt, tanto maiori suggillatione carnalem illum inurunt amorem.[22]

The passage from the *Amores* which Salutati has in mind is

---

believe Ovid is commending vice are simply seeing their own reflection in a mirror, not seeing Ovid's poem.

[22] ". . . we have three books by Ovid which are entitled Amores or, as they are commonly called, Without Title. In which, though he does not swerve from his customary sweetness and elegance of style, he sings and describes many turpitudes of love, celebrating as most beautiful disgraceful acts that are known to be most impure. To which I might easily reply, urging what the author himself says, when he refutes objections immediately after the prologue in his first chapter: that he does nothing unless it leads him bound and captive behind the triumphal chariot of love; by this remark suggesting that the servitude of lovers is vile and open, as in many cases, and that the slavery to vices is open and manifest to the eyes of all. And the same for other matters which he pursues throughout the book: the viler they are, the greater the livid marks of mockery by which they brand carnal love." *De Laboribus Herculis*, ed. B. L. Ullman (Turici, 1951), I, 69.

in the second elegy of the first book. Ovid begins the elegy by describing how he is unable to sleep, how he tosses and turns in agony because he is wounded and tormented by the arrow of Love. He considers the possibility of rebelling and refusing to submit to Cupid, but decides that, like an ox or horse, he will be punished less if he bears his burden willingly. And so he tells Cupid that he is a willing captive, painting a little vignette in which he follows Cupid's dove-drawn chariot as a captive slave:

En ego confiteor! tua sum nova praeda, Cupido;
    porrigimus victas ad tua iura manus.
nil opus est bello—veniam pacemque rogamus;
    neo tibi laus armis victus inermis ero;
necte comam myrto, maternas iunge columbas;
    qui deceat, currum vitricus ipse dabit,
inque dato curru, populo clamante triumphum,
    stabis et adiunctas arte movebis aves.
ducentur capti iuvenes captaeque puellae;
    haec tibi magnificus pompa triumphus erit.
ipse ego, praeda recens, factum modo vulnus habebo
    et nova captiva vincula mente feram.
Mens Bona ducetur manibus post terga retortis,
    et Pudor, et castris quidquid Amoris obest.
omnia te metuent; ad te sua bracchia tendens
    vulgus "io" magna voce "triumphe!" canet.
blanditiae comites tibi erunt Errorque Furorque,
    adsidue partes turba secuta tuas.
his tu militibus superas hominesque deosque;
    haec tibi si demas commoda, nudus eris.[23]

[23] "Look, I confess! I am new prey of thine, O Cupid; I stretch forth my hands to be bound, submissive to thy laws. There is no need of war—pardon and peace is my prayer; nor will it be praise for thine arms to vanquish me unarmed. Bind thy locks with the myrtle, yoke thy mother's doves; thy step-sire himself shall give thee fitting car, and in the car he gives shalt thou stand, while the people cry thy triumph, and shalt guide with skill the yoked birds. In thy train shall be captive youths and captive maids; such a pomp will be for thee a stately triumph. Myself, a recent spoil, shall be there with wound all freshly dealt, and bear my new bonds with unresisting heart. Conscience shall be led along, with hands tied fast behind her back, and

What Salutati sees in this passage is ostensible praise of Love, which is ironically undercut by the terms in which the praise is cast. Love is unreasonable, accompanied by Error and Furor; the virtues of modesty and good sense are enemies of love and must be deadened if Cupid is to be served. Love's captives are thus described as the thralls of an evil God, and Ovid employs *vituperatio* by indirection. He is using comic irony to expose the folly of those who deviate from the dictates of reason and morality. Pretending to show that the service of Love is good, he instead shows it to be bad. And the humor is increased because it is at the author's own expense. Throughout the love books Ovid strikes poses which make him the butt of his own jokes; he himself is the negative moral *exemplum*, the model for behavior which should be avoided.

The fourteenth-century adaptations of Jacques d'Amiens, *L'Art d'Amors* and *Li Remedes D'Amors* further suggest that where praise of a virtuous ideal was not explicitly indicated, there was also a tendency to believe that *laus* was present by indirection, that Ovid recommends *caritas* by implication while condemning lust. Since Jacques d'Amiens is adapting rather than translating, he occasionally halts his narrative and pauses briefly to explain what he thinks Ovid really meant. One of the most interesting of these didactic passages appears in Section II of *Li Remedes D'Amors*, where he explains that the word "love" may be used in two senses:

> Amors en II pars est partie:
> amors qui loist et ne loist mie;

Modesty, and all who are foes to the camp of Love. Before thee all shall tremble; the crowd, stretching forth their hands to thee, shall chant with loud voice: 'Ho, Triumph!' Caresses shall be at thy side, and Error and Madness—a rout that ever follows thy train. With soldiers like these dost thou vanquish men and gods; strip from thee aids like these, thou wilt be weaponless." All citations and translations from Ovid herein are from the Loeb Classical Library editions: *Heroides and Amores*, trans. Grant Showerman (London, 1931); *The Art of Love and Other Poems*, trans. J. H. Mozley (London, 1934).

> amors qui loist est carites,
> et, si con dist l'auctorites,
> karites cou est dex meisme;
> celle amors doit estre hautisme
> qui diu meisme est apielee
> par le raison que i'ai moustree.[24]

And he goes on to say that charitable love demands that a man give his love primarily to God, loving Him with all his heart and all his soul and all his power, that a man love his neighbor as himself, and that he keep the commandments. But the other sense of the word "love" refers to love which is contrary to charity:

> Or vous dirai l'autre partie
> de celle amor qui ne loist mie:
> Di com li philosophes dist
> qui cele amor aussi descrist,
> amors est abis de corage,
> a une volente volage,
> acordans a raison contraire;
> si faite amors pas ne doit plaire,
> car contre diu est vraiement. . . .[25]

Sinful love of the second type brings the lover pain, anxiety, and suffering. Ovid, therefore, wished to expose it in order to save men from their profane desires and lead them back to righteous love. The condemnation of *amor* as *cupiditas* carried with it the commendation of *amor* as *caritas*.

Comic irony and moral satire are, then, the hallmarks of the love books of the Renaissance Ovid. These books fall into two sequences; one sequence is encompassed in the

[24] "Love is divided into two parts: love which is allowed, and love which is not allowed at all; charity is permissible love, and, so the authorities say, God Himself is charity; this love ought to be highest, which God Himself has willed, for the reasons I have shown."

[25] "Now I will tell you the other division, of that love which is not permitted at all: as the philosophers who also described this love say, love destroys intentions, tending toward a willful flightiness which is in agreement with topsy-turvy reason; so making love should bring no pleasure, for it is truly against God. . . ."

three books of the *Amores*, where Ovid pretends to narrate the progress of his love affair with Corinna, from the initial triumph of Love to his unhappy discovery that Corinna is equally generous to other lovers. The other sequence results from the combination of the *Ars Amatoria* and the *Remedia Amoris*, the former advising young men and women of the best ways to succeed in love, the latter proposing methods by which they may escape from love. Both sequences have the same general development; they progress from involvement in love to disenchantment with it. They differ in that the *Amores* are narrative and dramatic, the *Ars* and *Remedia* expository and didactic. In the former Ovid himself strikes the pose of the unfortunate lover and pretends to tell of his experiences; in the latter he assumes the position of the sage counselor, pretending to draw upon his vast past experience in order to write a rule book of love. The *Ars* and *Remedia* are precept, the *Amores* example.

In the elegies of the *Amores* the young Ovid indulges in high comedy at his own expense, inviting the reader to laugh with him at the ridiculous situations in which his own impudence and folly place him. Only a naive reader would consider the *Amores* autobiographical, however. Their situations are lifelike, it is true, but they are also too neatly ordered and too extravagant to reflect actual history. In elegy seven of Book III, for example, Ovid tells how he was seized with a fierce longing to make love to Corinna; he rushed to see her, kissed her, clambered into bed with her —only to find, to his intense disgust and Corinna's still greater disgust, that his body was as impotent as his mind was lustful, even though Corinna did her best to arouse him; the annoyed mistress finally rushes off to bathe herself, lest her maid discover what a feeble lover she has. The situation is ridiculous, so ridiculous that few would believe Ovid to be confessing his own experience. The *Amores* are the Augustan equivalent of a slick-paper *True Confessions,* told by a man of wit and intellect, but about as likely to be true.

Part of the comic irony of these elegies arises from Ovid's occasional admissions that he *is* weak and foolish. He pretends that he is frankly telling what has happened to him, admits that his adventures and advances are wrong, hopes that his confession may serve some purpose, but disarmingly adds that he has not the strength to forge ahead on the narrow and rugged path of virtue even though the path of dalliance is sometimes equally rugged and hard:

> Non ego mendosos ausim defendere mores
>> falsaque pro vitiis arma movere meis.
> confiteor—siquid prodest delicta fateri;
>> in mea nunc demens crimina fassus eo.
> odi, nec possum, cupiens, non esse quod odi;
>> heu, quam quae studeas ponere ferre grave est!
> Nam desunt vires ad me mihi iusque regendum;
>> auferor ut rapida concita puppis aqua.[26]

(II.iv.1-8)

The point is, of course, that what the poet says of himself is true of all lovers: all know that lust is wrong, and they indulge their desires out of weakness rather than out of strength. Thus their self-indulgence is ultimately more painful than pleasurable. The admission that reason is a better pilot is not far beneath the surface of the *Amores*.

Another form of irony, related to the irony inherent in the lover's recognition that the lust he pretends to advocate is actually wrong, arises from the inherent contradictions of the arguments he uses to gain his ends. In the second elegy of Book II, for example, he attempts to persuade the eunuch who guards his mistress to close his eyes to the affair they are conducting and open the door to her bedroom. The eunuch refuses, and the poet accuses him of being an in-

---

[26] "I would not venture to defend my faulty morals or to take up the armour of lies to shield my failings. I confess—if owning my shortcomings aught avails; and now, having owned them, I madly assail my sins. I hate what I am, and yet, for all my desiring, I cannot but be what I hate; ah, how hard to bear the burden you long to lay aside! For I lack the strength and will to rule myself; I am swept along like a ship tossed on the rushing flood."

former, insidiously adding that informers bring nothing but trouble both to themselves and to lovers:

> vidi ego conpedibus liventia crura gerentem,
>   unde vir incestum scire coactus erat.
> poena minor merito. nocuit mala lingua duobus;
>   vir doluit, famae damna puella tulit.
> crede mihi, nulli sunt crimina grata marito,
>   nec quemquam, quamvis audiat, illa iuvant.
> seu tepet, indicium securas prodis ad aures;
>   sive amat, officio fit miser ille tuo.[27]

(47-54)

The persuasive lover is, of course, attempting to place the blame on the informer when it is obvious that it instead falls squarely on the partners to the love affair. And, without really wishing to, he admits that such affairs are really wrong and notes one reason why they are wrong: "vir doluit, famae damna puella tulit." Having made this admission, he contradicts it only a few lines later when he protests that the indulgence of lust is totally innocent and modest:

> Non scelus adgredimur, non ad miscenda coimus
>   toxica, non stricto fulminat ense manus.
> quaerimus, ut tuto per te possimus amare.
>   quid precibus nostris mollius esse potest?[28]

(63-66)

The very imagery he uses to suggest that lust is harmless implies that it is not, that it may instead by predatory, violent, and dangerous. In spite of the ingenuity of the lover's

---

[27] "I have seen in shackles the livid legs of a man who had forced a husband to know himself a cuckold. The punishment was less than he deserved. His evil tongue brought harm to two; the husband suffered grief, the wife the loss of her good name. Believe me, accusations are welcome to no husband, nor do they please him, even though he hear. If he is cool, you bring your traitorous tales to careless ears; if he loves, your service only makes him wretched."

[28] " 'Tis no crime we are entering on; we are not coming together to mingle poisons; no drawn sword flashes in our hands. What we ask is that you will give us the means to love in safety. What can be more modest than our prayers?"

arguments, the guard is not won over. For the arguments are ultimately self-contradictory and self-destroying.

Nor does self-contradiction occur only within individual arguments. The *Amores* are full of high comedy at the expense of the lover, comedy which arises from the incompatible poses which he strikes as the occasion warrants. He continually reveals himself to be an unethical Machiavellian, albeit a gay one, a devious liar, albeit a courageous one. Quite early in his courtship of Corinna, he presents himself to her as follows:

> Accipe, per longos tibi qui deserviat annos;
>   accipe, qui pura norit amare fide!
> si me non veterum commendant magna parentum
>   nomina, si nostri sanguinis auctor eques,
> nec meus innumeris renovatur campus aratris,
>   temperat et sumptus parcus uterque parens—
> at Phoebus comitesque novem vitisque repertor
>   hac faciunt, et me qui tibi donat, Amor,
> et nulli cessura fides, sine crimine mores
>   nudaque simplicitas purpureusque pudor.
> non mihi mille placent, non sum desultor amoris:
>   tu mihi, siqua fides, cura perennis eris.[29]

(ɪ.iii.5-15)

Later, in the fourth elegy of Book ɪɪ, upon which Donne drew for the "I can love both fair and brown" of *The Indifferent*, the lover indicates that he would have been closer to the truth had he said "mihi mille placet." Or again, when his mistress suspects him of an affair with her maid, he defends himself in tones of outraged innocence:

---

[29] "Take one who would be your slave through long years; take one who knows how to love with pure faith! If I have not ancient ancestry and a great name to commend me, if the author of my line was but a knight, and my fields are not renewed with ploughshares numberless, if both my parents guard frugally their spending—yet Phoebus and his nine companions and the finder of the vine are on my side, and so is Love, who makes me his gift to you, and I have good faith that will yield to none, and ways without reproach, and unadorned simplicity, and blushing modesty. I am not smitten with a thousand—I am no flit-about in love. . . ."

Ecce novum crimen! sollers ornare Cypassis
   obicitur dominae contemerasse torum.
di melius, quam me, si sit peccasse libido,
   sordida contemptae sortis amica iuvet! . . .
per Venerem iuro puerique volatilis arcus,
   me non admissi criminis esse reum![30]

(II.vii.17-20, 27-28)

Thus the seventh elegy concludes. The eighth begins:

Ponendis in mille modos perfecta capillis,
   comere sed solas digna, Cypassi, deas,
et mihi iucundo non rustica cognita furto,
   apta quidem dominae, sed magis apta mihi—
quis fuit internos sociati corporis index?
   sensit concubitus unde Corinna tuos?[31]

(II.viii.1-6)

The irony of such juxtapositions—and there are many more besides those mentioned above—exposes the character of the lover as lacking in both *simplicitas* and *pudor*. Daringly impudent, but bungling even in his audacity, he is more laughable than admirable.

Most comic of all, however, are the ironies which expose the ultimate futility of Ovid's affair with Corinna. He begins it, as we have seen, with protestations of undying fidelity. But these alone are not enough to keep the relationship alive, and the lover wishes to do more with Corinna than give her adoring worship. But once Corinna has yielded, dangers become apparent. She begins to consider the pos-

---

[30] "And look now, a fresh charge! Cypassis, the deft girl that tires your hair, is cast at me, accused of wronging her mistress' couch. Ye gods grant me better, if I have a mind to sin, than find my pleasure in a love of mean and despised lot! . . . By Venus I swear, and by the bows of her winged boy, I am not guilty of the charge you bring!"

[31] "Perfect in setting hair aright in a thousand ways, but worthy to dress only that of goddesses, Cypassis, you whom I have found in our stolen delight not only wholly simple, apt for your mistress' service, but more apt for mine—who is the tattler has told of our coming together? Where did Corinna get wind of your affair with me?"

44

sibility of becoming a courtesan, since that profession provides both wealth and pleasure (I.viii, I.x). The poet, a poor scholar, cannot afford to pay for his pleasure, and he is faced with the threat that richer men than he may be more successful in seduction. Later his mistress becomes pregnant and nearly kills herself by attempting abortion (II.xiii, II.xiv). Finally, the truth is out. Corinna is as committed to the joys of lust as her lover himself, and she is also as unfaithful to him as he is to her. Faced with the logical consequence to which his own Machiavellian philosophy of love leads, he does not find it either attractive or pleasant. He has lost at his own game, converted his mistress to his own position, and made of himself a cuckolded lover. He is now disillusioned with love and disgusted at the degradation it has produced in him; he resolves to abandon it:

Multa diuque tuli; vitiis patientia victa est;
    cede fatigato pectore, turpis amor!
scilicet adserui iam me fugique catenas,
    et quae non puduit ferre, tulisse pudet.
vicimus et domitum pedibus calcamus amorem;
    venerunt capiti cornua sera meo.
perfer et obdura! dolor hic tibi proderit olim;
    saepe tulit lassis sucus amarus opem.
Ergo ego sustinui, foribus tam saepe repulsus,
    ingenuum dura ponere corpus humo?
ergo ego nescio cui, quem tu conplexa tenebas,
    excubui clausam servus ut ante domum?
vidi, cum foribus lassus prodiret amator,
    invalidum referens emeritumque latus;
hoc tamen est levius, quam quod sum visus ab illo—
    eveniat nostris hostibus ille pudor![32]

(II.xi.a.1-16)

[32] "Much have I endured, and for long time; my wrongs have overcome my patience; withdraw from my tired-out breast, base love! Surely, now I have claimed my freedom, and fled my fetters, ashamed of having borne what I felt no shame while bearing. Victory is mine, and I tread under foot my conquered love; courage has entered my heart, though late. Persist, and endure! this smart will some day

And he concludes his resolution with self-congratulation: "non ego sum stultus, ut ante fui!"[33] But the irony of his discovery that he has been a fool for committing himself to lust is not the final irony of the *Amores*. The last turn is given when he makes the further discovery that he cannot stop loving his mistress after all, that he has become too involved to escape. He does not even plead with her to abandon her other lovers; he only asks that she pretend, for his sake, that she doesn't have them:

> indue cum tunicis metuentem crimina vultum,
> et pudor obscenum diffiteatur opus;
> da populo, da verba mihi; sine nescius errem,
> et liceat stulta credulitate frui! . . .
> mens abit et morior quotiens peccasse fateris,
> perque meos artus frigida gutta fluit.
> tunc amo, tunc odi frustra quod amare necesse est. . . .[34]

(III.xiv.27-30, 37-39)

Thus he makes of himself an even greater fool than he once was. The love which once seemed so full of pleasure is now compromised by pain. Corinna is a mirror image of himself, and the reflection is not a pleasant one.

In the *Ars Amatoria* and *Remedia Amoris* the pretense is different, but comic irony remains pervasive. The *Ars* pretends to provide precepts for succeeding in love, but, as in

---

bring thee good; oft has bitter potion brought help to the languishing. Can it be I have endured it—to be so oft repulsed from your doors, and to lay my body down, a free born man, on the hard ground? Can it be that, for some no one you held in your embrace, I have lain, like a slave keeping vigil, before your tight-closed home? I have seen when the lover came forth from your doors fatigued, with frame exhausted and weak from love's campaign; yet this is a slighter thing than being seen by him—may shame like that befall my enemies!"

[33] "I am not a fool, as I once was!" (III.xi.a.32)

[34] "Put on with your dress a face that shrinks from guilt, and let a modest aspect deny the harlot's trade. Cheat the people, cheat me; allow me to mistake through ignorance, to enjoy a fool's belief in you. . . . My mind fails me and I suffer death each time you confess your sin, and through my frame the blood runs cold. Then do I love you, then try in vain to hate what I love perforce. . . ."

the *Amores,* the arguments for lust are continually undercut by ironic techniques of juxtaposition and self-contradiction. And as in the *Amores* lust is exposed as dangerous, vicious, foolish, and debasing. But whereas the lover of the *Amores* remained caught in the net which he had woven for himself, Ovid provides in the *Remedia* a set of rules by which lovers can escape from their folly. The *Ars* pretends to present positive precepts, which turn out to be negative instead; the *Remedia* contains negative precepts which are actually positive.

The program of these love books is threefold: first, to explain how love can be won; second, to treat the more difficult problem of how love can be kept once it has been won; and third, to suggest ways in which love can be remedied when the lover is unsuccessful or disillusioned. The first and second books of the *Ars* treat the first two problems from the man's side; its third book provides precepts for women on these subjects. Part three of the program is, of course, the province of the *Remedia.* Ovid's solution of these three major problems in love might be summarized as follows: Love is (1) won by lies and deception; (2) kept by humiliation and self-deception; (3) remedied by strength of will and reason. These basic rules do not differ radically from those which the lover of the *Amores* applied —or did not apply in the case of the third. The art of love in either book is artifice.

The precepts on winning love are characterized by duplicity, cynicism, and frank naturalism. Ultimately, however, Ovid's pose of frank realism is used to suggest that love is more dangerous and devious than desirable; for he often juxtaposes a cynical precept with an illustrative example which undercuts it, a precept advocating duplicity with a hint that women as well as men can practice deception. He advises the shy lover, for example, that women are more lustful and passionate than men; they only seem less lusty because they are better dissemblers:

> Utque viro furtiva venus, sic grata puellae:
> Vir male dissimulat: tectius illa cupit.

Conveniat maribus, nequam nos ante rogemus,
  Femina iam partes victa rogantis agat.
Mollibus in pratis admugit femina tauro;
  Femina cornipedi semper adhinnit equo.
Parcior in nobis nec tam furiosa libido:
  Legitimum finem flamma virilis habet.[35]

(1.275-282)

And he goes on to illustrate his cynical counsel with a series of examples: Byblis, Myrrha, Pasiphae, Aerope, Medea, and Phaedra; each of these women loves violently, and their affairs are tainted by death and brutality. Ovid concludes:

Omnia feminea sunt ista libidine mota;
  Acrior est nostra, plusque furoris habet.
Ergo age, ne dubita cunctas sperare puellas. . . .[36]

(1.341-343)

It would take a hardy and enthusiastic lover to seek out feminine lust after such precepts and examples; they suggest that impassioned lust is dangerous, and women's lust is especially dangerous; there is heavy irony in the ingenuously understated conclusion of line 343; the conclusion which seems to follow from the examples is not *age*, but *fuge*.

Once the lover accepts Ovid's advice that all women want to yield, his next step is to persuade the woman of his choice that *she* should yield to *him*. In taking this step, the lover's best allies are lies and deception. Above all, he must promise gifts that he will never give and commend her on a beauty that she does not have. The latter is perhaps easier, since women are vain and will believe the most outrageous

[35] "And as stolen love is pleasant to a man, so is it also to a woman; the man dissembles badly: she conceals desire better. Did it suit us males not to ask any woman first, the woman, already won, would play the asker. In soft meads the heifer lows to the bull, the mare always whinnies to the horn-footed steed. In us desire is stronger, yet not so frantic: the manly flame knows a lawful bound."

[36] "All those crimes were prompted by women's lust; keener is it than ours, and has more of madness. Come then, doubt not that you may win all women. . . ."

lies about their loveliness. The art of promising is much more dangerous, for women are as wily and greedy as men: "invenit artem/ Femina, qua cupidi carpat amantis opes."[37] Only a skilled craftsman in the art of love will manage to win his beloved over without giving her a gift.

But such cynical advice is constantly undercut by admissions that there are, after all, moral standards which should be honored; they simply do not apply to love:

> ... innocue vivite: numen adest;
> Reddite depositum; pietas sua foedera servet:
>   Fraus absit; vacuas caedis habete manus.
> Ludite, si sapitis, solas impune puellas:
>   Hac minus est una fraude tuenda fides.
> Fallite fallentes: ex magna parte profanum
>   Sunt genus: in laqueos quos posuere, cadant.[38]
>
> (1.640-646)

Not only does this passage remind Ovid's reader that virtue is better than vice, but it also implies that moral standards apply to love as well as to the rest of life. The surface statement is, of course, that the wise man is moral in everything except love. But Ovid goes on to justify deception and dishonesty in love because it gives women their just deserts; since they lie and deceive, they should be repaid in kind. And this justification of masculine deception, based as it is on the assumption that deception in love is wrong and deserves to be punished, leads only to the conclusion that the man who deceives in love also is doing wrong and deserves to be punished. Deception, apparently advocated, is revealed instead as a vicious circle; both partners will deceive and both will be punished by being caught in the other's trap.

---

[37] "A woman knows the way to fleece an eager lover of his wealth." (1.419-420)

[38] ". . . live innocently, gods are nigh; return what is given to your keeping; let duty keep her covenant; let fraud be absent; keep your hands clean of blood. If you are wise, cheat women only, and avoid trouble; keep faith save for this one deceitfulness. Deceive the deceivers; they are mostly an unrighteous sort; let them fall into the snare which they have laid."

When Ovid gives his precepts on keeping love once it has been won, the irony only increases. The lover seems indeed to be caught in a trap, and Ovid humorously describes ways in which he may catch himself still more inextricably. Nor does Ovid pretend that love is not often painful, humiliating and futile; but once caught, the lover cannot bear to give up the thing which punishes him; and Ovid mockingly advises him to be brave and persist while simultaneously implying that love is not worth the burdens and misery which such persistence produces:

> Credita non semper sulci cum foenore reddunt,
>> Nec semper dubias adiuvat aura rates;
> Quod iuvat, exiguum, plus est, quod laedat amantes;
>> Proponant animo multa ferenda suo.
> Quot lepores in Atho, quot apes pascuntur in Hybla,
>> Caerula quot bacas Palladis arbor habet,
> Littore quot conchae, tot sunt in amore dolores;
>> Quae patimur, multo spicula felle madent.
> Dicta erit isse foras, quam tu fortasse videbis:
>> Isse foras, et te falsa videre puta.
> Clausa tibi fuerit promissa ianua nocte;
>> Perfer et inmunda ponere corpus humo. . . .
> Nec maledicta puta, nec verbera ferre puellae
>> Turpe, nec ad teneros oscula ferre pedes.[39]

(II.513-524, 533-534)

As in the *Amores*, the lover discovers that in order to hold his beloved, he must deceive himself about the quality of

---

[39] "Not always do the furrows repay their trust with interest, not always does the wind assist perplexed vessels; what aids lovers is but little, more there is to thwart them; let them make up their minds to many a trial. As many as the hares that feed on Athos, or the bees on Hybla, as many as the berries that the blue-gray tree of Pallas bears, or the shells that are on the shore, so many are the pains of love; the darts that wound us are steeped in poison. She will be said to have gone abroad, though you perchance will see her: believe she has gone, and that your eyes deceive you. On the promised night her door will be shut against you: endure to lay your body even on unclean ground. . . . Think it not shameful to endure a woman's abuse or blows, nor to give kisses to her tender feet."

her love for him and endure humiliation patiently. Having practiced deception and dishonesty in order to acquire his mistress, he must practice self-deception in order to keep her; for the wheel has now swung around, and she has an opportunity to deceive a lover whom she knows she has trapped.

The wheel swings most rapidly when the man has been unfaithful to his mistress. In his usual ingenuous manner, Ovid tells lovers that he believes promiscuity to be a good thing, normal and natural for both men and women. *He* would be the last one to advocate constancy in love; he only advocates prudence in inconstancy:

> Nec mea vos uni damnat censura puellae:
>> Di melius! vix hoc nupta tenere potest.
> Ludite, sed furto celetur culpa modesto:
>> Gloria peccati nulla petenda sui est.
> Nec dederis munus, cognosse quod altera possit,
>> Nec sint nequitiae tempora certa tuae.[40]
>
> (II.387-392)

But only a few lines later he admits that the reason for prudence in promiscuity is that the inconstant lover is always punished, and justly punished:

> Laesa Venus iusta arma movet, telumque remittit,
>> Et, modo quod questa est, ipse querare, facit.[41]
>
> (II.397-398)

Promiscuity is revealed to be as dangerous as lust, for the lover will be made to feel the pain which he has inflicted on the mistress to whom he has been unfaithful; following his example, she will practice promiscuity as well. The unfaithful lover will soon find himself a cuckolded lover. Again, Ovid's advice is full of contradiction and of irony.

[40] "Yet my ruling does not condemn you to one woman alone: heaven forfend! even a young bride can hardly secure this. Have your sport, but let modest deception veil the fault; seek no vainglory from your sin. Give no gift whereof the other might learn, and have no fixed seasons for your wantonness."

[41] "Venus when injured wages righteous war, and flings the weapon back; she makes you complain yourself of what she complained of but now."

Having revealed the humiliation and folly to which lustful love leads, Ovid describes in the *Remedia* the ways by
which a lover can escape from the source of his pain. But
before he begins to describe various kinds of remedies, he
gives the best advice of all: the wise lover will stop love before it starts. He will pause to consider what pain lust
brings, and such reasonable honesty will prevent him from
indulging in it at all:

> Quale sit id, quod amas, celeri circumspice mente,
>   Et tua laesure subtrahe colla iugo.
> Principiis obsta; sero medicina paratur,
>   Cum mala per longas convaluere moras.
> Sed propera, nec te venturas differ in horas;
>   Qui non est hodie, eras minus aptus erit. . . .[42]
>
> (89-94)

But for those lovers who have not practiced such wisdom,
Ovid suggests a series of slower and more difficult remedies
which will help them to escape from the quagmire in which
they are caught. First and foremost, they should keep busy;
love thrives on idleness, and it dies quickly in the heart of
the lover who turns his attention to practical and worldly
affairs. Secondly, the lover may take a long trip so that he
can no longer see the woman who tortures him; once he is
no longer near her, his passion will begin to die. Thirdly,
he should avoid thinking or talking about his mistress, and
when he does think of her, he should meditate upon her
flaws and upon the pain which she causes him. Finally, if he
is still too caught in his passion, he should look for another
mistress and vent it on her; this final piece of advice is somewhat ironic, however, since it only proposes a new disease
as a remedy for an old one. Ovid admits that much of his
advice will seem drastic to lovers, since they hate to escape

---

[42] "Consider in swift thought what kind of thing it is you love, and
withdraw your neck from a yoke that may one day gall. Resist begin-
nings; too late is the medicine prepared, when the disease has gained
strength by long delay. Ay, and make haste, nor wait on the coming
hours; he who is not ready to-day will be less so to-morrow. . . ."

from love nearly as much as they want to; and he advises them, if they find his precepts too hard, to continue indulging their passions if they cannot tear themselves away; if they indulge themselves long enough, they will become dissatisfied with love of their own accord, for "copia tollat amorem" ("abundance destroys love," 541). As all the love books of Ovid attempt to suggest, an intense acquaintance with lust is enough to cure anyone of it.

The Roman Ovid and the Renaissance Ovid probably are not dramatically different at all. When he describes his affair with Corinna or gives lessons on the art of love, the Roman Ovid is unquestionably writing tongue in cheek at least part of the time, as his careful control of ironic juxtaposition suggests. The Renaissance reader probably carried these hints a bit further and saw a subtle moral purpose in his ironies: they were intended to point up the inconsistencies and contradictions which characterize lustful love, the follies and humiliations which lustful lovers endure, so that men would avoid it and would find a better kind of love instead. Ovid was a moral satirist, and to imitate Ovid meant to write of sexual passion, usually with satiric undertones.

iii The Petrarchan Strand

Critical commonplace has taught us to think of Ovidianism and Petrarchanism as two vastly different poetic modes, and indeed they are. But they also have important things in common. They are restricted to the same subject matter, love. More particularly, they both follow the same plot line, for they both describe a way in which love may be abused and a way in which its abuse may be rectified or remedied. In other words, their subject is profane love and its correction. More important, however, the Renaissance reader thought they shared not only the same subject matter, but also the same attitude toward that subject matter. Both were then read from the perspective of Christian moral theology, and both were thought to express its assumptions about the nature and purpose of love: profane love should be corrected because it draws man's love away from God and turns it instead toward earthly objects to an inordinate and excessive degree. So aware were sixteenth-century readers of these resemblances that commentators on Petrarch quoted or referred to passages in Ovid in order to illuminate or explain passages in the *Canzoniere*.[43] Thus we must, to some extent, readjust our thinking and see Ovidianism and Petrarchanism as complementary rather than opposed to one another.

But they also have important areas of unlikeness which enable them to complement one another. In the first place, they differ in emphasis; although Renaissance readers believed that both Ovid and Petrarch condemned sinful love, it was perfectly clear that Ovid was more concerned with abuses of physical love (or lust) and Petrarch with spiritual abuses (or idolatry), although neither dealt with one exclusively. And in the second place, Petrarch and Ovid show a considerable difference in tone and technique. Petrarch writes under the aegis of the tragic mask and Ovid under the comic, although both put the same plot on the boards. Ovid is satiric and ironic where Petrarch is serious and straightforward; Ovid deals in giggles and Petrarch in sighs and tears; Ovid would correct by indirection and Petrarch by direction. But far from being incompatible, taken together these two traditions cover the whole range of possibilities for dramatizing profane love.

Much of the confusion which arises in discussions of Renaissance love poetry seems to derive from a loose usage of the phrase "Petrarchan love." Ubiquitous as Petrarchanism was in the sixteenth century (the *Canzoniere* alone went through eighty-seven editions), we ought to be fairly precise; and if we are to be precise about what the *Canzoniere* meant to those who imitated it or rebelled against its conventions, then we need to consult those many six-

---

[43] See, e.g.: Giovanni Andrea Gesualdo, *Il Petrarca con l'espositione di m. Giovanni Andrea Gesvaldo* . . . (Venetia, 1581), 15v, 23r, 46v, and *passim*; Alessandro Vellutello, *Il Petrarcha con l'espositione d'Alessandro Vellvtello* . . . (Venetia, 1532), 1v, 15r, 26r, 55r, 88r, 128r, and *passim*.

teenth-century editions of it which contained commentaries.[44] When we do so, we discover that part of the ambiguity and elusiveness of "Petrarchan love" results from the assumption that there is a single entity which those two words describe. There is not simply one kind of Petrarchan love; there are several, for the story of love told in the *Canzoniere* is a developing one, not a static one. This series of songs and sonnets was understood in the Renaissance as a description of the way in which sinful love could gradually be transformed into holy love. Thus it is most profitable to distinguish between two basic kinds of "Petrarchan love."

Initially the love which Petrarch feels for Laura is of the type which modern theologians would call *eros*, which Petrarch and his immediate posterity would call inordinate and sinful passion or idolatry, and which I shall call "profane Petrarchan love." It is a violent and restless love, incapable of satisfaction, deaf to reason, close to madness. Although the lover recognizes that his feeling is sinful and offers only the alternatives of damnation or repentance, he is for a long time so completely consumed by it that he is unable to conquer it and achieve repentance. This emotional conflict is the most characteristic quality of profane Petrarchan love, and, consequently, its most characteristic mood is misery and unhappiness, expressed through sighs and tears.

In the *Secretum Meum*, three confessional dialogues between himself and St. Augustine which Petrarch wrote before the death of Laura but which were not published until

[44] The meaning of the *Canzoniere* was expounded and explicated by four major sixteenth-century commentators—Dolce, Gesualdo, Bembo, and Vellutello. I refer chiefly to Vellutello, however, because his edition was by far the most popular; it went through twenty-one editions. All four editors follow the standard practice of the time; they print each poem and then comment on it at length. Most sixteenth-century editions of Petrarch had this kind of commentary, and thus we can assume with some safety that the reader would know the standard learned interpretation as well as the text. In *Il Petrarchismo Italiano nel Cinquecento* (Milan and Naples, 1957), Luigi Baldacci discusses the various commentaries in some detail.

after his death, the attitude toward profane love which informs the *Canzoniere* is clarified. For in the third dialogue, Petrarch discusses his love with Augustine, and the latter carefully explains to him why it is sinful. As in the other two dialogues, the discussion is somewhat comic, for Petrarch consistently believes himself to be more virtuous than he actually is, and the wise and clever Augustine consistently reveals the weakness of his arguments and the extent of his error and self-deception; throughout the dialogues Augustine is represented as a guide to Truth who has been sent to illuminate the mind of the erring Petrarch. Thus he exposes Petrarch's pretense that his love is good by saying:

> Nothing so much leads a man to forget and despise God as the love of things temporal, and most of all this passion that we call love; and to which, by the greatest of all desecrations, we even gave the name of God, without doubt only that we may throw a heavenly veil over our human follies and make a pretext of divine inspiration when we want to commit an enormous transgression.[45]

Augustine is not, of course, condemning all human love, but only that form which pretends to be holy and sacred and is not. More explicitly, Petrarch's error is that his love is inordinate and idolatrous: he has loved Laura more than God Himself, thus inverting the moral order of the universe. Augustine accuses:

> She has detached your mind from the love of heavenly things and has inclined your heart to love the creature more than the Creator: and that one path alone leads, sooner than any other, to death.
> *Petrarch.* I pray you make no rash judgment. The love which I feel for her has most certainly led me to love God.

[45] *Petrarch's Secret*, trans. William H. Draper (London, 1911), 131-132.

S. Augustine. But it has inverted the true order.

Petrarch. How so?

S. Augustine. Because every creature should be dear to us because of our love for the Creator. But in your case, on the contrary, held captive by the charm of the creature, you have not loved the Creator as you ought.

(124-125)

And finally, Augustine points out the misery, sorrow, and pain which Petrarch's dedication to love has brought him, and says "If all this seems to you the token of but a moderate passion, then at least I shall be quite certain you are the victim of no moderate delusion" (136). As we shall see, the conflict between Augustine and Petrarch in the *Secretum* is the same as that which occurs in the *Canzoniere*; and the conflict is resolved in the same way in both works: Petrarch is eventually converted to the Augustinian position.

Within the *Canzoniere*, Petrarch's reformation and re-direction of his love for Laura occurs only after her death, when he is deprived of the source of his temptation; only then does he manage at last to achieve completely his liberation from sinful love and substitute for it love of God. In this second form of love, which we might call "holy Petrarchan love," his love for Laura is not totally banished; rather, the lover gradually recognizes that her love for God and her goodness and virtue should be an example to him, and thus his love for her aids the transformation of his feeling. But through her death he is taught the lesson of *contemptus mundi*, and he recognizes that love must be directed toward immortal things, such as the image of God which was reflected in her. His first kind of love for Laura is *cupiditas*. The second kind of love, directed toward her piety and goodness and ultimately toward God Himself, is *caritas*. Both are typical of the "Petrarchan lover," but the former is that of the Petrarchan lover in his early unre-deemed state and the latter that of the Petrarchan lover whose passion has been purified and made holy.

We can observe the operation of the early profane form of Petrarchan love in the second sonnet in the *Canzoniere,* where the poet describes in retrospect how love once struck him unawares:

Per fare una leggiadra sua vendetta,
E punire in un dí ben mille offese,
Celatamente Amor l'arco riprese,
Come uom ch'a nocer luogo e tempo aspetta.

Era la mia virtute al cor ristretta
Per far ivi e ne gli occhi sue difese,
Quando 'l colpo mortal lá giú discese,
Ove solea spuntarsi ogni saetta.

Però, turbata nel primiero assalto,
Non ebbe tanto né vigor né spazio
Che potesse al bisogno prender l'arme,

O vero al poggio faticoso et alto
Ritrarmi accortamente da lo strazio,
Del quale oggi verrebbe, e non pò, aitarme.[46]

The commentator Vellutello reads this sonnet as the poet's account of the way he fell prey to "lo suo amoroso errore,"

---

[46] To make a charming vengeance of some blow
And punish in one day a long disgrace,
Surreptitiously Love resumed his bow
Like one who to do harm bides time and place.

My virtue was constrained inside my heart
To raise there its defence, and in the eyes,
When the mortal attempt struck by surprise
Where used to be defeated every dart.

Therefore, bewildered in the first assault,
It did not find enough vigour or room
To emerge all in arms and face its doom,

Or to draw me to the high difficult
Hill shrewdly, away from the agony
From which it would but cannot rescue me.

All citations from Petrarch's *Canzoniere* are taken from *Petrarch: Sonnets and Songs,* translated by Anna Maria Armi. Copyright 1946 by Pantheon Books, Inc., reprinted by permission of Random House, Inc. I have also followed this edition's method of numbering the songs and sonnets.

Vellutello's favorite phrase to describe Petrarchan love in its profane stage; he says that it tells "how the poet became oppressed by the insidiousness of love" and describes the way in which concupiscible and irrational love attacks a man so that he falls prey to "passioni e perturbationi"; Vellutello summarizes the moral as follows:

> Soleua prima nel suo cuore ogni saetta spuntarsi, perche ad ogni altro amore haueua sempre, mediante la sua virtu, dato repulsa. La qual virtu, in altro non consiste, che in repugnar ad ogni dishonesto e non ragioneuole appetito. Ne maggiori difese contra di quelli possiamo far al cuore che reconciliarlo ben con Dio, come uuol Il. Poe. inferire, ch' egli, essendo ne giorni santi, uoleua fare. Ne quali almeno, ogni buon Christiano debbe quanto puo a suoi passati errori cercar di rimediare, e giusto 'l suo potere por freno a quelli, ne quali per l'auenir potrebbe incorrere.[47]

Later Vellutello says in his discussion of sonnet LXV that the poet made his great mistake in not finding a remedy for his love at the very beginning instead of letting it grow into an almost incorrigible habit, and he cites Ovid's *Remedia Amoris* as justification for his view that love is best nipped in the bud before it burgeons. (55r)

Petrarch's love for Laura in its early stages is, then, profane because it is excessively passionate, irrational, and inordinate. More particularly, however, it is profane because it involves both lust and idolatry. At one moment the poet says:

[47] "Formerly he used to blunt every arrow in his heart, because to every other love he had, by means of his virtue, given repulse. The which virtue consists in nothing other than in repudiating every dishonest and unreasonable appetite. We are able to make the greatest defense against these in our heart by reconciling it well with God, as the poet means, it being a holy day, he wished to do. In these ways at least, every good Christian ought, as much as possible, to remedy his past sins and justly [use] his power to restrain those which he may commit in the future." Vellutello, *op.cit.*, 3r.

... mi nacque un ghiaccio
Nel core; et evvi ancóra,
E sará sempre fin ch'i' le sia in braccio.[48]

(CXIX)

And the poet is frequently lost in admiration of his lady's physical beauty in his early days, perhaps just as frequently as he admires her spiritual beauty. Lust is not, however, his chief sin, and it is only a minor theme in the *Canzoniere*.

More serious is the sin of idolatry which he recognizes that he has committed after Laura's death has convinced him that the object of his worship was but a mortal thing:

Quel ch'i' fo, veggio, e non m'inganna il vero
Mal conosciuto, anzi mi sforza Amore,
Che la strada d'onore
Mai no 'l lassa seguir chi troppo il crede;
E sento ad ora ad or venirmi al core
Un leggiadro disdegno, aspro e severo,
Ch'ogni occulto pensero
Tira in mezzo la fronte, ov'altri 'l vede;
Ché mortal cosa amar con tanta fede,
Quanta a Dio sol per debito convensi,
Più si disdice a chi più pregio brama.
E questo al alta voce anco richiama
La ragione sviata dietro a i sensi:
Ma perch'ell'oda, e pensi
Tornare, il mal costume oltre la spigne,
Et a gli occhi depigne
Quella che sol per farmi morir nacque,
Perch'a me troppo, et a se stessa, piacque.[49]

(Stanza 6, Canzone CCLXIV)

[48] ... in my heart an ice rose high,
An ice that here is grown
And here shall grow till in her arms I lie.
[49] I see what happens, nor am I deceived
By a mistaken truth, but pushed by Love
Who closes the road of
Honour to those who toward him have been
Too faithful, and at each hour comes to move

Vellutello interprets this stanza as meaning just what it says, that the Love by which the poet was pushed was an amorous error which he now repents, and that it was an error because it was excessive and inordinate:

> . . . dice sentirsi adhor adhor uenir al cuore, un leggiadro, aspro e seuero sdegno, il qual li fa dimostrar nel uolto, ou' altri puo uedere, il desiderio ch'egli ha di potersi dal suo amoroso error liberare. Perche amar con tanta fede cosa mortale, quanto per debito solamento si conuien a Dio, come uuol inferire che da lui M. L. amata era, piu si disdice a chi brama piu pregio. . . .[50]

Petrarch's love for Laura, although it does occasionally express itself in a desire for physical consummation, is far from promiscuous. "Petrarchan love" is limited to one woman, and hence Petrarch sings the praises of Laura and Laura alone over a period of twenty-one years. Such fidelity to one woman is not inherently wrong, of course; what makes it wrong in this case is that initially the spirit in which the fidelity is given is sinful. In the early stages of his love the poet made a god of his beloved and gave her the fidelity

---

> My heart to gentle scorn severe and grieved
> Which brings my thoughts above,
> On my forehead where my secrets are seen:
> To love a mortal thing beyond the mean,
> With a faith that to God only pertains
> Is less becoming when praise we desire.
> And this does with loud voice also require
> That reason bear the senses' chains;
> But although it does mean
> To return, the bad custom drives it on,
> And paints to it like sun
> One who was born only to make me die
> Because she pleased to mine and to her eye.

[50] "He says that from hour to hour he feels come to his heart a graceful, sharp, and severe disdain, which also shows itself in his face, where others may see it, the desire that he has to be able to free himself from his error in love. For to love a mortal thing with so much faith, which is appropriate only to God (as he means Madonna Laura was loved by him), is still more unbecoming to those who more wish praise . . ." (105v).

which he should have given only to God. The error of such idolatry is one of the main themes of the *Canzoniere*.

In the early parts of the *Canzoniere*, which deal with the condition of profane love, a major subsidiary theme is the conflict between reason and passion. Much of the lover's misery derives from this conflict, for he is pulled in two directions by two powerful and opposing standards of value. Reason recognizes the sinful nature of his love and urges repentance, and yet passion overcomes this reasonable demand. Sometimes this conflict is dramatized as a struggle between heart and soul, as in the following sonnet, which takes place after an attempted but unsuccessful rebellion against the blind god of love:

> Fuggendo la pregione ove Amor m'ebbe
> Molt'anni a far di me quel ch'a lui parve,
> Donne mio, lungo fôra a ricontrarve
> Quanto la nova libertá m'increbbe.
>
> Diceami il cor che per sé non saprebbe
> Viver un giorno; e poi tra via m'apparve
> Quel traditore in sí mentite larve
> Che piú saggio di me inganato avrebbe.
>
> Onde piú volte sospirando in dietro
> Dissi:—Oimè!, il giogo e le catene e i ceppi
> Eran piú dolci che l'andare sciolto.—
>
> Misero me, che tardo il mio mal seppi!
> E con quanta fatica oggi mi spetro
> De l'errore ov'io stesso m'era involto![51]
>
> (LXXXIX)

[51]   Fleeing the prison where Love made me wait
So many years, only his whim to please,
Ladies, it would be tedious to relate
How this new freedom deepened my unease.
The heart was telling me that such a task
It could not bear; then I saw him go by,

62

The yoke is sweet and yet he knows it is wrong to bear it; he tries to cast it off and yet cannot because he has let his love grow too great, greater than the reason which should conquer it. Still able to recognize his state of sin, too weak to do anything about it, and yet fully aware that he alone is responsible for his miserable condition, he can only shout cries of pain.

Not only must the poet suffer because he is aware of his state of error and sin, but he must also suffer because the lady refuses to return his love. At rare moments her disdain produces a complementary scorn in him, which would aid him in remedying his condition if he persisted in it:

> Femina è cosa mobil per natura;
> Ond'io so ben ch'un amoroso stato
> In cor di donna picciol tempo dura.[52]

> (CLXXXIII)

But such *contemptus feminae* is infrequent. More often the lover is simply made miserable by her refusals. He weeps, sighs, and protests that her scorn will kill him:

> Né, però che con atti acerbi e rei
> Del mio ben pianga e del mio pianger rida,
> Poría cangiar sol un de' pensier mei.

> The betrayer, in such a deceptive mask,
> That would have seduced one wiser far than I.
> Hence often sighing behind him I said:
> —Ah me! the yoke, the fetters and the chains
> Were sweeter than to go without your reins.—
> Unlucky, that too late I knew my ill!
> How painfully I try to free my will
> From the pitfall that I myself have laid.

Vellutello explains this sonnet as a description of the way an initial error brings misery, but nevertheless remains a beguilingly evil prison from which it is difficult to escape; and a continued commitment to sin turns the heart to stone. (69r)

[52]   A woman is by nature a frail thing;
         And I know well that an amorous state
         Within a woman's heart lasts little time.

Non, perché mille volte il dí m'ancida,
Fia ch'io non l'ami, e ch'i' non speri in lei;
Che s'ella mi spaventa, Amor m'affida.[53]

(CLXXII)

But all such protests, all such insistences that he will remain confirmed in his idolatrous worship, are met with the same response. Laura will not return his impassioned love.

The lover does not, however, remain forever in this state of profane love, which brings him only sorrow and misery. After the death of Laura all his attempts to repent and to escape from love, described time after time in the early parts of the *Canzoniere*, at last achieve fruition. And with a recognition and repentance of his sinful love comes a recognition of the value of Laura's disdain, against which he has previously protested. Such disdain is not a mere love convention, a way of titillating the lover and making his love burn more brightly, but rather a conformity to the established moral order of the world and a way of gradually aiding the salvation of the lover. Petrarch states this value in sonnet CCLXXXIX, which occurs after Laura's death:

L'alma mia fiamma oltra le belle bella,
Ch'ebbe qui 'l ciel sí amico e sí cortese,
Anzi tempo per me nel suo paese
È ritornata, et a la par sua stella.

Or comincio a svegliarmi, e veggio ch'ella
Per lo migliore al mio desir contese,
E quelle voglie giovenili accese
Temprò con una vista dolce e fella.

Lei ne ringrazio, e'l suo alto consiglio,
Che col bel viso, e co' soavi sdegni,
Fecemi, ardendo, pensar mia salute.

[53] Yet, though by actions cruel and unkind
       She mourns my fortune, laughs at my despair,
       She shall not change one thought within my mind.
       Nor, though she kill me thousand times a day,
       Shall I cease to love her, to hope in her;
       For if she frightens me, I trust Love's way.

> O leggiadre arti, e lor effetti degni,
> L'un co la lingua oprar, l'altra col ciglio,
> Io gloria in lei et ella in me virtute![54]

Laura has refused to grant him her love because she has realized that his own love is sinful and that the only way to aid in his redemption is to deny him. By refusing she does, in one sense, grant him love, but it is charitable love rather than the passionate idolatry which he gives her. She returns love for love, but not like for like. Eventually her disdain achieves its purpose, although only in retrospect after her death, and the poet's salvation is completed:

> Come va 'l mondo! or mi diletta e piace
> Quel che piú mi dispiacque; or veggio e sento
> Che, per aver salute, ebbi tormento,
> E breve guerra per eterna pace.
>
> O speranza, o desir, sempre fallace,
> E de gli amanti piú ben per un cento!
> O quant'era il peggior farmi contento
> Quella ch'or siede in cielo, e 'n terra giace!
>
> Ma 'l ceco Amor, e la mia sorda mente
> Mi traviavan sí, ch'andar per viva
> Forza mi convenia, dove morte era.

[54]   My lofty flame, more than the fairest fair,
That here had heaven as a courteous friend,
Before her time has reached her journey's end,
And returns to her land her star to share.

Now I begin to wake, I understand
That she for our own good fought my desire,
And made my youthful wishes to retire,
Tempering them with a look hard and bland.

I thank her soul and her holy device
That with her face and her sweet anger's bolts
Bid me in burning think of my salvation.

O lovely arts bringing worthy results,
One working with the tongue, one with the eyes,
I for her glory, she for my vocation.

Vellutello reads this sonnet on the value of Laura's disdain quite simply and straightforwardly, seeing it as an account of the way in which the first youthful error was corrected and base love was transformed into a higher love. (126v)

Benedetta colei ch'a miglior riva
Volse il mio corso, e l'empia voglia ardente,
Lusingando, affrenò, perch'io non pèra.[55]

(ccxc)

His own love for her is transformed. Having once worshiped a mortal being instead of the immortal and eternal
God, he now speaks with a religious contempt for the transient world and has turned his mind toward heavenly things.
Profane love has now become holy love, and the death of
Laura and the death of *eros* have saved him from spiritual
death.

Thus the *Canzoniere* is built upon the opposition between two kinds of love, *cupiditas* and *caritas*, the former
urged by passion and the latter by reason; both of these can
properly be called Petrarchan, one of them being characteristic of the early parts of the sequence and the other the
culmination toward which the whole sequence works. Petrarch's love develops from sinful love of mortal things,
whether of the lady's beauty or of the lady herself *in toto,*
into a proper love of God and of mortal things only for the
eternal *imago Dei* which resides in their mortal garb.

The manner of the *Canzoniere*, an aspect perhaps even
more influential than its moral meaning, reflects this development. One of its chief characteristics is the use of antithesis, a characteristic which grows naturally out of the conflicts expressed within the whole work—conflicts of reason

[55]   What is the world! Now I am charmed and pleased
        By what displeased me most; I see and feel
        That to be saved I was tormented, and teased,
        Given short war for an eternal weal.

        O hopes, o wishes treacherous and mad,
        The greatest price that all lovers are worth,
        How much worse had it been to make me glad,
        Of her who sits in heaven, sleeps in earth!

        But the blind love and my own deafened mind
        Had me so stranded, that led by sheer force
        I had to go where Death wants us to lie.

        Blessed be she who to the better shores
        Turned my direction and flattered my blind
        Hot will and checked it, so I may not die.

66

and passion, of sinful love and divine. The lover can say of his mixed emotions:

> Amor mi sprona in un tempo et affrena,
> Assecura e spaventa, arde et agghiaccia,
> Gradisce e sdegna, a sè mi chiama e scaccia,
> Or mi tène in speranza et or in pena. . . .[56]
>
> (CLXXVIII)

The use of oxymorons, considered almost the hallmark of Petrarchanism, is in the poetry of Petrarch himself a very effective means of expressing the confusion of the lover in the face of an emotion which he simultaneously hates and enjoys. Oxymorons such as "living death" or "sweet pain" are much more than mere wit; they have emotional and moral appropriateness as well.

The images and conceits which the poet uses are another means of expressing his sense of conflict over the love which he feels. Sometimes he is an insect which irrationally seeks the flame which burns him and causes his death (XIX). Sometimes he is a frail boat tossed back and forth in a storm (LXXX). Sometimes he wishes that he could be transformed into the cold, hard passivity of marble or diamond (LI). Or else he is a martyr dying from his lady's disdain but still faithful to her (XII). His lady is a sweet warrior (XXI). He is a besieged city in which his heart has committed treason (CCLXXIV). The God of Love is a tyrant from whom he unsuccessfully tries to rebel (LXXXIX). He weeps and sighs continually, and his sighs are gales and his tears floods of rain (CCXXXV). He can never escape from Laura because her face is painted on his heart (XCVI). But he can sometimes ease his pain by singing about it (XXIII). Such conceits are, of course, endless, and those mentioned above occur and recur and become transmogrified in many other sonnets. But however extravagant or repetitive, they are

---

[56] Love at the same time goads me and restrains,
Confirms and frightens me, inflames and freezes,
Accepts and spurns, holds me close and released,
Now he nurses my hopes and now my pains. . . .

usually effective, since they are so thoroughly expressive of the confused and uncontrollable emotion which the poet wishes to describe.

Petrarchan love is a mercurial complex of many things, but it is possible to summarize at least some of its major characteristics. At the outset the lover's passions focus on a mortal woman whom he admires to an extent that approaches idolatry, but this love is, after her death, gradually transformed from profane love into love of God. During the time that he is involved in profane love, the lover recognizes that it is sinful and wishes to repent of it, but is unable to do so because his passion is stronger than his reason. Although his lady's disdain nearly kills the lover and arouses him to vehement protests in the early poems, in the end it becomes clear that she has aided in his achievement of salvation through her refusal to reciprocate his love and through her exemplary piety. The prevailing tone is one of misery and suffering, grief and pain. The prevailing technique is the use of antithesis to express the lover's conflict and an egocentric self-analysis of emotions and responses. As the very first sonnet suggests, the purpose of the sequence is moral and exemplary; the poet describes his youthful error in the hope that others will avoid it, since its only fruit is shame and repentance, and will realize that whatever pleases on earth is only a short dream.[57]

iv   The Platonic Strand

There are some indisputably Platonic elements in the *Canzoniere*, but they are not so much systematized as susceptible to systematization.[58] The poet's gradual reformation through love and his final contempt for the mortal and earthly and transient are both impeccably Platonic dogmas. Subsequent Platonizers could easily read more Platonism

[57] See Vellutello's comment on Sonnet I.

[58] Petrarch knew very little Greek, and very little Plato was available in Latin; thus his knowledge of Platonism was limited. For a discussion of the Platonic elements in the *Canzoniere*, see Robert V. Merrill, "Platonism in Petrarch's *Canzoniere*," *MP*, XXVII (1929), 161-174.

into Petrarch's work than was actually there, and several of them did.[59] Because of the great Platonic wave which arose in Florence toward the end of the fifteenth century and swept into France and to a lesser extent England, Platonism seeps into sonnet sequences which take their initial inspiration from Petrarch.[60] So Petrarchanism and Platonism are easily confused, with no small historical justification. But at least for historical convenience, they should be kept separate. Holy Petrarchan love and Platonic love are much alike, yet enough distinctive characteristics may be added to Platonic love to warrant its separate definition.

But we cannot study the *Symposium* itself in order to find out what Platonic love meant in the Renaissance, as we can study the *Canzoniere* to define Petrarchan love or the *Amores* and *Ars Amatoria* to understand Ovidian love. For so many reinterpretations stood between the Renaissance man and the *Symposium* and so few Renaissance men were fluent enough in Greek to read it that the primary source was seen by most only from a dim and cloudy distance. Consequently, if we wish to recover Donne's Plato, we must survey the motes in the middle distance rather than the master himself.

The multiplicity of motes complicates matters a bit, and to generalize in a few pages about "Donne's Plato" is perhaps foolhardy. Any one or two or three of several great Platonists could have inspired Donne: Bembo, Ficino, Leone Ebreo, Castiglione, LaPrimaudaye, Pico. He could even have gotten his Platonism from Augustine or Cicero, from Desports or Ronsard or Spenser, perhaps even out of the air without ever reading a Platonic word. But Donne, intellectual that he was, probably went to the philosophers of the Academies; and since what few allusions he makes in his poetry are usually to Italian writers, the safest specu-

[59] See, e.g., Gesualdo, 7r, 12v, 19v, 21v, 48r, 57v, and *passim*; Bembo, *Il Petrarca con Dichiarationi non piu Stampate* (Venetia, 1564), 83, 96 [misprinted in this edition as 69], 99, 318, and *passim*.
[60] See Robert V. Merrill, with Robert J. Clements, *Platonism in French Renaissance Poetry* (New York, 1957).

lation is that he read the Christian Platonists of the Florentine Academy.

To further complicate matters, Platonic teachings about love tend to be ambiguous, for Platonism lends itself easily toward either what Charles Williams has called the Way of Affirmation or the Way of Negation.[61] Because the Platonist argues that man may move up toward God from things on earth by climbing the ladder of love, Platonism may at times seem to emphasize the importance and value of earthly and human love. But because, on the other hand, it also teaches that Ideas (or God, in the Christian Platonism which flourished during the Renaissance) are infinitely more real and valuable than anything on earth, it may also seem to stress the importance of surmounting mere earthly and human love, and it may even see human love as a dangerous distraction. Hopkins' sonnet on mortal beauty maintains the poise between these two extremes very nicely:

> To what serves mortal beauty/—dangerous; does
> set danc-
> ing blood—the O-seal-that-so/ feature, flung
> prouder form
> Than Purcell tune lets tread to?/ See: it does
> this: keeps warm
> Men's wits to the things that are;/ what good means—
> where a glance
> Master more may than gaze,/ gaze out of coun-
> tenance.
> Those lovely lads once, wet-fresh/ windfalls of
> war's storm,
> How then should Gregory, a father,/ have glean'd
> else from swarm-
> ed Rome? But God to a nation/ dealt that day's
> dear chance.

[61] Basically these are two ways of knowing God which Williams traces through history in *The Descent of the Dove* (New York, 1956); the following is as close as he comes to a brief definition: "The one Way was to affirm all things orderly until the universe throbbed with vitality; the other to reject all things until there was nothing anywhere but He." (58)

To man, that needs would worship/ block or
    barren stone,
Our law says: Love what are/ love's worthiest,
    were all known;
World's loveliest—men's selves. Self/ flashes
    off frame and face.
What do then? how meet beauty?/ Merely meet it;
    own,
Home at heart, heaven's sweet gift;/ then leave,
    let that alone.
Yea, wish that though, wish all,/ God's better
    beauty, grace.[62]

To avoid oversimplifying, it is helpful to remember that the very emphasis on the ladder of love led the Renaissance man to think hierarchically: one kind of love is good, another is higher, and another is highest; but each is good and necessary.

Thus Platonic love has a practical level during the Renaissance. On this level one purpose of love is to populate the earth. Since all men yearn for the eternal, they try to satisfy their desire by having children. The doctrine is familiar to us as what Diotima calls (in Jowett's translation) "birth in beauty," and Ficino elaborates on it further:

We all desire to have goods, and not only to have them but to have them eternally. The single goods or mortals change and fade and they would all quickly disappear if new ones were not continuously made in place of those which leave. Therefore, so that goods may somehow endure for us forever, we desire to recreate those which pass away. That re-creation is effected by generation. Hence has been born in everyone the instinct for generation. But since generation, by continuation, renders mortal things like divine, it is certainly a divine gift.[63]

[62] *Poems of Gerard Manley Hopkins*, ed. W. H. Gardner (Oxford, 1948).
[63] *Commentary on Plato's Symposium*, ed. and trans. Sears Reynolds Jayne, *University of Missouri Studies*, XIX (1944), 202-203.

Ficino later distinguishes this kind of love from lust, which seeks only self-gratification (233).

According to Platonic tradition, Renaissance lovers could also be two-in-one and one-in-two in another sense as well. Not only might they unite with one another physically, but they could also achieve a spiritual or intellectual union through sympathy and understanding. Unlike physical love, this kind of relationship can occur between members of the same sex or men and women who are not married to one another; but like righteous physical love, its motivation is unselfish. La Primaudaye describes it as it occurs between friends:

> To love (saith *Cicero*) is nothing else but to be desir-ous to profite and pleasure another without hope of recompence. For otherwise friendship would be a meere merchandise, whereas it ought to be as free as charitie. *Socrates* also saide, that the end of friendship was, that of two soules one should be made in wil and affection, and that none should love himselfe better than his friend. . . . Whereby it appeereth unto us, that a friend is a seconde selfe, and that whosoever would take upon himselfe this title in regard of another, he must transforme himselfe in his nature whom he pur-poseth to love, and that with a stedfast and setled mind to continue so forever. Hereupon one of the ancients speaking of him that loveth perfectly, saith, that he liveth in another mans bodie. (131)

For La Primaudaye, such friendship is also the foundation of marriage (480).

Sometimes the notion that the lover gives up his soul to live in another is described in the terms of religious ecstasy; Romei cites Plato as saying in the *Convivio*

> . . . that Loue, with such a strong knotte knitteth louers together, that of twoo hee maketh one alone, willing to inferre, that those, who absolutely giue themselues ouer in prey to amorous passions, are after such a sorte

ententiue on their louing cogitations, as it may be affirmed, that the soule disioyned from the body, liueth in the beloued: and therefore no meruaile, though the bodies of Louers depriued of vitall vigor, do consume and languish. . . . (67-68)

Ficino sees Plato as saying something slightly different. Love may be either simple, when it is not returned, or reciprocal. When it is simple, the soul of the poor lover wanders homeless, since the beloved will not accept it, and the soulless lover is himself dead (144). But when love is reciprocal, the death of self which inevitably occurs in charitable love is ultimately creative rather than destructive, for it produces a multiplication of identities. Ficino grows quite ecstatic as he describes the wondrous process whereby lovers lose themselves in order to find themselves, dying in order to live:

> O, happy death, which is followed by two lives. O, wondrous exchange in which each gives himself for the other, and has the other, yet does not cease to have himself. O, inestimable gain, when two so become one, that each of the two, instead of one alone, becomes two, and as though doubled, he who had one life before, with a death intervening, has now two. For a man who dies once and is twice resurrected has exchanged one life for two and his single self for two selves. (145)

Obviously this exchange of identities has an ethical value in addition to the metaphysical satisfaction which it provides; for such lovers succeed in conquering their self-love and give one another the gift-love which God gives man; the metaphysical pleasure is their reward for their *imitatio Dei*.

If Platonic love leads men to moral improvement in that it leads them to imitate divine love, it also improves them morally because it leads them toward God. When this process is described simply, the lover is said to be loving the *imago Dei* when he loves the physical or moral beauty of his beloved:

> The lover . . . beholding beauty as the Image of Di-
> uinitie, raiseth vp by that meanes his minde to medi-
> tate on that beauty which is perfect and celestial. This
> diuine louer desireth that his deere affected should be
> set on fire, with so holy, chast, and immaculate a loue
> towards him. With such loue, not onely yong men, but
> olde, religious, and men married may be inamored;
> and it is the highest and most perfect degree of
> temperature.[64]

Ficino describes the process in a somewhat more complicated fashion: the lover climbs a ladder on three rungs, rising from the body to the soul to the Angelic Mind, ultimately reaching God Himself; the image of God is present
in all three, though less in the body than in the soul or Angelic Mind, and the lover can gradually grow to know God
directly by first experiencing His presence in the universe
He has created (215).

But there is another side to Platonism. It can be ethereal
as well as practical. At times Platonists may seem to har-
bor the ungrateful desire to kick out from under themselves
the ladder on which they have climbed, for the image of
God exists in earthly things only darkly, as in a mirror. The
lover is seeking God when he loves, after all; as Bembo's
hermit, a development from Diotima, preaches in *Gli
Asolani*:

> O Lavinello, what do you think is this eternal orb of
> the sun before you, which ever shines so steadily, so
> surely, with such unwearied radiance? or that other sis-
> ter light which never is the same? . . . They, my son,
> are none other than His charms who apportions these,
> as well as everything besides, and sends them as His
> messengers inviting us to love Him. For wise men say
> that of our two constituents we take the body, that

[64] Romei, 34. Romei delineates two other kinds of love: Chaste
love is directed toward the Idea of beauty and does not rise beyond
it to God, and righteous corporeal love seeks eternity through the
production of children within marriage.

fleeting, inharmonious mixture of water, fire, earth, and air, from our progenitors, but take the pure immortal soul from Him whom it desires to rejoin.[65]

But if the lover is really seeking God when he loves mortal things, the hermit adds, then it is only natural for him eventually to wish to find God alone, as he exists above and beyond the earthly world: ". . . when our minds perceive these secondary beauties, they are pleased and gladly study them as likenesses and sparks of it, but they are never wholly satisfied with them because they yearn for that divine eternal loveliness which they remember and for which they are ever secretly spurred on to search (183-184)." And so the Platonist can teach that mortal beauty is ultimately unsatisfying and unworthy, that only divine Beauty is a suitable object for man to love.

If the Platonists, when they pursue the Way of Negation, can speak eloquently of the insufficiency of earthly love and earthly beauty, they can speak still more eloquently of the joys of Celestial Love. For God and Love are one, and that One is also perfect and eternal, even beyond eternity and perfection. The man who leaves earthly joys and soars through the great darkness toward that illimitable light, though he may be rejecting much that is very good, is finding a love which so far surpasses earthly love that the hermit can only define it by negatives, by saying how it differs:

> There none encounter rivalries, suspicions, or jealousies since, however many love Him, many more may love Him also and enjoy their love as thoroughly as one alone would do; that infinite Godhead can satisfy us all and yet remain eternally the same. There none need fear treachery or harm or broken faith. Nothing unsuitable is sought, or granted, or desired. The body receives what is sufficient, as Cerberus is thrown a biscuit lest he bark; and the soul enjoys what it requires most. Nor is anyone forbidden to seek what he loves or denied the power to attain that delight to which his

[65] Trans. Rudolf B. Gottfried (Bloomington, Ind., 1954), 179.

love impels him. Nor do men go by land and sea, or climb on walls or roofs, to find what they desire. Nor is there need of arms or messenger or escort; for God is all that each can see or wish. Neither anger nor scorn nor repentance nor change nor joy deceptive nor vain hope nor grief nor fear is found there. There neither chance nor fortune can prevail. There all is full of certainty, content, and happiness. (192-193)

Clearly, when such an ascent is achieved, little more than this can be said. And that is why, though the vision of God alone is the ultimate goal of the Platonists, so much Platonic poetry remains in the earthly sphere, describing love between human beings. A poet may affirm the beauty of God as reflected in His creation by himself creating verbal beauty to describe it, but he cannot recreate the uncreated Word; he may attempt to capture divine beauty in its finite immanence, but he can never capture the Infinite Beauty through mere finite words.

These then are the three great traditions available to sixteenth-century love poets. In these pages which follow, I have used these three traditions and the types of love typical of each as a convenient way of dividing Donne's love poems into similar groups, although in some cases Donne's approach is so original that the decision to discuss a poem in one chapter or another has been almost arbitrary. *The Extasie*, for example, seems to use Ovidian irony to portray an idolatrous relationship which masquerades as Platonic idealism. It is analyzed in Chapter IV, although it could have fallen in Chapter III or V, because the main emphasis of this book is on the kinds of love which Donne dramatizes and his attitude toward them.

As he wrote of lust and idolatry and idealized love, Donne inevitably looked back to these three traditions, sometimes borrowing or imitating but more often innovating or revolutionizing. His "philosophy of love," on the other hand, seems to be essentially conservative. He could invent a new stanza form, a new way of putting images together, a new tone of voice in which to speak of love. But he could not invent new kinds of love, for lust and idolatry and charity are old as Ovid and Petrarch, old as St. Augustine, old as the Old Testament and the New, old as man himself. And he ultimately judges these varieties of amatory experience from the hierarchical perspective of the ordinary sixteenth-century man: lust is bad and idolatry is worse; charitable love for other human beings is good and divine love still more intensely satisfying. But he is an extraordinary poet because he also momentarily captures these varieties of emotional experience from the inside.

III · THE SCIENCE OF LUST

When senses, which thy souldiers are,
We arme against thee, and they fight for sinne....

At times Donne's lovers sound very enthusiastic about sexual love. In poems like *Communitie, The Sunne Rising,* or
Elegies XVIII and *XIX* the speakers sing in Dionysiac cho-
rus that physical union is the major end and sole delight of
love. Sometimes they add that variety is the spice of love. But
at other times, as in *Loves Alchymie* or *Farewell to love,*
Donne creates lovers who sound very disillusioned indeed.
If we do not assume that Donne is dramatizing a variety of
character types who strike various conventional poses—the
youthful man about town, the iconoclastic rebel, the world-
weary habitué, the pagan sensualist—we are puzzled by
Donne's apparent inconsistency. Even if we do make that
assumption, it is still easy to assume that Donne at heart
embraces one extreme or the other, either ascetic revulsion
or profane joy.

But no single speaker speaks for Donne, who, if his later
sermons are any evidence, would condemn both extremes.
Donne argued from the pulpit that sexuality is not inherently sinful, as the ascetic would say, but the abuse of it is,
and that abuse, the sin of lust, is dramatized in the enthusiastic sensualists. The disillusionment of *Farewell to love* is
the natural result of overrating sex as these moral icon-
oclasts do. Both, from Donne's point of view, are wrong, for
sexual love can be both chaste and good when it is a complement to the love of God, and it is not inferior to virginity.
The senses may be soldiers within the militant church,
Donne's view runs, but they can also be armed against God
and fight for sin; sexual pleasure is good when it serves the
right ends, wrong when excessive or too self-gratifying.

That Donne later preached this view from the pulpit and
that it was widely accepted when he wrote his love poetry
does not, of course, necessarily prove that it informs his
love poetry. But a close examination of individual poems

confirms evidence from the history of ideas, showing that in his love poems Donne did draw on conventional beliefs about the nature and purpose of love.

One indication that Donne assumes traditional beliefs to be true is the prevalence of religious imagery; in poem after poem Donne projects lovers who use the language of theology to describe their amatory success. The lover in *Elegie III*, for example, says to his mistress:

> Although thy hand and faith, and good workes too,
> Have seal'd thy love which nothing should undoe,
> Yea though thou fall backe, that apostasie
> Confirme thy love; yet much, much I feare thee.

Such lines as these are characteristic of Donne's wit, of his ability to yoke opposites together by violence and thereby to give an impression of outrageously clever impudence. But the lines are also witty in the sense of comic, and their comedy arises because the opposites remain opposite. The elegy as a whole is a lover's expression of dissatisfaction with the impermanence of the sexual seal and the amatory faith and good works which he has won, turning on the implication that a sexual seal of love is one thing, the seal of grace quite another, the one being physical and temporal and the other divine and spiritual; the religious imagery, simultaneously suggesting the likenesses and differences between profane love and sacred, recalls the more satisfying love he might have chosen. Because the folly of his choice is pointed up by the imagery he uses to describe it, the lover is a comic figure.

That most of these poems draw upon the Ovidian tradition provides another clue as to the attitude toward sexual gratification which they express. Donne's indebtedness to Ovid is considerable; sometimes he borrows lines, sometimes situations, sometimes themes. If Ovidian poetry was often read as philosophy-teaching-by-bad-example, then Donne's Ovidian poems probably are also the monologues of men who are meant to be negative moral *exempla*, models for what is to be avoided; and the spirit of comic irony which is so pervasive in Donne's love poetry corroborates the hypothesis that Donne's Ovid is Ovid the moral satirist.

To be sure, the Ovidian spirit which animates much of Donne's love poetry is always partially transmuted by an individual mind which is also a Renaissance mind. Donne condenses, complicates, and adds his own characteristic note of logical argument. The poems fall into three groups, Ovidian to varying degrees. In one group Donne plays a logic game, and the comic irony results because the logic used to defend lust is contradictory or fallacious. Casuistical lovers take the offensive in order to seduce or to justify their seductions, but in the process they continually undercut their own arguments; they disprove what they are trying to prove. In a second group the Ovidian irony arises from situational comedy rather than a logic game; Donne depicts lovers who have devoted themselves to preaching inconstancy and who suddenly discover, to their surprised discomfort, that their own doctrines have rebounded upon them, that their mistresses are as unfaithful as they have been taught to be. The lovers realize painfully that promiscuity may be justifiable in theory, that it may be delightful when they themselves practice it, but that it is much less delightful when their mistresses practice it. Like all cuckolds, they are embarrassed by their situation. In such poems as these, even if we did not know that the Renaissance Ovid was a satirist, we could not long escape the recognition that Donne is being ironic.

At the farthest reach and most thoroughly transmuted through the influence of Renaissance notions are the third group of poems, which follow the Ovidian tradition of *remedia amoris* but are pervaded by a Christian sense of the moral repulsiveness of lust. In these poems the lovers cannot seem to escape from the awareness that they have willfully chosen to defy divine providence and incur divine wrath. The tone shifts, in this third group, from impudent gaiety to grim misery. Their lament is concisely summarized in the initial lines of *Loves exchange*:

Love, any devil else but you
Would for a given soul give something too.

Such poems as *Farewell to love*, although of an Ovidian genre, contain a stronger sense of the essential sinfulness of lust than any poem written by the Augustan Ovid is or could be. The lovers in these poems speak with a tone of black disillusionment and dissatisfaction, both with sex and with themselves. The joys of lust seem to them a hollow dream, created to tempt men into sin and self-destruction.

i *Militant Logic*

Many of the *Songs and Sonets* and *Elegies* preach promiscuity on the basis of a single central doctrine: inconstancy in love is justified by the laws of the natural universe. Whether preaching to the world or to a reluctant mistress, the lovers in these poems support their arguments by appealing to nature and to logic. The thesis of these sermons in favor of lust and promiscuity is that change and flux dominate the natural world—rivers run, the heavens revolve, and animals seek the mate closest at hand. From this premise reached by inductive observation, it is easy for the lovers to conclude that they and their mistresses, as a part of the natural world, are bound only by the law of freedom in love and may change their affections as often as they please. A corollary conclusion also follows from this, of course; sometimes the lovers also argue that any attempt to achieve permanence in love is a violation of natural law, that the desire to establish a lasting relationship or to remain faithful to a single mate is a result of the tyrannous accretions of custom. A desire for constancy is not inherent in natural man.

These lovers do not try to seduce women by arousing them with words or by turning their heads with flattery. They try to *prove* that promiscuity is justifiable. Their logic marches onward from premise to conclusion with militant vigor, and at first glance their conclusions seem well-nigh indisputable, since the casuistry of their arguments is well-hidden. No doubt the fair sex was perplexed, but that is just the effect which the lovers wish to achieve.

In these poems Donne is playing off against each other two possible attitudes toward nature, one conservative and one liberal or libertine, which were in the air at the time. At its best the liberal view is represented by Montaigne, at its worst by Machiavelli. Essentially, it preaches individualism and relativism; each man's nature, it says, gives him his own law and this law must be obeyed (Montaigne) or manipulated (Machiavelli). To Montaigne Nature was gentle, and the urge to defy custom or civil law was not, therefore, particularly dangerous. But to Machiavelli Nature was selfish and brutal, offering plentiful possibilities of exploitation to the strong. If we can judge by the introduction to *The Jew of Malta*, the Machiavellian view of Nature was not looked upon with a friendly eye in Renaissance England; its message of liberation from moral limitations seemed dangerous and evil. Shakespeare's Machiavellian villain Edmund states its case even more famously:

> Thou, Nature, art my goddess; to thy law
> My services are bound. Wherefore should I
> Stand in the plague of custom, and permit
> The curiosity of nations to deprive me,
> For that I am some twelve or fourteen moonshines
> Lag of a brother? Why bastard? Wherefore base?
> When my dimensions are as well compact,
> My mind as generous, and my shape as true,
> As honest madam's issue? Why brand they us
> With base? with baseness? bastardy? base, base?
> Who, in the lusty stealth of nature, take
> More composition and fierce quality
> Than doth, within a dull, stale, tired bed,
> Go to th' creating a whole tribe of fops
> Got 'tween asleep and wake? Well then,
> Legitimate Edgar, I must have your land.

(I.ii.1-16)

This Nature to which Edmund appeals is the Nature of the

beast, gratifying his desires because his desires seem to be their own sanction, refusing to be governed by the laws of society. Ultimately, the liberal view tends toward the position, later to be systematically formulated by Hobbes, that nature is a state of disorder or war, that the Law of Nature is not in harmony with the Law of Reason but is based on struggle and fear. And by that time the liberal view is used to support conservative or reactionary political doctrines, whereas conservative Nature provides the foundation for political liberalism.

The attitude toward nature which the libertine view defies and contradicts is the conservative position of the Roman jurists, of the Church Fathers, of Hooker, and of the typical Renaissance Englishman. According to this hierarchical view, even beasts obey the reasonable Law of Nature and man obeys it too, although in a different way because his conscious rationality makes him superior to beasts. The Law of Nature has been in existence since the world was created and "is as it were an authentical or an original draught written in the bosom of God himself. . . ."[1] Not only is it eternal and immutable, but it is also rational and orderly. By observing the Law of Nature, itself a reflection of the will of God, and by discovering the principles which guide it, natural man formulates moral truths and moral laws:

> The general and perpetual voice of men is as the sentence of God himself. For that which all men have at all times learned, Nature herself must needs have taught; and God being the author of Nature, her voice is but his instrument. By her from Him we receive whatsoever in such sort we learn. Infinite duties there are, the goodness whereof is by this rule sufficiently manifested, although we have no other warrant . . . by force of the light of Reason, wherewith God illumineth every one which cometh into the world, men

[1] Richard Hooker, *Of the Laws of Ecclesiastical Polity*, Everyman's edition (London, 1907), I, 160.

being enabled to know truth from falsehood, and good from evil, do thereby learn in many things what the will of God is. . . .[2]

Thus, in following the Law of Reason and the Law of Nature, man works toward the perfection of his being. If any part of nature violates the natural order and the Law of Reason, however, then the result is chaos, struggle, and fear. And one of Donne's lovers, in a conservative mood, appeals to the belief that order is natural as he addresses his mistress in *Elegie XV*:

> Sooner I'll thinke the Sunne will cease to cheare
> > The teeming earth, and *that* forget to beare,
> Sooner that rivers will runne back, or Thames
> > With ribs of Ice in June would bind his streames,
> Or Nature, by whose strength the world endures,
> > Would change her course, before you alter yours.

Donne's poems of promiscuity seem to contradict blatantly the conservative attitude toward nature which was generally accepted in Renaissance England and to set forth the libertine view. Donne has created a rogue's gallery of lovers who insist that the unrestrained gratification of sexual passion is more natural than ordinate love. The Nature to which they appeal for support is unlike that of Montaigne, for it is far from gentle; these lovers see brutal selfishness as the chief characteristic of natural love. From this libertine position they argue that traditional morality, "the general and perpetual voice of men," is itself unreasonable and tyrannous. The *consensus gentium* about what is right, when tested against the passions of the lovers, seems totally wrong.

But these Ovidian poems, although they seem to present logical justifications for lust by appealing to a libertine view of nature, are full of bad logic and undercutting ironies. Because the lovers use logic, they invite their arguments to

---

[2] *Ibid.*, I, 176-177.

84

be tested on that basis, and the arguments fail the test. The lovers lose their own debates with tradition, and their militant logic boomerangs against them. They are not meant to be dangerous, but comically innocuous, threats to the conservative belief that natural order exists and is good.

The song *Confined Love* formulates a typical pronouncement of the credo of promiscuity, and we can learn much about the tone, logic, and irony of Donne's poems of promiscuity by examining it. The poem is at once a philosophical defense of the libertine position and an immodest proposal addressed to a woman who has scruples about being unfaithful to her husband, but on both counts it is a failure, for the proposer repeatedly borrows from the very moral traditions which he is trying to overturn; logically his argument is inconsistent, and psychologically it errs by reminding the woman of the inescapable dominance of moral law. In each stanza the speaker chooses to use a word with strongly negative emotional charges—"false" in the first, "beasts" in the second, and "greediness" in the third—and the net result is to make his point of view seem degrading and distasteful. Few women would listen and say "yes."

Confined Love

> Some man unworthy to be possessor
> Of old or new love, himself being false or weake,
> Thought his paine and shame would be lesser,
> If on womankind he might his anger wreake,
> And thence a law did grow,
> One might but one man know;
> But are other creatures so?
>
> Are Sunne, Moone, or Starres by law forbidden,
> To smile where they list, or lend away their light?
> Are birds divorc'd, or are they chidden
> If they leave their mate, or lie abroad a night?
> Beasts doe no joyntures lose
> Though they new lovers choose,
> But we are made worse then those.

85

Who e'r rigg'd faire ship to lie in harbors,
And not to seeke new lands, or not to deale withall?
Or built faire houses, set trees, and arbors,
Only to look up, or else to let them fall?
  Good is not good, unlesse
  A thousand it possesse,
  But doth wast with greedinesse.

The initial stanza simultaneously attacks constancy in love and the husband of the woman to whom the poem is addressed. Trying to suggest that promiscuity will liberate her from unfair masculine tyranny, the speaker says that monogamy was instituted by a man who was too false or weak to practice genuine "love." He was unworthy of his old beloved because he wanted to be false to her, and yet he could not practice the disloyalty which he felt because he was too weak to win a new mistress. Poised in this frustrating position, he decided to vent his wrath upon the women who created it, and so he imposed a law that each woman should "know" only one man. Since he himself was capable of acquiring only one woman, he decreed that his own incapacity was equivalent to moral rectitude.

Although psychologically clever, the speaker's account of the origin of moral law is obviously a mixture of whimsicality, *argumentum ad hominem*, and superb audience adaptation. The quotation from Hooker a few pages earlier typifies the universally accepted belief that moral laws existed from the beginning because they were written upon the heart of God and were made immanent in His creation, clearly present for all creatures to observe and follow. The speaker is mocking this orthodox view by saying that moral laws were created *ex nihilo* by a mythical tyrant who used injustice to hide his own weakness. His amusingly blasphemous inversion is not really meant to be believable, for his real purpose is to discredit the husband of the woman addressed by implying that he is a tyrant who must be either false or weak if he expects her to be faithful to him. She ought to rebel against his injustice, using the speaker as her ally. Yet even the libertine speaker himself cannot escape the sanctions of the Law of Nature. When he condemns the mythical tyrant who instituted monogamy by calling him "false," making "false" synonymous with "inconstant," he brings all the negative associations of inconstancy perilously close to the surface and undermines his own argument in favor of it.

That psychological error is followed by another in the next stanza, where he tries to argue that the law immanent in Nature commands promiscuity rather than constancy. All natural things, he says, are subject to change: the sun, moon, and stars move about the heavens and shine on all parts of the earth indifferently; birds and beasts abandon their mates and choose new ones freely and guiltlessly; and therefore the lover believes that man, as a part of the natural order, should conform to the changefulness apparently ordained for all creatures. In assuming that what is sanctioned for beasts and heavenly bodies is also sanctioned for human bodies, he is ignoring the doctrine that nature is composed of hierarchies and that laws vary according to each creature's place in the hierarchy. But as he says to his lady, "If beasts can be promiscuous, we can too," he again arouses an unpleasant group of associations; "beast" has strongly pejorative connotations, and when the lover asks his listener to act like one, he also suggests that such behavior is degrading and bestial. In the last line he tries to recover from his error in making such a comparison, but it is a weak recovery. When he complains that human beings differ from beasts because "we are made worse" (we can have less fun because we are supposed to follow stricter laws), he only weakens his case by recalling hierarchical values, even if he also protests that they curtail his pleasure.

In the third stanza the speaker turns to another well-worked Ovidian argument, the doctrine of use. According to this doctrine, no good thing is really good unless it is used; things which are greedily hoarded are fruitlessly wasted, and their waste is unnatural and wrong. There is simply no point in rigging a ship which is not sailed, in planting a garden which no man sees, or in building a house where no man lives. And the implication is, of course, that there is no point in being a woman or a man without using the sexual capacities of manhood or womanhood. When not extended to apply by analogy to sex (to which it would not normally apply, since man is not an inanimate object), this doctrine is quite close to orthodoxy, and again the lover cannot present it without assuming moral traditions to be true. His appeal depends on the belief that greed is essentially sterile and selfish and therefore sinful. But in an argument so rigorous he can hardly apply a double standard, saying that someone else's greedy fidelity is wrong, while his greedy desire for physical gratification is right.

Beyond this inconsistency, however, the lover goes on to draw a broader generalization from his evidence than actually follows. His argument has been that things ought to be put to use so that they can fulfill the purpose for which they were created—a ship, for example, ought to be sailed. But he goes on to argue that human beings need to be "possessed" by thousands in order to be good, although presumably they, like ships, can fulfill their purpose just as well if they are the property of only one person; all he may validly infer is that human sexual capacities must be used, not that they must be used with thousands. Since the woman addressed presumably has already been possessed by one person, hence her reluctance to accept his proposal, the lover cannot afford to restrict his argument to make it valid; but the conclusion that he wishes his listener to accept— that sexual promiscuity is ordained by nature—does not follow from his premises. And again the lover has made a psychological miscalculation as well as a logical one, for most women would probably be repelled by the suggestion that they should be possessed by thousands. Both the verb and the number would make the lover's proposal seem undesirable.

The source from which he has borrowed his philosophy of use also suggests that promiscuity is not quite so liberating as the lover wishes to suggest. His argument, probably

as ancient as the first seduction, has its most widely available literary source in a speech by Dipsas, a character
whom Ovid describes in the eighth elegy of the first book of
the *Amores*. Dipsas is an aged prostitute who, no longer
able to practice her profession successfully, now earns her
living by being a bawd. Ovid describes the invidious sermon which she gave his mistress as he eavesdropped behind
closed double doors, and the doctrine of use provides one
of her weightier arguments:

> labitur occulte fallitque volubilis aetas,
>   et celer admissis labitur annus equis,
> aera nitent usu, vestis bona quaerit haberi,
>   canescunt turpi tecta relicta situ—
> forma, nisi admittas, nulla exercente senescit,
>   nec satis effectus unus et alter habent. . . .[3]
>
> (49-54)

When the doctrine of use appeared in *Confined Love*, most
people who read the poem would probably have realized
that the lover was presenting the case of Dipsas without the
benefit of footnotes, and their realization would only cor-
roborate the other hints that Donne is being ironic. The
lover's argument for promiscuity becomes by implication
an argument for prostitution and the lover himself a bawd.
Both the flaws in his logic and the invidiousness of his
source effectively undermine his case for libertine
naturalism.

In the little poem *Communitie* we find the same kind of
logic game as in *Confined Love*, although it is now used
with a slightly different purpose and effect. *Communitie*
is addressed, not to a recalcitrant mistress, but to a benighted world which unthinkingly accepts the voice of the
consensus gentium. Pretending to be reasoning out the case

[3] "The stream of a lifetime glides smoothly on and is past before
we know, and swift the year glides by with horses at full speed. Bronze
grows bright with use; a fair garment asks for the wearing; the aban-
doned dwelling moulders with age and corrupting neglect—and
beauty, so you open not your doors, takes age from lack of use. Nor,
do one or two lovers avail enough. . . ."

for and against unrestricted sexual gratification, the speaker
finally concludes that both women and lust are morally neutral or indifferent. This poem is the kind of intellectual experiment which Donne must have enjoyed passing around
at the Inns of Court, for in it the speaker seems to squeeze
an impudently false conclusion out of true premises by using perfectly valid logic. *Communitie* is an ingenious *tour
de force*, a logical exercise which challenges the reader to
see if he can discover the trick in the argument. If we do not
join in the game, we miss much of the fun of the poem.

Communitie

Good we must love, and must hate ill,
For ill is ill, and good good still,
But there are things indifferent,
Which wee may neither hate, nor love,
But one, and then another prove,
As wee shall finde our fancy bent.

If then at first wise Nature had
Made women either good or bad,
Then some wee might hate, and some chuse,
But since shee did them so create,
That we may neither love, nor hate,
Onely this rests, All, all may use.

If they were good it would be seene,
Good is as visible as greene,
And to all eyes it selfe betrayes:
If they were bad, they could not last,
Bad doth it selfe, and others wast,
So, they deserve nor blame, nor praise.

But they are ours as fruits are ours,
He that but tasts, he that devours,
And he that leaves all, doth as well:
Chang'd loves are but chang'd sorts of meat,
And when hee hath the kernell eate,
Who doth not fling away the shell?

The first stanza is used to throw the reader off his guard and even to mislead him as to the nature of the poem. It consists of statements so universally accepted that they would seem almost naive truisms: We must love goodness and hate evil, and there are also "things indifferent" which are not absolutely good or evil and the moral worth of which is apparent only when they are "proved" or tested. When the corollary is added that the moral worth of these "things indifferent" may change according to time and place, we have the reasoning upon which much of Hooker's *Ecclesiastical Polity* is founded. Few Renaissance readers would be likely to disagree at this point in the poem. In the first stanza the speaker poses as full of morality and high seriousness, but even when wicked conclusions begin to emerge from these pious premises, he keeps up his tone of innocent objectivity.

In the rest of the poem he blends these moral truisms with rational logic and comes up with a defense of amoral and irrational behavior. Women, created morally indifferent because they are neither absolutely good nor absolutely bad, should be neither loved nor hated; rather, all men may "use" all women just as they may "prove" other "things indifferent." That women, by virtue of being human, are not completely good or bad is also a truism which most Renaissance readers would accept, but since the speaker is pretending to proceed by rigorous logic, he cannot simply assert that women fall in the class of "things indifferent." He must prove it, for otherwise the conditional argument which he presents in the second stanza is meaningless. He has said, in effect, that *if* women are neither good nor bad, all men may use them at will as things indifferent. But he must affirm the antecedent and show his affirmation to be true before the desired conclusion will follow.

This he attempts to do in the third stanza. His proof, which is presented in a quasi-logical manner, runs:

> If women were good, their goodness would
> be self-evident.

Their goodness is not self-evident.
Therefore, they do not deserve praise. [*I.e.*, they are
    not absolutely good.]

If they were bad, they would destroy
    themselves and others.
They do not destroy themselves and others.
Therefore, they do not deserve blame. [*I.e.*, they are
    not absolutely bad.]

Through this proof, although it contains some controversial statements, the speaker makes his assertion that women are in the class of things indifferent seem more convincing. Again, his argument is based upon two truisms which the average man would find perfectly acceptable, that "Good is as visible as greene," and that "Bad doth it selfe, and others wast. . . ."

Now the argument is complete. After having gratified and deceived the high-minded reader by spouting pious truisms, the speaker goes on to fling their unpleasant naturalistic implications before his astonished eyes. Abstract diction becomes concrete in the final stanza, and moral generalizations give way to a verbal vision of rapacious sexual gluttony. Women, hitherto shown to be morally indifferent, are now made as morally neutral as the fruits of the jungle are to natural man. Like other vegetable life, they may be tasted, devoured, or ignored, and their shell cast aside once they have been devoured.

Unlike *Confined Love*, the logic of *Communitie* is far from shabby. Given the truth of the premises, the speaker's conclusions seem to follow necessarily. Yet the premises are truisms which are undeniable, and the conclusions are almost repulsively brutal. Nor is there any effort to hide their brutality. Rather, promiscuity, which seems so logically justifiable, is described in images designed to make it seem as naturalistically amoral and crudely irresponsible as possible. It is as if the speaker wished to say to a conservative and pious audience: "These moral truisms are what you believe, and yet they can be used, through perfectly valid logic, to justify conclusions which you find morally repulsive. See what I can do with them! Now what are *you* going to do?" The poem is, in short, a characteristic example of Donne's witty audacity and insolent ingenuity.

But Donne's readers would no doubt have recognized that the speaker is using the cleverest of word games, equivocation, that he is whimsically changing the meanings of the key words in his argument in order to squeeze his amoral conclusion out of his moral premises. One can imagine another young lawyer at the Inns of Court reading the poem, recognizing the challenge to discover the trick in the argument, and saying something like this: "Ah yes, but 'prove' and 'use' do not mean the same thing, as you try to pretend; you cannot say that we are obliged to consume 'things indifferent' just because we are obliged to test them. And further, 'things indifferent' are not amoral, as you try to imply; you begin by using the phrase in its commonplace sense, which assumes that there are things whose goodness or badness may change according to their context and situation; but this sense does not assume that notions of goodness and badness are totally irrelevant, only that they are relative and that things may be blamed or praised as circumstances warrant; but you, changing the meaning later in the poem (and cleverly refusing to use the phrase again lest your reader recognize your equivocation), try to show that because women are neither absolutely good nor absolutely bad, one is justified in treating them as if they were worthless; all you are permitted to conclude, if you do not shift the meaning of 'things indifferent,' is that all men must test the worth of each woman (not consume, but test) in order to determine whether the particular circumstances of her condition and nature make her good or bad or perhaps a mixture of both. It is very ingenious, the way you try to hide all this inconsistency by your complex series of syllogisms, which make the poem seem logically impeccable. But it won't work in the long run, for moral truth is one thing and sin is another, and no amount of ingenuity can make them seem identical for very long. That is undoubtedly the point of the first two lines, which are your own private joke, your way of hinting that the advocacy of sin is all a game. For, as you say, 'Good wee must love, and must hate ill,/ For ill is ill, and good good still. . . .' "

Like *Confined Love* and *Communitie*, *The Indifferent* is the statement of a man who believes that promiscuity or inconstancy is the law of the natural universe; but unlike them, it is not based solely on appeals to logic, although it is equally militant in its advocacy of lust. As has long been recognized, in this poem Donne is drawing directly upon the fourth elegy of the second book of Ovid's *Amores*. There Ovid simply asserts the promiscuity of his love for women without any attempt to justify it. It is a simple fact of his existence that he can find something to lust after in any woman he happens to run across, and the whole elegy is simply a cleverly arranged catalogue of the myriad types he can love. Donne, however much he may echo Ovid's delight in variety and the immediacy which results from direct address in the second person, complicates his poem by making it more than a mere listing of different feminine anatomical types, color schemes, and personality syndromes.

The Indifferent

I can love both faire and browne,
Her whom abundance melts, and her whom want
    betraies,
Her who loves lonenesse best, and her who
    maskes and plaies,
Her whom the country form'd, and whom the town,
Her who beleeves, and her who tries,
Her who still weepes with spungie eyes;
And her who is dry corke, and never cries;
I can love her, and her, and you and you,
I can love any, so she be not true.

Will no other vice content you?
Wil it not serve your turn to do, as did
    your mothers?

Or have you all old vices spent, and now would
    finde out others?
Or doth a feare, that men are true, torment you?
Oh we are not, be not you so,
Let mee, and doe you, twenty know.
Must I, who came to travaile thorow you,
Grow your fixt subject, because you are true?

Venus heard me sigh this song,
And by Loves sweetest Part, Variety, she swore,
She heard not this till now; and that it should be
    so no more.
She went, examin'd, and return'd ere long,
And said, alas, Some two or three
Poore Heretiques in love there bee,
Which thinke to stablish dangerous constancie.
But I have told them, since you will be true,
You shall be true to them, who'are false to you.

Ovid's elegy is simply a point of departure. Donne's speaker, equally anxious to boast about his eclectic interests, succeeds in outdoing the promiscuity of Ovid's poem by adding that he also prefers his women to be inconstant. The audacity of "I can love any" is surpassed by the audacity of the qualification: "I can love any, so she be not true." And he also outdoes Ovid's witty iconoclasm in another way: in *The Indifferent* the speaker makes a conscious effort to invert traditional morality with apparent effortlessness. The lover begins his impudent second stanza by equating constancy with vice, asking women in general why they don't content themselves with some other vice besides that of remaining faithful to their lovers and demanding the same in return. Appealing to tradition, he argues that they should follow the examples of their mothers, gleefully combining an insult to the sacred cow of Motherhood with another inversion of the *consensus gentium*, for he assumes that custom or precedent teaches immorality rather than morality. Or, he adds insolently, perhaps women have simply exhausted the fascination of other sins by overindulging in them, so that the vice of constancy seems new and interesting to them. At any rate, he himself will suffer any indignity from the hands of women, except the request that he be loyal to any single one of them.

In the final stanza the inversion of commonplace assumptions about what is morally right is completed by the lover's assertion that Venus is on his side. Venus is here presented not even as *Venus vulgaris*, the goddess of generation, but rather as a goddess of inconstancy who is shocked to discover that her standards are being overthrown by a few peculiar and fanatical heretics. Concerned about this rebellion against the religion of love which she has hitherto believed to be universally established, she scurries about to investigate and quickly proclaims anathema upon the heretics. They will be punished for their deviation from the conventions of love by being forced to admit their existence even if they refuse to conform to them; even though some lovers attempt "to stablish dangerous constancie," they will simply have to be constant to people who are false to them.

Through adding the lover's insulting and dialectical defense of promiscuity in the second stanza and the verdict of Venus in the third, Donne has obviously complicated Ovid's elegy. But through the addition of these stanzas he has done still more to the concepts of promiscuity upon which Ovid's poem is based. Donne's lover is more audacious; he believes not only that inconstancy is delightful, but also a law to which all human beings should conform and normally do. He pretends to speak not only for himself, as Ovid does, but for all mankind as well. He gaily turns the assumptions of traditional morality upside down: the virtue of fidelity is a vice, the religion of love is a religion of lust, and the heretics are those who believe that promiscuity is evil. Such an inversion is at its most humorous, of course, when there is a rigid and widely accepted system of morality to be turned upside down. A poem like *The Indifferent* grows most naturally in an era like the Renaissance, when absolute moral standards were thought to reign absolutely. That fact accounts for part of the difference between Ovid's elegy and Donne's adaptation of it. And as in *Communitie* and *Confined Love*, the lover and his patron goddess cannot totally overturn the *consensus gentium* after all, for they must borrow some of its assumptions and vocabulary. The lover and Venus may believe that constancy is a vice, but both also believe that "heretics" must be punished, that those who are constant are "true," and those who are inconstant are "false."

These three poems, together with several others like *Womans constancy* and *Elegie XVII*, share a common point of view and method of justification, different as they are from one another in other ways. All seem to present a naturalistic philosophy of lust, affirming that variety and self-gratification are the shaping principles of the universe and that it is good that it should be so. All set out to contradict what is normally thought about the order of the universe and the nature of man, and the tone of objectivity in which outrageous pronouncements are made seems to cover a boyishly gleeful delight in smashing the icons which stuffy elders worship. That the speakers so consciously strike a pose, however, is enough to prevent the cautious reader from taking them for representatives of Donne's own point of view. There is a literary source behind them, and that source is the Renaissance Ovid.

But when Donne adopts an Ovidian pose, he also adapts it by complicating and sharpening the comic irony. Although Ovid plays frequently with the ironies of iconoclasm and self-contradiction, he does not call attention to moral tradition nearly so extensively as Donne. As a rule, Ovid asserts promiscuity as a fact of his nature and lies about his libertinism when he finds himself in awkward situations, which occur rather frequently. Ovid, as a lover, is simply a fool. The lovers whom Donne creates are wise fools. Their defenses of lust and promiscuity are far more learned and ambitious than anything which Ovid attempted, and they are far more conscious of a need to justify themselves before the frowning jury of moral tradition.

97

Hence, they present intricate proofs of the righteousness of libertinism, but they never fully succeed in escaping from the moral traditions which they try to deny. Because they pretend to be logical and objective, their self-contradiction is all the more destructive. The ultimate implication of poems like *Communitie* or *Confined Love* is that libertinism is, after all, logically indefensible and moral tradition inescapable.

The comedy of these poems, as of most of Donne's Ovidian poetry, is double. We are amused, on the one hand, by the sheer intellectual virtuosity of the arguments; their quickness and cleverness astonishes and delights us. On the other hand, however, the lovers are amusing because they are not quite clever enough; ultimately they only disprove what they are trying to prove and prove what they are trying to disprove. In the tenth paradox of the *Paradoxes and Problemes*, Donne discusses the relationship between fools and laughter with something more than mock seriousness, and his discussion neatly describes this satiric comedy which pervades his Ovidian poems:

> I alwayes did, and shall vnderstand that *Adage*:
> *Per risum multum possis cognoscere stultum*,
> that by much *laughing* thou maist know there is a Foole, not, that the *laugher*s are *Fooles*, but that among them there is some *Foole* at whom *wisemen* laugh: which moued *Erasmus* to put this as his first *Argument* in the mouth of his *Folly*, that *she made Beholders laugh*: for *fooles* are the most laughed at, and laugh the least themselues of any.

For all their wit, many of Donne's lovers are made to take themselves and their arguments very seriously, and they become all the more ridiculous because they do not realize how laughable they are. In these poems Donne is purging vice through laughter, laughter at men who shout that they are right while all the world recognizes that they are wrong.

ii *Logic's Countermarch*

In other poems Donne treats the essential ridiculousness of the pose of promiscuity more directly and obviously. Using the irony of situational comedy, he dramatizes a series of lovers who have suddenly realized that their mistresses can be as changeable as themselves and who do not altogether enjoy their realization. Because they believe promiscuity to be a "natural law" which reigns universally, they must also believe that it is a law which governs women. Yet, having found a woman whom they like and for whom they have invested considerable time and energy, they find themselves wishing that the law of promiscuity were not so universally binding after all. They find their naturalism rebounding upon them, their premises being carried to their logical conclusion with a vengeance; and they are not really happy with their discovery that the militant logic of inconstancy can countermarch and attack its originators.

In these poems too, Donne is drawing on themes, situations, and satiric techniques which he has learned from Ovid. When, in the second book of the *Ars Amatoria*, Ovid prescribes methods for making love affairs last, he comes eventually and inevitably to the problems which arise when a chosen mistress shares her favors with other men. Ovid argues that this is her right. The wise lover will accept it as such and attempt to ignore the fact of her infidelity, since to face it is so uncomfortable. This advice, that the lover should try to blind himself to the fact that he has been cuckolded, is comic enough. But Ovid goes on to admit that he himself cannot follow it. He simply cannot help being jealous and angry:

> Rivalem patienter habe, victoria tecum
> > Stabit: eris magni victor in arce Iovis.
> Haec tibi non hominem, sed quercus crede Pelasgas
> > Dicere: nil istis ars mea maius habet.
> Innuet illa, feras; scribet, ne tange tabellas:
> > Unde volet, veniat; quoque libebit, eat.
> Hoc in legitima praestant uxore mariti,

Cum, tener, ad partes tu quoque, somne, venis.
Hoc ego, confiteor, non sum perfectus in arte;
  Quid faciam? monitis sum minor ipse meis.
Mene palam nostrae det quisquam signa puellae,
  Et patiar, nec me quolibet ira ferat?
Oscula vir dederat, memini, suus: oscula questus
  Sum data; barbaria noster abundat amor.
Non semel hoc vitium nocuit mihi: doctior ille,
  Quo veniunt alii conciliante viri.
Sed melius nescisse fuit: sine furta tegantur,
  Ne fugiat, ficto fassus ab ore pudor.
Quo magis, o iuvenes, deprendere parcite vestras:
  Peccant, peccantes verba dedisse putent.[4]

(II.539-558)

Although Ovid pretends that he is lacking in sophistication and tolerance because he himself hates rivals, that most other men are able to be more large-minded than he, he is of course describing the more typical nature when he describes his own. He admits, in effect, that the desire for fidelity is even more natural than lust, and the *consensus gentium* about what is right in love turns out to be sensible as well as right.

Several of Donne's poems are based on this Ovidian situation, and they too are miniature situational comedies, though each varies its treatment of the theme. In *Elegie*

---

[4] "Endure a rival patiently: victory will be on your side; you will stand a victor on the citadel of great Jove. Think that no man, but the Pelasgian oaks are saying this: naught of greater import than this does my art contain. Does she beckon? bear it; does she write? touch not her tablets; let her come whence she will; let her go whither she pleases. Husbands afford this liberty to their lawful wives, when thou, soft sleep, comest to their aid. In this art, I confess, I am not perfect; what am I to do? I fall short of my own counsels. Shall anyone in my presence make signs to my mistress? shall I endure it? shall wrath not drive me where it will? Her own husband, I remember, had kissed her: I complained of the kisses; my love is full of savagery. Not once only has this fault done me harm: wiser he by whose complaisance other men come to his mistress. But ignorance were better: allow deceptions to be hid, lest the shame of confession fly from her dissembling countenance. Wherefore all the more, O lovers, detecting your mistresses; let them err, and erring think they have deceived."

III, Change, the speaker realizes, as Ovid does, that rivals in love are inevitable. Although he also follows Ovid in attempting to overcome his discomfort with cheerful sophistication, he does not really succeed in sounding very cheerful about his own method of solving their common dilemma—to escape from his potentially fickle mistress by imitating her fickleness. He too cannot help being jealous and angry, and he too tries to desensitize himself to the prodding of moral realities. But he gradually drops Ovid's tone of breezy good humor and sounds first bitter, then defensive. His solution is perhaps tougher and more aggressive than Ovid's, but that is only because his greater discomfort demands a sturdier armor.

ELEGIE III

Change

Although thy hand and faith, and good workes too,
Have seal'd thy love which nothing should undoe,
Yea though thou fall backe, that apostasie
Confirme thy love; yet much, much I feare thee.
Women are like the Arts, forc'd unto none,
Open to'all searchers, unpriz'd, if unknowne.
If I have caught a bird, and let him flie,
Another fouler using these meanes, as I,
May catch the same bird; and, as these things bee,
Women are made for men, not him, nor mee.
Foxes and goats; all beasts change when they please,
Shall women, more hot, wily, wild then these,
Be bound to one man, and did Nature then
Idly make them apter to'endure then men?
They'are our clogges, not their owne; if a man bee
Chain'd to a galley, yet the galley'is free;
Who hath a plow-land, casts all his seed corne there,
And yet allowes his ground more corne should beare;
Though Danuby into the sea must flow,
The sea receives the Rhene, Volga, and Po.
By nature, which gave it, this liberty

Thou lov'st, but Oh! canst thou love it and mee?
Likenesse glues love: and if that thou so doe,
To make us like and love, must I change too?
More then thy hate, I hate'it, rather let mee
Allow her change, then change as oft as shee,
And so not teach, but force my'opinion
To love not any one, nor every one.
To live in one land, is captivitie,
To runne all countries, a wild roguery;
Waters stincke soone, if in one place they bide,
And in the vast sea are more putrifi'd:
But when they kisse one banke, and leaving this
Never looke backe, but the next banke doe kisse,
Then are they purest; Change'is the nursery
Of musicke, joy, life, eternity.

The predominant mood in this poem is indecisiveness.
The lover, although he has no evidence that his mistress is
unfaithful, recognizes that her infidelity will come inevitably, since change is the law of nature. But amatory change
seems both necessary and unpleasant. Should he decide to
embrace it as a good or condemn it as an evil? The lover
hesitantly wavers between these two poles and finally concludes by deciding to accept the fact of change and call it
joyous. He determines to move on from one potentially unfaithful mistress to another, thereby avoiding cuckoldry
and maintaining his "purity." But after all the revelations
of the inherent joylessness of amatory change which he has
given, his decision to continue his commitment to change
hardly seems full of the joyousness which he attributes to
it in the end. Rather, he seems a man who is trying very
hard to whistle in the dark and pretend that his notes are
not flat.

The poem begins by announcing its Ovidian theme in a
way that could only be done in a Christian era. His mistress
has given their love for one another the double seal of faith
and good works, seals normally so efficacious that they are
not easily broken. In fact, their love is so miraculous that

even apostasy, which is after all only a falling back, would be yet another seal. Yet after these playful suggestions that sex is good, in whatever metaphors one describes it, he admits that it is also dangerous. For the lover knows that if he enjoys the seals which his mistress has given him, other men may too, and his mistress may not remain faithful to him.

The next eighteen lines contain the lover's analysis of the nature of women. Following the doctrines of libertine naturalism, he sees them as inherently lustful and promiscuous, like all other animals. But women, he says, even outdo other beasts, for they are more lustful than goats and more wily in fulfilling their lust than foxes. This follows from the nature which "wise Nature" has given them; they are made "apter to'endure then men" and have practically unlimited capacities for fulfilling their lustful desires. Men have no choice, therefore, but to accept the inevitability of feminine promiscuity; women are available to all men in the same way that any ploughed field will receive seed corn or that an ocean welcomes all rivers indifferently. Women have infinite capacities for inconstancy, and they love this liberty to change which is theirs by nature.

This discussion of the nature of women, founded upon an appeal to the libertine concept of nature, is quite similar to that used in *Confined Love*. But the lover in *Elegie III* has already accomplished his seduction, and now the libertine argument operates to his disadvantage. As he realizes in line 22, his mistress cannot love both promiscuity and him. If a woman is interested in a man only to fulfill her lust and any man will do, then *she* can eat the kernel and fling away the shell when it is no longer of any use. The lover realizes that he, as an individual personality, shrinks into nothingness before the drives of nature. He can perhaps be an object of lust, but he cannot be loved.

The militant logic of natural change has created his dilemma, and now he must decide what is to be done about it. Should he imitate the promiscuity of his mistress? Now that he is about to suffer from it, he finds it hateful. If likeness glues love, and if the only way their love can be cemented is by his becoming like her in promiscuity, then he feels that they might as well not love. Why have a relationship based upon an agreement that they will both be unfaithful to one another? But should he, on the other hand, remain loyal to a single mistress who is not loyal to him? That is like being chained to a galley which is free, like being a captive confined in one country.

The lover attempts to escape the horns of his dilemma and of cuckoldry by choosing a middle course. He will accommodate himself to the fact of natural change by changing occasionally, but not with the promiscuity of which women are capable. He argues that waters stink and become stagnant if they remain in one place; if they fall into the vast sea, they also become putrified. He will neither choose only one woman nor the vast sea of them; like a river he will meander slowly from mistress to mistress and never look back to see his former mistress in another man's arms. Having at last decided on intentional blindness, he can forget that only a few lines earlier he said of change, "More then thy hate, I hate'it." Instead, he can affirm that "Change'is the nursery / Of musicke, joy, life, and eternity."

The lover's sophistical solution of his dilemma is no doubt meant to seem comical, comical with all the irony of the Ovidian tradition. Through his very choice of the river image to describe his love, he contradicts himself, since he has already proved in lines 19 and 20 that all rivers eventually flow into the sea anyway. Thus his own putrifaction seems inevitable. He hates change and yet embraces it, trying to blindly forget that he hates it. He is acutely uncomfortable because his mistress will treat him as a mere animal, and yet his naturalistic philosophy maintains that human beings are nothing but mere animals. He knows that his philosophy does not justify jealousy, and yet he feels it. He knows that "To runne all countries" is "a wild roguery," and yet that is just what he is going to do, and call it purity to boot. He is painfully unhappy about his situation, and yet he never gets out of it. He is clutching at a straw in the last line of the poem and does not succeed in convincing either himself or the reader that it really is a log. The words he uses to describe the potentialities offered by change, "musicke, joy, life, eternity," sound wryly discordant, for the reader has been made to realize fully what the speaker realizes only partially, that he will never reach these four ideals by meandering from mistress to mistress.

Though the lover chooses to try to escape from his frustration by blinding himself and then embracing the very kind of love that causes it, Donne suggests through the imagery of the poem that another route and a better love are possible. *Elegie III* begins with a witty yoking of sex and religion, and it concludes with the equally paradoxical assertion that change is the nursery of eternity. But Donne's wit is more than just intellectual play; it serves as much to show *discordia discors* as *discordia concors*. Two loves, *caritas* and *cupiditas*, are yoked by violence together. The speaker, devoted to *cupiditas*, attempts to persuade himself that its tyrannous transiency can be overcome, that he can achieve the security of *caritas* through persistent self-gratification. And yet as we read the poem his final defensive assertion of the joyousness of change seems ridiculously incongruous; the Renaissance reader, probably even more aware of the incongruity because more accustomed to thinking of profane and sacred love as two disparate realms, would recall instead that *caritas*, with its faith and altruistic good works, and not *cupiditas*, is the nursery of joy, life, and eternity. Donne's wit is functional, its function is irony, and that irony reveals the value of righteous love while the speaker pursues its opposite.

In *Elegie VII* Donne also draws upon the Ovidian irony that a man who embraces impermanent love embraces his own punishment. Taking the same situation that he used in *Elegie III*, a man's recognition that the militant logic of lust can countermarch to attack its proponents, Donne now imagines a different kind of lover and a different kind of reaction. The speaker of *Elegie VII* does not try to fool himself, either about the potential infidelity of his mistress or about the pleasures of promiscuity; he confronts the facts, and his confrontation produces self-hatred and bitterness. The moral order which was implicitly suggested through the imagery of *Elegie III* is now stated explicitly by a man who sees that, through painful justice, he is only harvesting what he has sown.

ELEGIE VII

Natures lay Ideot, I taught thee to love,
And in that sophistrie, Oh, thou dost prove
Too subtile: Foole, thou didst not understand
The mystique language of the eye nor hand:
Nor couldst thou judge the difference of the aire
Of sighes, and say, this lies, this sounds despaire:
Nor by the'eyes water call a maladie
Desperately hot, or changing feaverously.
I had not taught thee then, the Alphabet
Of flowers, how they devisefully being set
And bound up, might with speechlesse secrecie
Deliver arrands mutely, and mutually.
Remember since all thy words us'd to bee
To every suitor; *I, if my friends agree*;
Since, household charmes, thy husbands name to teach,
Were all the love trickes, that thy wit could reach;
And since, an houres discourse could scarce have made
One answer in thee, and that ill arraid
In broken proverbs, and torne sentences.
Thou art not by so many duties his,
That from the worlds Common having sever'd thee,
Inlaid thee, neither to been seene, nor see,
As mine: who have with amorous delicacies
Refin'd thee'into a blis-full Paradise.
Thy graces and good words my creatures bee;
I planted knowledge and lifes tree in thee,
Which Oh, shall strangers taste? Must I alas
Frame and enamell Plate, and drinke in Glass?

Chafe waxe for others seales? breake a colts force
And leave him then, beeing made a ready horse?

The lover identifies his philosophy and personality in the
first three words of the poem: he is "Natures lay Ideot."
He is a libertine naturalist, but he is also an amateur and
even a fool when he tries to live by his philosophy. His
amateurish blunders, however, have not occurred for lack of
research on his subject; he has followed the techniques for
deceiving suspicious husbands taught by the master himself.
In I.iv of the *Amores*, for example, Ovid tells his mistress to
try to arrive before her husband at a banquet to which all
three have been invited, just in case the two of them may
have a chance to meet. But at dinner, in the presence of the
husband, they will communicate by "The mystique language of the eye nor hand":

> me specta natusque meos vultumque loquacem;
> > excipe furtivas et refer ipsa notas.
> verba superciliis sine voce loquentia dicam;
> > verba leges digitis, verba notata mero.
> cum tibi succurret Veneris lascivia nostrae,
> > purpureas tenero pollice tange genas.
> siquid erit, de me tacita quod mente queraris,
> > pendeat extrema mollis ab aure manus.[5]

> (17-24)

Having learned them from Ovid, the lover has in turn
taught his mistress the tricks of love which make possible
the sports of love, in spite of household spies.

Nor has the lover blundered because he did not have a
sufficiently pliable pupil to teach. He found his student in
a state of rustic naiveté and almost complete innocence.
She once responded to the speeches of would-be seducers

[5] "Keep your eyes on me, to get my nods and the language of my
eyes; and I shall say to you words that speak without sound; you will
read words from my fingers, you will read words traced in wine.
When you think of the wanton delights of our love, touch your rosy
cheeks with tender finger. If you have in mind some silent grievance
against me, let your hand gently hold to the lowest part of your ear."

by saying that their offers were agreeable to her if they seemed agreeable to her family. Her wit once reached only to playing word-games to discover her husband's name. She had no fluency of speech, and when she responded to some gentleman's brilliant and lengthy discourse, she could reply only by stammering and stuttering proverbs and truisms. From such abject provincialism, the lover redeemed her by his teaching; and since she, as she is now, is actually his own creation, she is more justly the property of her lover than the property of her husband. For her husband chose her, went through the marriage ceremony, and sheltered her only so that she stayed just as she was. She was once a simple wife. Now she is refined into a "blisfull Paradise" in which the tree of knowledge and the tree of life have been planted.

But again Donne's imagery is an ironic complement to the situational irony. As the remainder of the poem reveals, the beloved is no paradise at all. Or rather, she is a sexual paradise, a garden of Earthly delight which is not enclosed; but in the biblical sense, she is a paradise lost, a paradise in which the fall from innocence has taken place. She was almost completely innocent before her lover recreated her, but now that she has acquired knowledge and tasted evil, she has also acquired new capacities for rebelling against her own creator-lover, who forgot that she was also endowed with free will. And so, as the lover realizes, she may seem as blissful to other men as she has seemed to him. The speaker's blunder was not choosing an unteachable pupil, but in choosing an apt one and teaching her too well. In fact, of course, his blunder was in teaching her at all, and his error is pointed up by the inverted religious imagery.

However enjoyable the destruction of innocence was for the lover, its consequences are painful. As re-creator, tempter, and destroyer, he was in the role of master. He assumed a diabolically God-like position when he planted "knowledge and lifes tree," and he claimed his mistress's "graces and good words" as his own. But in assuming the role

108

of master over his beloved, he instead ironically made himself a servant to other men; believing he was creating her for his own use, he instead trained her for the use of others. Like a skilled artisan, he has framed enamel and plate and himself must drink in glass; he is a secretary who has softened wax so that others may imprint their seals, a groom who has trained a horse for other men to ride. Ultimately he reaps pain rather than enjoyment from his endeavor, self-abasement rather than self-importance. He hoped to make evil a good, and in diabolic manner he has instead turned good to evil.

In *Elegie III* and *Elegie VII* Donne has taken an Ovidian theme and increased the irony already inherent in it by creating naturalistic lovers who feel misery or confusion when they realize that their philosophy of love is a two-edged sword. *Elegie XX, Loves Warre*, depicts a similar situation; the lover in this poem also realizes that his beloved is at least potentially inconstant, since all women are naturally inconstant. But rather than abandon her or reflect upon his misery, he chooses to stay with her and enjoy her companionship, hoping that he will be able to monopolize her affections as long as he is near enough to stand guard. On the surface, at least, *Elegie XX* is full of exuberance and optimism, whereas the other two elegies express confusion, pessimism, and dissatisfaction. In tone, it is the closest of the three to Ovid himself.

In *Loves Warre* Donne blends the Ovidian theme of potential cuckoldry with another standard Ovidian theme, the *miles amoris*. In the ninth elegy of Book I of the *Amores* Ovid ingeniously describes many ways in which the soldiers of love and war are similar: both the lover and the soldier should be young; both have to endure many hardships, yet victory is always uncertain; both have to sneak past guards and sentinels, and the lover must fight his rivals just as the soldier does his enemies; the lover must besiege the doors of an unwilling mistress just as the soldier must batter the gates of resisting cities. In short, Ovid emphasizes that both the lover and the soldier need bravery, perseverance, and energy. The irony of the elegy depends on the tacit recognition that the lover sleeping on the doorstep of his lady's house cuts a somewhat sillier figure than the brave lieutenant keeping watch at the door of his captain's tent.

Donne borrows a few Ovidian comparisons to begin his elegy; the initial lines draw on Ovid's

> mittitur infestos alter speculator in hostes;
> in rivale oculos alter, ut hoste tenet.
> ille graves urbes, hic durae limen amicae
> obsidet; hic portas frangit, at ille fores.[6]

(17-20)

But after compressing together images of love and war, Donne's lover goes on to explain why military combat is inferior to love's war. Unlike Ovid, who ostensibly writes to arouse from their laziness men too slothful to love, this lover tries to defend the pursuit of glory in love and to arouse his mistress so that he can make a conquest. Ovid's praise of love by comparing it with war is obviously ironic, whereas Donne's *miles amoris* seems quite serious when he attacks war and defends love, saying that the one brings misery and the other pleasure, that soldiers kill men and lovers create them.

ELEGIE XX

Loves Warre

Till I have peace with thee, warr other men,
And when I have peace, can I leave thee then?
All other Warrs are scrupulous; Only thou
O fayr free Citty, maist thyselfe allowe
To any one: In Flanders, who can tell
Whether the Master presse; or men rebell?
Only we know, that which all Ideots say,
They beare most blows which come to part the fray.

---

[6] "The one is sent to scout the dangerous foe; the other keeps eyes upon his rival as on a foeman. The one besieges mighty towns, the other the threshold of an unyielding mistress; the other breaks in doors, the one, gates."

France in her lunatique giddiness did hate
Ever our men, yea and our God of late;
Yet she relyes upon our Angels well,
Which nere returne; no more then they which fell.
Sick Ireland is with a strange warr possest
Like to an Ague; now raging, now at rest;
Which time will cure: yet it must doe her good
If she were purg'd, and her head vayne let blood.
And Midas joyes our Spanish journeys give,
We touch all gold, but find no food to live.
And I should be in the hott parching clyme,
To dust and ashes turn'd before my time.
To mew me in a Ship, is to inthrall
Mee in a prison, that weare like to fall;
Or in a Cloyster; save that there men dwell
In a calme heaven, here in a swaggering hell.
Long voyages are long consumptions,
And ships are carts for executions.
Yea they are Deaths; Is't not all one to flye
Into an other World, as t'is to dye?
Here let mee warr; in these armes lett me lye;
Here let mee parlee, batter, bleede, and dye.
Thyne armes imprison me, and myne armes thee;
Thy hart thy ransome is; take myne for mee.
Other men war that they their rest may gayne;
But wee will rest that wee may fight agayne.
Those warrs the ignorant, these th'experienc'd love,
There wee are alwayes under, here above.
There Engins farr off breed a just true feare,
Neere thrusts, pikes, stabs, yea bullets hurt not here.
There lyes are wrongs; here safe uprightly lye;
There men kill men, we'will make one by and by.
Thou nothing; I not halfe so much shall do
In these Warrs, as they may which from us two
Shall spring. Thousands wee see which travaile not
To warrs; But stay swords, armes, and shott
To make at home; And shall not I do then
More glorious service, staying to make men?

111

Speaking to a mistress who has perhaps asked why he has not proved his worth on a military expedition like other men, the lover begins by arguing that he has not even won "peace" with her yet, and even when he has defeated his rivals and made his conquest he dare not leave her and fight other battles. He must continue to stay with her and guard her in order to be sure that she does not grant another victory to someone else in his absence. A mistress, he says, is a "fayr free Citty" in the warfare of love, and this war is without scruples. Since the unwritten international law of love's war permits her to transfer affections and privileges as often as she pleases, she is free to yield if another conquering hero comes along when he is gone. But if he cannot deny the natural law which grants her freedom from moral scruples about infidelity, he can encourage her to remain loyal to him by staying near her.

His pronouncement that "All other Warrs are scrupulous" also points in another direction, however, meaning that all combat besides love raises scruples and troubles the conscience; and so he goes on to explain his dislike of military warfare, citing specific illustrations of its doubtful moral value. In Flanders, for example, it is nearly impossible to decide which side is in the right; one cannot say whether the ruling power is guilty of tyranny or whether the people are guilty of rebellion; but, he adds with a smile, we *do* know that any mediator who attempts to bring peace would receive assaults from both sides and fare worse than either antagonist. France has recently been ravaged with political and religious civil war, and England has maintained a somewhat compromising position in relation to its outcome. Although France is England's historic enemy and although their natural enmity has been increased through the Huguenot Henry's conversion to Roman Catholicism on the principle that "Paris is worth a mass," Elizabeth is giving Henry financial aid in order to play France off against Spain. In spite of their hatred of the English nation and its religion, Frenchmen love English angels so well that they never pay them back; Elizabeth's policy has thus produced "fallen angels." Beneath the levity is the implication that the glory of war and the integrity of international politics are tarnished by betrayal, hypocrisy, and compromise. Even if the Irish war is more justifiable, since Ireland needs to be purged of insurrection and rebellious double-dealing by having a vein in its vain head opened, this war is best described through the imagery of disease. And although England deserves to win in Ireland, her policies of pirating Spanish wealth are overgreedy, for like Midas she becomes rich in the sterile symbol of wealth, gold, while her people starve. Finally, the individual soldier who takes part in England's sea expeditions lives in a "swaggering hell," confined in fragile and disease-ridden ships and carried to hot dry climates which reduce him to ashes and dust before his time.

After justifying himself by dwelling so long on the miseries of war, in the last twenty lines the speaker eloquently praises love's war. Through ingenious and witty metaphors, the combat which takes place on the couch is described in terms drawn from the battlefield. In love's war the lover wins a pleasing death, the death of sexual consummation. The arms in which he will be clad are not harsh and metallic, but rather the soft arms of his mistress. Nor is there anything to fear from the weapons which will be used to inflict death, since the lovers will be making men rather than killing them. But beneath this witty description, there are suggestions of the latent destructiveness of sex. If its wounds are not literally mortal, they are often spiritually mortal, as the pun on death implies. If its weapons give pleasure rather than pain, they still are weapons in a struggle which is selfish and sometimes brutal. There are hints that love's war too can be predatory, confining, and ague-like, "now raging, now at rest. . . ."

In this poem Donne has created a Falstaff-like realist who speaks partial truths with irresponsible gaiety. Although his motive is seduction, he presents the undeniable proposition that creation is greater than destruction; and he manages to equate military cowardice with moral courage, arguing that war is full of treason and compromise, while love demands total and uncalculating commitment. But there are nevertheless dark spots beneath the brightness and charm of his pose. Since the lover is afraid to leave his mistress alone among his rivals because she may betray his love by granting hers to other men, he admits that treason is possible in love too. Although he says that "All other Warrs are scrupulous" but love knows no laws, he himself feels scruples about leaving his mistress behind to receive the assaults of other *milites amoris*. Likewise, he later says of war and love, "There lyes are wrongs; here safe uprightly lye. . . ." While punning he is also admitting that there are at least some sanctions in war (lying is wrong) which help prevent treason or make it clearly wrong when it occurs, but the misfortune of love is that there are no moral laws which will help prevent betrayal by either party since self-gratification is its only guide. Love, although it is said to be superior to war, does not lack the potentialities for betrayal and compromise which the lover finds so contemptible in war. Taken alone, *Elegie XX* might seem a light-hearted *jeu d'esprit* in which Donne outdoes Ovid in ingeniously extending the metaphor of love's war. But this lover is in a sense a youthful and undaunted forerunner of the lovers in *Elegies III* and *VII*; he knows he is taking up a risky game and may suffer betrayal and infidelity, and he innocently decides the pleasure is worth the risk.

In all three poems Donne creates lovers who have substituted lust for love and who, to a greater or lesser degree, sense that they have erred. The strident and forced gaiety of *Elegie III*, the scornful self-contempt of *Elegie VII*, and the mild suspicion of *Elegie XX* all indicate that these lovers recognize that lustful love cannot meet the pragmatic test: it cannot make them completely happy, and it may make them miserable. Each reacts differently. One tries to repress his recognition, another sardonically ridicules himself, and another actually succeeds in temporarily forgetting it. Their reactions vary as their objectivity varies. But most of Donne's contemporary readers would, I think, see them

114

as the most objective, the speaker of *Elegie VII*, sees himself. All, though they do not all realize it fully, are "Natures lay ideots."

At about the same time that he wrote his elegies, Donne was probably also writing his *Satyres*. And in *Satyre II*, after listing nearly every form of sinner he can think of, the curmudgeonly scholar who acts as Donne's mouthpiece in the poem comments, "But these punish themselves." *Communitie* states a similar belief: "Bad doth it self, and others wast. . . ." These elegies dramatize this same moral principle. In a poem like *Elegie VII* Donne is depicting a lover at the very moment when moral traditions have caught up with him, confronted him, and proved the inherent practicality of the moral laws of love. But in all three the lovers, by preaching promiscuity, have punished themselves, for all dread the possibility that their mistresses may practice what they themselves have preached.

iii *Disillusionment and* Remedia Amoris

The third step is, of course, complete disillusionment with lust, and in *Loves Alchymie* and *Farewell to love* Donne imagines lovers who take it. These poems are the Donnean equivalent to the Shakespearean "Th' expense of spirit in a waste of shame/ Is lust in action. . . ." They see lust as a filthy quagmire in which man foolishly permits himself to be caught; although he is lured into it because it seems to promise excitement and pleasure, once he has entered its forbidden boundaries he discovers instead that he is being sucked down into a hell which was disguised as a heaven. Whereas the earlier poems dramatized the folly of lust through comic irony and satire, these are straightforward assertions that lust is an evil. The only logical conclusion is *remedia amoris*.

Poems like *The Sunne Rising* or *Elegies XVIII* and *XIX*, all of which focus on sexual consummation, seem superficially to be at the other end of the continuum. But even in them intense delight in physical gratification is not the predominant mood. *The Sunne Rising* comes closest. It is a genre poem, an *aubade*, built upon a situation treated most famously by Ovid in I.xiii of the *Amores*, by Chaucer in *Troilus and Criseyda*, and by Shakespeare in *Romeo and Juliet*. It takes place as the lover wakes up in the morning in bed with his mistress and discovers that the sun is shining in his eyes and that the night of love is now over. With no small petulance and annoyance, he makes an address "Ad Solem" (as Donne's poem is frequently titled in the manuscripts), telling it to go away and to stop interfering with his pleasure. Prior to Donne, at least, the sun is made the villain of the melodrama, but it is the villain who triumphs in the end, for day breaks to separate the pair in spite of the lover's exhortation. Ovid concludes his own elegy with a wryly humorous comment on the futility of his attempts to stop the course of nature for his own benefit: "nec tamen adsueto tardium orta dies!" ("and yet the day arose no later than its wont!").

Thus there were potentialities for comic irony within the genre which Donne did not even choose to exploit in *The Sunne Rising*. Rather, by force of wit, the annoyed lover dominates the sun throughout. Of the sun's beams, which the sun arrogantly believes reverend and strong, the lover impudently says, "I could eclipse and cloud them with a winke. . . ." At the conclusion the sun is accused of being aged and tired; and the lover mockingly tells it that the world has been, therefore, contracted to a tiny size, in fact to the size of the lover and the beloved (who are themselves the whole world). The sun too is contracted, to the size of their bed and bedroom, and its duty to warm the world is thus reduced to the easy task of heating this tiny Everywhere:

> Thine age askes ease, and since thy duties bee
> To warme the world, that's done in warming us.
> Shine here to us, and thou art every where;
> This bed thy center is, these walls, thy spheare.

Unlike Ovid or Troilus or Romeo, this lover refuses to be the least bit disturbed by that busy old fool, the unruly sun.

His profane gaiety easily succeeds in making the sun seem tired and impotent in comparison with himself and his beloved. But in this poem wit and ingenuity are more predominant than sexual passion. The lover seems to delight most in his ability to triumph over the sun and thus outdo Ovid.

Fine as the poem is, it is not a typical example of Donne's poems of sexual love. For the other side of the question, one can look at an inferior (and therefore less noticed) poem, *Breake of day*, which uses exactly the same situation. This poem, however, is spoken by the woman, and her lover is about to abandon her. In *Breake of day* the tone is far from gay. It is, in fact, faintly tragic. The woman begins by stating her faith that love can triumph even over the break of daylight on the morning after, and she does so with a mixed tone of innocent happiness and apprehensive fear:

> 'Tis true, 'tis day; what though it be?
> O wilt thou therefore rise from me?
> Why should we rise, because 'tis light?
> Did we lie downe, because 'twas night?
> Love which in spight of darknesse brought us hether,
> Should in despight of light keepe us together.

But as the poem progresses it appears that the woman's statement of faith in the power of love is a vain hope rather than a reality. For the break of daylight is going to separate them rather than keep them together. Before the woman discovers that her lover is about to leave her, however, she surveys her situation by the light of day; and she says that if light, which usually can only spy, could also speak, the worst it could say of her is

> . . . that I lov'd my heart and honor so
> That I would not from him, that had them, goe.

The possessor of her heart and honor *is* going to go from her, however, even if she is not going to leave him, for he has business to do. The man is, of course, simply following Ovid's sensible advice in the *Remedia Amoris*, that atten-

117

tion to worldly business is the best cure for love: "Otia si tollas, periere Cupidinus arcus," "Take away leisure, and Cupid's bow is broken" (139). But the woman, who has not been forewarned that her lover would leave her on the morning after, accuses him of wrongdoing with some warmth:

> He which hath businesse, and makes love, doth doe
> Such wrong, as when a married man doth wooe.

And her accusation in these concluding lines turns the reader's sympathy toward her and away from the lover who can eat the kernel and fling away the shell.

Nor is intense joy in the physical the prevailing tone in the most frankly erotic poems that Donne ever wrote, *Elegies XVIII* and *XIX*. Both poems are inspired by lines 703-732 in the second book of the *Ars Amatoria*, where Ovid describes in voluptuous detail the best way to draw the most pleasure from sex. Donne imitates Ovid's frank forthrightness, but he captures little of the blend of lightness and eroticism which gives the prevailing tone in Ovid's account. Rather, Donne seems almost willfully and intentionally to blend in either crude and repulsive images or undercutting theological imagery, refusing to exploit the possibilities for expressing sensual delight offered by his Ovidian materials. Donne's treatment of consummation often seems heavy, sometimes even cynically or clinically cold, when compared with Ovid's. Where Ovid seems to write of the art of love, Donne seems to write of the science of lust.

Elegie XVIII, subtitled "Loves Progress," is principally concerned with stating an anti-Ovidian thesis about the progress of love-making. In lines 717-728 Ovid urges that much of the pleasure of sexual consummation derives from putting it off as long as possible. He warns his readers not to rush impatiently to fulfill their desires if they wish to enjoy themselves to the full and to give their partner maximum delight. Donne's poem is not so much advice to a pair of lovers as to other men; and it tells them, in effect, to get consummation over with as quickly as possible. The speaker admits that traditionally love begins with the face and moves downward, but he urges lovers to "Rather set out below; practice my Art. . . ." And he prefers his own art to Ovid's counsel of slowness because it teaches "the nearer way." The speaker freely admits that, by using his art, lovers do not dwell luxuriously upon beauty; and he admits by implication that lust is not interested in beauty, but only in predatory and rapacious gratification. The poem deals in sexual passion, but it does not express the desire to prolong pleasure forever which characterizes genuinely erotic poetry. Nor does it encompass that form of lust which faintly approaches love—lust which wishes the other partner to share equally in sexual pleasure. In *Elegie XVIII* the woman is a patient etherized upon a table. The treatment may be practical and efficient, but it is hardly joyous.

Beyond this, however, the elegy does not begin to express the passions of lust until thirty-five or so lines have passed by. The counsel on the proper way to progress in love is preceded by a lengthy philosophical disquisition on "the right true end of love." This introduction argues that men love material goods for their usefulness rather than their accidental qualities; in women, likewise, virtue or beauty are accidents, and the useful essence is to be found in "the Centrique part." The lover even confesses that the Cupid who presides over the right true love which he advocates is an infernal God:

> Search every spheare
> And firmament, our *Cupid* is not there;
> He's an infernal god and underground,
> With *Pluto* dwells, where gold and fire abound:
> Men to such Gods, their sacrificing Coles
> Did not in Altars lay, but pits and holes.

This Cupid, however appropriate, is hardly a propitious or attractive deity to invoke. And, finally, there is the brutal ugliness of the poem's conclusion.

> Rich Nature hath in women wisely made
> Two purses, and their mouths aversely laid:

They then, which to the lower tribute owe,
That way which that Exchequer looks, must go:
He which doth not, his error is as great,
As who by Clyster gave the Stomack meat.

Elegie XIX, which seems somewhat more spontaneously gay, is also not without grim undercurrents and a satiric tone. This poem is a speech in which a lover urges his mistress to undress quickly and completely in order that the pair may enjoy the fruits of love unimpeded. Approximately twenty lines are devoted to the lover's anticipatory eagerness as he watches his mistress gradually unclothe herself, garment by garment. After she is fully undressed, the lover philosophizes for approximately twenty more lines on the value and quasi-religious significance of nakedness. The result is that the last half of the poem is a ridiculously pedantic anticlimax. A few lines will suffice to illustrate:

O my America! my new-found-land,
My kingdome, safliest when with one man man'd,
My Myne of precious stones, My Emperie,
How blest am I in this discovering thee!
To enter in these bonds, is to be free;
Then where my hand is set, my seal shall be.
     Full nakedness! All joyes are due to thee,
As souls unbodied, bodies uncloth'd must be,
To taste whole joyes.

The strained intellectuality of these lines sounds almost like a satire on amatory hyperbole, and in general the last half of the poem seems unsatisfactory as a song of seduction.

The final lines of the poem further buttress this incipiently negative attitude:

Then since that I may know;
As liberally, as to a Midwife, shew
Thy self: cast all, yea, this white lynnen hence,
There is no pennance, much less innocence.
     To teach thee, I am naked first; why than
What needst thou have more covering then a man.

The reference to midwives seems a harsh reminder that children as well as pleasure result from such unions. And this reminder is juxtaposed to the statement that "There is no pennance, much less innocence."[7] The lover is making a rather clear admission that their behavior is wrong, albeit with a black delight which recognizes itself as black and pronounces blackness good. If the speaker finds joy in lust, he also says such joy is sinful and that sinning is good. But embracing a sin and knowing it is sin is very different from saying that it is not sinful at all. It is as if Donne wished to say in *Breake of day* and *Elegies XVIII* and *XIX* that there is no doubt that lust is frequently and strongly felt, but that there is also no doubt that, despite its pervasiveness and intensity, it is often violent, selfish, and cruel.

There is no doubt, at any rate, that this is the attitude toward lust in *Loves Alchymie* and *Farewell to love*. The first frankly asserts that lust is as disappointing and ugly as it is universal. In the second, disillusionment is so complete that a firm resolution to escape is possible.

Loves Alchymie is a thoroughly grim, pessimistic, and despair-filled poem. Its power rests upon the paradox that the lover hates the lust which he feels and yet hates equally the naive belief that love can be anything but lust. So, although he is thoroughly disillusioned by the false promises of joy which lust seems to offer, he decides to embrace the source of his disillusionment rather than believe a lie.

Loves Alchymie

Some that have deeper digg'd loves Myne then I,
Say, where his centrique happinesse doth lie:
    I have lov'd, and got, and told,
But should I love, get, tell, till I were old,
I should not finde that hidden mysterie;
    Oh, 'tis imposture all:

---

[7] This reading has the overwhelming manuscript authority and is, therefore, more probably the right one; but Grierson preferred to print the slightly milder "There is no pennance due to innocence" of a few less reliable manuscripts and the 1669 edition.

And as no chymique yet the'Elixar got,
    But glorifies his pregnant pot,
    If by the way to him befall
Some odoriferous thing, or medicinall,
      So, lovers dreame a rich and long delight,
      But get a winter-seeming summers night.

Our ease, our thrift, our honor, and our day,
Shall we, for this vaine Bubles shadow pay?
    Ends love in this, that my man,
Can be as happy'as I can; If he can
Endure the short scorne of a Bridegroomes play?
    That loving wretch that sweares,
'Tis not the bodies marry, but the mindes,
    Which he in her Angelique findes,
    Would sweare as justly, that he heares,
In that dayes rude hoarse minstralsey, the spheares.
    Hope not for minde in women; at their best
    Sweetnesse and wit, they'are but *Mummy,* possest.

This poem has obvious connections with *Elegie XVIII,* for it too maintains that love consists of digging for "the Centrique part." But *Loves Alchymie* also adds that digging for the centric part brings neither happiness nor fulfillment. Instead love offers only false promises, which are of two kinds, one described in the first stanza and the other in the second—fulfillment in physical union and fulfillment in love between minds. Sexual love is real, but it brings no satisfaction; spiritual love is not real and therefore can bring none either.

The lover begins by charging anyone who knows more about love than himself, who has "Deeper digg'd love's mine," to explain wherein consists its essential happiness. He himself has loved women, possessed them, and counted over his possessions; and yet his experience has only convinced him that, no matter how often he repeated it, he would never find any essential happiness in it. Love's joy is a mystery which will remain hidden from him forever or else, and more probably, it is simply an imposture like alchemy. No alchemist has ever found the *elixir vitae*, for which he continually searches and experiments, and no alchemist ever will, since it does not exist; yet the alchemist who accidentally produces some trivial thing which seems sweet-smelling or medicinally beneficial glorifies his alchemical vessels, alchemy, and himself. His accidental discovery is trivial, but the alchemist, ignoring the discrepancy between his expectations and actuality, makes himself happy by pretending that the inconsequential results of his labor are worthwhile. Lovers too pursue nonexistent joys; they dream of a "rich and long delight," and they pretend that the cold short pleasures of "a winter-seeming summer's night" are satisfying.

The speaker has, however, no doubt in his own mind about the extent to which the accidental joys of physical love can satisfy. He sees them as the shadow of a vain bubble; the theoretical essential joy of love (something more than mere lust) is as false as the *elixir vitae*—it is a vain bubble. The accidental joys of physical love which are acquired in pursuing the bubble are even more false, for they are only shadowy reflections of something which does not exist; shadows of real things are unreal enough, but the joys of physical love are as deceptively unreal as the shadow of a non-existent bubble. And yet, the speaker says, men sacrifice their ease, thrift, honor, and life for "this vaine Bubles shadow." It seems as if love is only lust, which is not worth the expense of spirit it demands. The speaker contemptuously notes that his own servant can acquire such amatory bliss by simply going through a marriage ceremony, can no doubt acquire it more cheaply and easily than he himself.

But despite the fact that the lover believes physical love to be unsatisfying and costly, he goes on in the concluding lines of the poem to assert that it is the only "love" possible. Harshly skeptical of Platonic love, he sardonically charges that anyone who is naive enough to marry because he thinks he loves the lady's angelic mind is also sufficiently self-deceived to mistake the "rude hoarse minstralsey" of the marriage music for the music of the spheres. No one should hope to find mind in a woman; even at their best sweetness and wit, they are only physical creatures. And the love of women is nothing but lust, nothing but the possession of mummy (dead flesh used as a medicine), which leaves a bitter taste in the mouth but gives a temporary cure for the disease of lust.

It would be difficult to find a more repelling image to describe the act of making love. The image of mummy, which gives the poem its title in most of the manuscripts, fittingly sums up the speaker's reaction to his own amatory experience. He has hoped to find happiness, and instead he has found that love is nothing but mere physical gratification, whatever others may say about love between minds. Spiritual love is nonexistent, and lust is only a communion with lifeless flesh. The speaker's dilemma is that of a man too sensual and cynical to discover Platonic love, too honest to extol physical love as a beautiful or even adequate substitute. He lives in a universe where only lust is real. And he is thoroughly repelled by its reality and ugliness.

In *Farewell to love*, which is really a farewell to lust, reasons for dissatisfaction are made still more explicit. The *Farewell* is a *remedium amoris* which recounts love's progress in reverse. In this poem a lover recalls the various hopes and expectations with which he viewed love *a priori* and contrasts them with the "sorrowing dulnesse" which occurs *de facto*. This process of making explicit and conscious his reasons for disappointment with lust enables the lover to resolve to abandon love altogether, for lust only does damage without fulfilling the promised compensation of pleasure.

Farewell to love

Whilst yet to prove,
I thought there was some Deitie in love
So did I reverence, and gave
Worship; as Atheists at their dying houre
Call, what they cannot name, an unknowne power,
As ignorantly did I crave:
Thus when

Things not yet knowne are coveted by men,
  Our desires give them fashion, and so
As they waxe lesser, fall, as they sise, grow.

  But, from late faire
His highnesse sitting in a golden Chaire,
  Is not less cared for after three dayes
By children, then the thing which lovers so
Blindly admire, and with such worship wooe;
  Being had, enjoying it decayes:
      And thence,
What before pleas'd them all, takes but one sense,
  And that so lamely, as it leaves behinde
A kinde of sorrowing dulnesse to the minde.

      Ah cannot wee,
As well as Cocks and Lyons jocund be,
  After such pleasures? Unlesse wise
Nature decreed (since each such Act, they say,
Diminisheth the length of life a day)
  This, as shee would man should despise
      The sport;
Because that other curse of being short,
  And onely for a minute made to be
Eager, desires to raise posterity.

  Since so, my minde
Shall not desire what no man else can finde,
  I'll no more dote and runne
To pursue things which had indammag'd me.
And when I come where moving beauties be,
  As men doe when the summers Sunne
      Grows great,
Though I admire their greatnesse, shun their heat;
  Each place can afford shadows. If all faile,
'Tis but applying worme-seed to the Taile.

The first stanza describes the way in which a young man
who has experienced love in imagination and not in reality
tends to glorify what he does not know. The speaker says

that before he tested love, he thought there was something divine about it, and so he revered and worshiped it. And with the sharp self-scorn of retrospective evaluation, he compares the "ignorance" or blind unknowingness of his craving with the calling of a dying atheist for God. Both atheist and inexperienced lover long for something which seems vague (because they have not experienced it directly) but nevertheless real, and the object of their longing, when it is experienced directly, turns out to be a means of punishment.

The stanza concludes with a description of the way in which the degree of desire affects the apparent value of the thing desired. When a man has not known or experienced a thing he covets, the lover says, he fashions its image in his imagination; and as the desire diminishes or increases, so does the size and value of its imagined image. Thus presumably he, filled with an inordinate desire for love before he actually knew it, attributed a value to it which made it as great as his desire. But, as the next stanza shows, this was only the vanity of human wishes, for the thing which lovers blindly admire before experiencing it instantly decays in value as soon as they have it. A lover is like a child who admires a gaudy tinseled figure at a fair, but who quickly grows bored with it after only a few days. For love, like the figure at the fair, may have a glittering surface and may seem desirable for a few moments, but ultimately it reveals itself as a hollow sham. *A priori* love seems to offer pleasure to man's whole being, to his mind and all his senses, for it is experienced only in the imagination. But in reality, love "takes but one sense" instead of pleasing the whole being; and the pleasure it gives to that one sense is so lame and unsatisfying that only a "sorrowing dulnesse" is left in the mind after the brief moment of gratification.

In the third stanza the lover ponders this situation, wondering why love should offer such disappointment to man when it does not seem to do so to beasts. Cocks and lions are joyous after sexual consummation, but man is not. Why? The lover suspects that this is because "wise Nature"

126

has laid two curses on man, curses which are appropriate to his nature and destiny and which are not appropirate to beasts. In *Farewell to love* "naturalism" completes its full circle, for the natural laws to which the lover appeals are those of the orderly Law of Nature, not those of amoral and libertine nature; in this poem Nature is a preservative and conservative force, not a violent and destructive one, and Nature is also hierarchical, decreeing one set of laws for rational man and another set for animals.

Thus Nature has wisely placed two "curses" upon man's amatory experience, two curses which supplement one another and prevent man from destroying himself through inordinate desire. The first curse is the curse of depression after sexual consummation, the "sorrowing dulnesse to the minde." This curse is necessary because each act of sexual intercourse cuts a day off man's life, and depression after consummation prevents a man from wishing to repeat it too often; its purpose is to make man "despise the sport," and its purpose has been well fulfilled in the lover who speaks. The second curse on consummation, "that other curse of being short," is apparently the curse of brevity in pleasure.[8] This curse was instituted in order "to raise posterity"; that is, because sexual pleasure is brief and impermanent, men wish to repeat it in spite of the depression which follows; the desire for repetition with which man is cursed is Nature's way of ascertaining that posterity will be raised, that the earth will continue to be populated with human beings. Thus the two curses complement each other, one preventing man from seeking sexual consummation too often and

[8] The meaning of the last three lines of stanza three is the subject of considerable critical controversy; in Appendix IV of his edition, Redpath gives a rather complete summary of the positions which various critics have taken. My own view is that the manuscript reading of lines 29-30, "And onely for a minute made to be/ Eager, desires to raise posterity," is superior to Grierson's emendation ("And onely for a minute made to be, ⟨Eagers desire⟩ to raise posterity"). And my interpretation of the lines is similar to that which George Williamson sets forth in "Donne's *Farewell to Love*," *MP*, XXXVI (1938), 301-303. In any case, however, the controversy has little relevance to the total meaning of the poem.

the other urging him to repeat it often enough to populate the earth. But if Nature is wise in decreeing this preservative tension and it ultimately operates for the good of the human race, the individual man is hardly blessed by it. For he is driven by the second curse to repeat the brief and unsatisfying pleasure which shortens his life, and he is doomed by the first curse to suffer a long depression after his brief pleasure. Both curses operate together to make sexual gratification seem unsatisfactory and undesirable when regarded from a coolly rational point of view.

In the final stanza the lover regards it in precisely that way. Looking upon sexual experience rationally, he resolves to avoid it. Before he experienced love, his inordinate desire gave it fashion and its worth seemed great. Now his desire has fallen, and with it the worth of love. *De facto*, sexual consummation is worse than tinseled sham. It is a curse which offers no real or lasting joys, only depression and ultimately death. Since it is so, the lover determines that he will no longer desire what no man can ever obtain, satisfaction with lust. He will no longer run after the thing which only damages him. Henceforth when he is in the presence of beautiful women, he will look for a place which is shadowed from their radiant heat, just as men try to find shade to preserve themselves from the scorching flames of the hot summer sun. And if that fails, he says with reasoned but bitter determination, " 'Tis but applying worme-seed to the Taile." He is referring to the possibility of taking an anaphrodisiac, but he chooses to state that possibility in an image well-designed both to express his own repulsion to lust and to make lust seem repulsive and ugly.

Loves Alchymie and *Farewell to love* are the kind of poems which only a medieval or a Renaissance man could have written, for they are pervaded by a sense that lust is morbid and destructive, and this sense can only grow out of the feeling that lust is sinful—an expense of spirit in a waste of shame. Their forthright admission that lust is evil is quite un-Ovidian. Ovid is amused by the irrational behavior of lovers, the foolishness of their poses, the triviality of their concerns, the predicaments in which they are involved by their ridiculous and excessive commitment to a woman. But he is not overwhelmed by the ugliness of inordinate sexual desire as Donne, Shakespeare, Marston, Webster, and many another Renaissance man are. The difference between the treatment of love in Donne and in Ovid is the difference between an era in which divine providence provided the moral sanctions and an era in which they were provided by human reason. In Renaissance England to be virtuous was to be holy; in Augustan Rome to be virtuous was to be reasonable. In Ovid's era inordinate sexual desire was unreasonable. In Donne's era lust was both unreasonable and unholy.

IV · IDOLATRY AND SORROW

When want, sent but to tame, doth warre
And work despaire a breach to enter in,
When plenty, Gods image, and seale
Makes us Idolatrous,
And love it, not him, whom it should reveale. . . .

In other poems Donne turns away from Ovidianism and explores the nature and effects of idolatrous love, which occurs whenever men give something mortal and transient the total adoration due only to God. That Donne believed human beings could commit a spiritual sin by loving one another too much is clear from the *Sermons* and the *Holy Sonnets*. In *Holy Sonnet VIII* "faithfull soules" glorified in heaven look down at various sinners on earth and, among others,

> They see idolatrous lovers weep and mourne. . . .

Or in *XIII* the speaker courts Christ by using a Petrarchan pitch:

> . . . but as in my idolatrie
> I said to all my profane mistresses,
> Beauty, of pitty, foulnesse onely is
> A signe of rigour. . . .

But within the *Songs and Sonets* the word "idolatry" is used with specific reference to love only once. In *Loves exchange* the speaker sees his beloved's beauty as a means by which the God of Love causes people to break vows and violate the moral and natural order:

> This face, by which he could command
> And change the Idolatrie of any land,
> This face, which wheresoe'r it comes,
> Can call vow'd men from cloisters, dead from tombes. . . .

For in the *Songs and Sonets* Donne is more interested in

130

understanding and dramatizing an emotional condition than in giving it a name, and so his speakers quite naturally use the more inclusive and ambiguous word "love." Although traditional moral theology, with its emphasis on the sinfulness of idolatrous love, stands firmly behind these poems, it does not intrude upon their verisimilitude; Donne is imagining what it feels like to be an idolatrous lover from the inside, and he asks his audience to share his vicarious experience, to understand all if not to pardon all. No mean psychologist in his Ovidian poems, in these Petrarchan poems Donne's ability to depict the turbulent flow and ebb of human thoughts and emotions reaches its finest expression.

Yet Donne's readers would have quickly recognized an idolatrous lover by a number of clues. One strong indication that love is idolatrous is a lover's total commitment to the object of his love; it seems to him as if his beloved contains all the value to be found in the universe and as if the annihilation of her or of his love would be the end of the universe. Othello expresses this condition with terrible irony when he says of Desdemona: ". . . when I love thee not,/ Chaos is come again" (III.iii.91-92). The lover of Donne's *The broken heart*, mentally reviewing what it feels like to fall in love, says that grief fills the whole heart, leaving no room for anything else:

> Ah, what a trifle is a heart,
> > If once into loves hands it come!
> All other griefs allow a part
> > To other griefes, and aske themselves but some. . . .

The idolatrous lover is willing to sacrifice power, success, peace, or honor for the sake of his beloved. Whatever else it is, idolatry is monotheistic, and its one God is a jealous God.

A second clue that the love expressed in a particular poem is idolatrous is the use of religious imagery to describe a love affair which is more profane than sacred. Human love described through religious imagery is not necessarily idol-

atrous, of course. Lovers may use religious imagery metaphorically and mean it only metaphorically; Milton does
this when he says "Methought I saw my late espoused
Saint . . ." and Spenser does it in Sonnet XXII of the *Amoretti*:

> This holy season, fit to fast and pray,
> Men to devotion ought to be inclynd:
> Therefore, I lykewise, on so holy day,
> For my sweet saynt some service fit will find.
> Her temple fayre is built within my mind,
> In which her glorious ymage place is,
> On which my thoughts doo day and night attend,
> Lyke sacred priests that never thinke amisse.

But when the lovers forget that their religious metaphors
are only metaphors, as they may easily do in the total commitment of idolatry, loving one another as gods rather than
as the images of God, then the love dramatized is probably
idolatrous. And they reveal whether they take their metaphors literally or not by the inferences they draw from
them about justifiable moral behavior or by their reactions
when faced with evidence that their metaphors *are* only
metaphors and that they themselves are only human.

A third hint that the love described in a poem is idolatrous is that such love often produces grief. Sometimes the
lover recognizes that his passion is inordinate and suffers
from his awareness of his state of sin. Sometimes his mistress refuses to look upon him with equal love. But even if
the love is mutual, it can bring sadness ultimately. For the
idolator loves something mortal as if it were immortal, and
the object of such love usually reveals itself as subject to
human frailties or to mortality itself. The lover's discovery
of mutability and death in an object formerly seen as the
incarnation of all possible good can thus work a breach for
despair to enter. Or alternatively the profane Petrarchan
lover, because his love is irrational and inordinately passionate, easily becomes jealous or possessive, his fear growing out of a secret awareness that his love is founded upon
an earthly and therefore mutable base, but an awareness

contrary to his outward pretense that his love will last forever. Again, one might think of Othello. Whatever the situation, idolatry brings little peace, and that is why "tear floods and sigh tempests" are such constant companions in Petrarchan poetry.

As one might expect, however, Donne draws on the Petrarchan tradition in a variety of ways. Frequently he picks up one of its set themes, such as the cruel scorn of an unwilling mistress, and works witty variations on it, expecting his reader to recognize that the conventional treatment of the theme is being transformed or refreshed; such is the case, for example, in *Loves Deitie* or *The Apparition*. Sometimes his use of the tradition is completely conventional, as in *Twicknam Garden*, which is the monologue of a profane lover who, like Petrarch himself, recognizes that he is caught in an unworthy and unholy love and yet is unable to contain his passion or escape from it.

But in some poems, discussed in section iii of this chapter, Donne dramatically alters the Petrarchan tradition. Instead of presenting the condition of the idolatrous lover subjectively, as Petrarch and his imitators had done, he depicts it with the objectivity of comic irony. He thus in a sense blends two traditions, using Ovidian methods on Petrarchan matter. In *The Canonization* and *The Extasie* he creates lovers who worship one another and who also expect the world to worship them. But comic irony ripples beneath their declarations, rooted in self-deception, that their love offers a model for the world to imitate. In a somewhat different way the poems discussed in section iv also blend Ovidianism and Petrarchanism. These poems center in a theme common to both traditions, the remedy of love. The lovers of *The Blossome* and *Loves Diet* want to escape from the imperious ladies whom they have adored, for they recognize the error of their love and their advances have been answered only with scorn. So they resolve to run from Petrarchan love, but in a most un-Petrarchan direction. They plan to use an Ovidian remedy, promiscuity, to cure Petrarchan idolatry.

133

Poems like these, especially when combined with some of the sensual Ovidian ones, might lead us to believe that Donne wanted to ridicule or rebel against the Petrarchan tradition. But he did neither. He was simply against two things: bad poetry, which sometimes resulted when his contemporaries wrote stale and mechanical imitations of the Petrarchan style; and bad love, which he equated with emotional excess or sentimental hypocrisy, as did Petrarch himself. In a poem like *Elegie VIII*, he ridicules the former. It begins:

> As the sweet sweat of Roses in a Still,
> As that which from chaf'd muskats pores doth trill,
> As the Almighty Balme of th'early East,
> Such are the sweat drops of my Mistris breast,
> And on her ⟨brow⟩ her skin such lustre sets,
> They seeme no sweat drops, but pearle coronets.
> Ranke sweaty froth thy Mistresse's brow defiles,
> Like spermatique issue of ripe menstruous boiles. . . .

On and on the conventional comparisons are transmogrified or brutalized until the concluding outburst of annoyance:

> Leave her, and I will leave comparing thus,
> She, and comparisons are odious.

But Donne is simply disgusted with an abuse of the Petrarchan style. And when he uses Ovidian irony to mock the lovers of *The Canonization*, he is ridiculing bad love. When he poses lust as a remedy for idolatry in *Loves Diet*, he is assuming that, as sins go, lust is better—not because it is more "realistic," but because it is less grave. Petrarch would not quarrel with either poem, and Donne does not quarrel with the fundamental assumptions of Petrarchanism. Donne had, in fact, so much admiration for Petrarch that he adopted a line from the *Canzoniere* as his motto and inscribed it on the flyleaf of his books. He chose line 55 of Canzone CCVI, "Per Rachel ho servito, e non per Lia" (For Rachel I have served, and not for Leah), to indicate that his real devotion was to the contemplative life rather than

134

the active life.[1] It is a motto appropriate to either poet and one which suggests wherein their resemblance lies. Both did, though neither did so conspicuously, serve the contemplative life.

i Scorn

One of the set themes of the Petrarchan tradition which Donne used rather often was the disdain of the beloved and the lover's reaction to it. When Donne picked it up, it had already been used in a number of ways. The most common, perhaps, was the lover's hyperbolical assertion that his death was imminent if his beloved did not return his love and that she was acting like a cold-blooded murderess. But the *Canzoniere* alone suggests a good many other possibilities; there the poet describes a kaleidoscopic variety of reactions: he becomes angry, lapses into total despair, accuses women of being fickle, hates himself for loving wrongly anyway, accepts scorn as his due because he is unworthy, and admits that Laura's refusal is morally right. And throughout this variety of responses, the reader was expected to believe that Laura was right, not that she was motivated by cruelty or malice.

One of the most interesting examples of the way in which Donne used this set theme is *Loves Deitie*, for it combines within a single poem rebellion against love of a disdainful mistress and acceptance of the moral righteousness of her scorn. In his admission that she is right, the lover conforms to the basic assumptions of the Petrarchan tradition. But he voices his initial objections to her disdain in such a way that the poem sounds almost anti-Petrarchan. For in the beginning he has an anti-traditional bias, wishing to chip away from love the accretions of convention. And, further, he shows a kind of Ovidian naturalism as he argues that scorn is wrong because it is unnatural for love to be unreciprocated, in the process giving the word "love" enough

[1] Geoffrey Keynes, *A Bibliography of Dr. John Donne Dean of Saint Paul's* (Cambridge, Eng., 1958), 3d edn., 205-206.

twists to indicate that by love he means sex as well as affection.

Loves Deitie

I long to talke with some old lovers ghost,
    Who dyed before the god of Love was borne:
I cannot thinke that hee, who then lov'd most,
    Sunke so low, as to love one which did scorne.
But since this god produc'd a destinie,
And that vice-nature, custome, lets it be;
    I must love her, that loves not mee.

Sure, they which made him god, meant not so much,
    Nor he, in his young godhead practis'd it;
But when an even flame two hearts did touch,
    His office was indulgently to fit
Actives to passives. Correspondencie
Only his subject was; It cannot bee
    Love, till I love her, that loves mee.

But every moderne god will now extend
    His vast prerogative, as far as Jove.
To rage, to lust, to write to, to commend,
    All is the purlewe of the God of Love.
Oh were wee wak'ned by this Tyrannie
To ungod this child againe, it could not bee
    I should love her, who loves not mee.

Rebell and Atheist too, why murmure I,
    As though I felt the worst that love could doe?
Love might make me leave loving, or might trie
    A deeper plague, to make her love mee too,
Which, since she loves before, I'am loth to see;
Falshood is worse then hate; and that must bee,
    If shee whom I love, should love mee.

The mood which inspired this monologue seems to be similar to that which inspired La Rochefoucauld's maxim that "Il y a des gens qui n'auraient jamais été amoureux, s'ils n'avaient jamais entendu parler de l'amour." The poem

begins with the lover's explanation that he longs to pene-
trate the civilized façade of love and to see what its heart
of darkness is like; he longs to talk with a lover who died
before the God of Love began his tyrannous reign and before amatory conventions were established, for he wishes to
discover how love was expressed then. But the third and
fourth lines of the poem indicate that the lover approaches
his inquiry with a preconceived hypothesis: before the
reign of Cupid, love must have been reciprocal and men
simply did not love women who did not return their love.
Within the first stanza itself, however, the rebellion against
convention of the first four lines is turned into acceptance
and conformity. For in the last three lines the lover admits
that since Cupid is now the ruling monarch, since this God
has instituted laws governing the nature and progress of
love, and since custom has given tacit assent to them, he
will follow suit and continue to love a woman who does not
love him. In spite of his rebellion against convention, in the
phrase "that vice-nature, custome" the lover suggests an
important assumption upon which he will later act; nature
may be the governor, but custom is nature's lieutenant-
governor and even the final arbiter of moral law, because
natural law is implemented only through the *consensus
gentium.*

Although in this first stanza the lover has oscillated between conformity and revolt, concluding with conformity,
in the next two he returns again to the mood of rebellion.
He now begins to twist his previous acceptance of tradition
by appealing to the earliest era of love. As he tries to show
that reciprocal love has the earliest historical foundation, the
revolutionary nature of his argument gradually becomes clear.
Long ago human beings invented the God of Love, he says,
but they never intended their invention to become their
tyrant, nor did the God of Love rule like one in his early
years. Instead he indulgently brought men and women
(actives and passives) together so that they might mate.
And so the lover, recognizing only the early apostolic era
as the proper precedent, concludes that his love cannot

really be love until he makes love to his mistress and she makes love with him.

Continuing the analogy of the tyrannous accretions of tradition, he goes on in the next stanza to explain what they are and why revolt and reformation are justified. The God of Love has now multiplied his functions and become many Gods, the sum of which would equal Jove and his prerogatives. These added functions are "To rage, to lust, to write to, to commend," whereas, as the second stanza has indicated, the early God was concerned only with lust, only with fitting actives to passives. If only, the lover concludes, returning to his refrain, men were aroused to rebellion by this gluttony for power, he would not love her who does not love him. And now his meaning seems to be twofold—their love would be reciprocal, and it would also be sexual.

Until the last stanza we have been given little idea of the beloved's attitude; we know only that she has not returned his love, but we do not know why, although the lover's loud protests lead us to believe that she is as irresponsibly tyrannous and cruel as the modern God of Love and fickle Fortuna combined. But now, with a surprising change of direction, the lover's mood of iconoclasm and mockery vanishes, and he admits that his beloved's scorn is actually good. He reveals the until-now-suppressed fact that she "loves before," and he accepts traditional morality through his recognition that her infidelity would be worse than rejection, however much he might long for reciprocity. In spite of his protests and rebelliousness, he is willing to conform to the moral order of the universe, to prefer fidelity which involves suffering to infidelity which involves sin.

Loves Deitie begins with a tone of forceful rebelliousness, but as is so often the case with Donne's poetry, we must place greater weight on the mood of its conclusion. *Loves Deitie* is built upon a contrast between conformity and revolt, between tradition (both literary and moral) and reformation. But all its twists of logic and word-play, brought to support amatory rebellion and atheism, are denied by a sudden reversal at the end of the poem, when the

lover makes his wit bow and humbly submit to his beloved's
disdain, simply because (whatever proofs to the contrary
wit can offer) he knows full well that it would be wrong to
do otherwise. Thus the lover's search for what is behind the
conventions of love, with its excursion into the possibility
that love is nothing but pure sexuality, returns in the end to
full acceptance of "that vice nature, custome."

Loves Deitie, with its witty analysis and surprising conclusion, represents a delightful and light way of responding
to the mistress's disdain. *The triple Fool* gives an equally
light response which is even more conventionally Petrarchan. The lover admits gaily that he is foolish to love, that
he is silly to write poetry about it, but that he cannot help
himself:

> I am two fooles, I know,
> For loving, and for saying so
>   In whining Poetry;
> But where's that wiseman, that would not be I,
>   If she would not deny?

And, like a typical Petrarchan lover, he adds that writing
about his grief makes it less fierce:

> Griefe brought to numbers cannot be so fierce,
> For, he tames it, that fetters it in verse.

But the poem goes on to extend the conventional statement
that writing poetry eases the pain of love by showing that
ultimately it makes the poet-lover triply foolish. For someone else often makes a song of the love poem and thereby
increases both the grief and the love. Although Petrarchan
conventions have been extended, the extension is the sort
that we might expect of any imitator of Petrarch. The lover
conforms to the tradition in admitting that his love is foolish, extends it by showing that it is triply foolish. He is
perhaps more gay about being wrong in loving than the
average Petrarchan lover, but he freely admits that he is
wrong.

Other rogues in Donne's gallery respond somewhat differently. Some imitate the cruelty of their mistress and answer scorn with angry vindictiveness and cruelty. The most angry of all these is the speaker of *The Apparition*. The basis of the poem is the Petrarchan lover's conventional pose that the disdain of his mistress will kill him. Usually the lover who takes this pose goes on to spin pretty conceits on the beloved's paradoxical combination of beauty and cruelty. *The Apparition* is quite different. In this poem the Petrarchan pose is only a point of departure. Instead of dwelling on his beloved's cruelty, as the first line would lead us to expect, the speaker goes on to prove himself even more cruel than any Petrarchan mistress.

It begins with what promises to be a light and humorous touch:

> When by thy scorne, O murdresse, I am dead . . .

But the rejected and jealous lover goes on to promise that his ghost will haunt her when she, but a "fain'd vestall," lies in bed with her other lover. She will be frightened and try to wake him, but he will only think she wants to make love again and turn away, pretending to be soundly asleep. Such products of the fain'd ghost's imagination are unpleasant enough, but the promise he delivers to her is still worse. She will lie in bed "Bath'd in a cold quicksilver sweat," herself transformed into a ghost by fear. As for the speaker himself,

> What I will say, I will not tell thee now,
> Lest that preserve thee'; and since my love is spent,
> I'had rather thou shouldst painfully repent,
> Then by my threatnings rest still innocent.

These hate-filled lines are rather obscure, but they seem to mean something like the following: "I won't tell you in this poem what I am going to say when I come to haunt you because I'm afraid the advance warning may keep you safe from harm or fear then, which is the very reverse of the effect I wish to have on you. I no longer love you, and therefore I prefer that you then experience a painful sense of repentence for rejecting me and thereby killing me. My threats so far have made you reject my advances and thereby remain innocent; if you regret rejecting me, you will at least do something wrong." The speaker thus reveals himself as a coolly cruel man who wishes to return hurt with hurt, to exact a kind of unjust retributive justice.

The Apparition certainly is not one of Donne's greatest poems (although it is not a bad poem of its kind), but it gives a forewarning against a common temptation in interpreting Donne's Petrarchan poetry. It is easy to lump together the poems built around the theme of the mistress's scorn, poems such as *Twicknam Garden, The Funerall*, and *The Blossome*, and to see them as playful compliments addressed to Magdalen Herbert or perhaps the Countess of Bedford. If we were consistent in this practice, we would also have to include *The Apparition* on the same ground, although this is patently absurd. The poems built around the theme of scorn usually make more sense if we read them as literary rather than personal in their inspiration: Donne is taking a standard type of poem and using his wit to work variants on it. He could, and probably did, write poems which grew out of his private life as well, but we should see a poem as a "courtly compliment" only if it is complimentary.

The Funerall, built upon the same conceit as *The Apparition*, is similar to it. Again we find a careful and gradual unveiling of surprises and sudden revelations. Although this poem represents a burial ceremony in several senses, we do not realize all the implications of the title until we reach the last line. The poem begins as if the speaker is a dying man who at the moment of death looks back upon a happy love relationship, signified by the bracelet of hair about his arm. But as he continues to ponder on this outward sign, he wonders if his mistress might not have given it to him as a sign of her domination over him. When we reach the phrase "loves martyr" we see that the relationship was not what it seemed to be in the first stanza, but only in the last line of the poem does it become clear that

141

the speaker is a rejected lover who is dying from disdain and who is still not reconciled to his rejection. In ". . . since you would save none of mee, I bury some of you," we hear a milder version of the vindictive defiance which was the predominant tone of *The Apparition*. The word "bury" is a pun, meaning both the burial of the bracelet of hair with the lover's body and a symbolic sexual conquest of the beloved: "Since you rejected my seductive advances in life, I will succeed in burying at least some of you after I am dead."[2] *The Funerall* moves from apparent satisfaction with nonsexual adoration to an angry desire for physical triumph over the lady's scorn.

The Funerall

Who ever comes to shroud me, do not harme
        Nor question much
That subtile wreath of haire, which crowns my arme;
The mystery, the signe you must not touch,
        For 'tis my outward Soule,
Viceroy to that, which then to heaven being gone,
        Will leave this to controule,
And keepe these limbes, her Provinces, from dissolution.

For if the sinewie thread my braine lets fall
        Through every part,
Can tye those parts, and make mee one of all;
These haires which upward grew, and strength and art
        Have from a better braine,
Can better do'it, Except she meant that I
        By this should know my pain,
As prisoners then are manacled, when they'are
        condemn'd to die.

What ere shee meant by'it, bury it with me,
        For since I am
Loves martyr, it might breed idolatrie,

---

[2] Grierson, following the majority of the manuscripts, uses the reading "since you would save none of mee. . . ." But some of the manuscripts and all the early editions use "have" for "save," further suggesting a sexual reference in the line.

If into others hands these Reliques came;
    As'twas humility
To afford to it all that a Soul can doe,
    So, 'tis some bravery,
That since you would save none of mee, I bury
        some of you.

The lover of *The Funerall* reacts as he does because he is confused about the position in which his lady's refusals have placed him, and his confusion is focused in the bracelet of her hair which he wears. Because he is not sure whether his love exalts him or debases him, he sees the bracelet first as a mysterious and holy relic, then as a prisoner's manacles. His initial fanciful conceit on the wreath of hair as his "outward Soule" is a means of self-glorification, used to prove him a "saint" in the "religion of love." After his death, he says, his body will not undergo dissolution and decay because it will be preserved through the band which "crowns" his arm with a crown of love's martyrdom, and thereby he will meet one of the tests of sainthood. Her hair will work this miracle easily, for if his own body contains a wonder-working kind of hair, the sinewy thread of nerves which falls from his brain and gives his body life by tying it together, then *her* hair, which springs from an even better brain, will hold his body together even better after his death.

But at the conclusion of the second stanza the lover's mood shifts. It occurs to him that the bracelet of hair may not be so much a holy relic, an outward sign of her gift of grace, as an emblem of the pain which he has had to endure through his beloved's rejections and a sign of her cruel domination over him. For a man to let a woman dominate him so was, to Renaissance eyes, disgraceful. And thus he realizes momentarily that he may not be a saint in the religion of love, but a prisoner condemned to death through his love. Since his love is so conspicuously idolatrous, his meaning is probably double—death through disdain and the spiritual death of inordinate love. That her gift may be

143

an emblem of his spiritual imprisonment and destruction is such an unpleasant possibility, however, that the lover does not dwell on it long. He turns away from it after only three lines and refuses to consider any further the possible meanings of the "subtile wreath."

In the final stanza he tiredly concludes that, whatever its meaning, the bracelet should be buried with him. Whether an honor or a punishment, it is certainly dangerously potent, and it might lead others to admire his example and to become idolators too if it and his body were left above ground. In the last four lines this rueful recognition that he offers a negative *exemplum* to the world, in spite of his previous self-glorification, transforms itself into first self-hatred and then aggressive hostility. In saying of the "subtile wreath" that it was humility "To afford to it all that a Soule can doe," he means that by humbling himself before his mistress and her gift, he was actually debasing himself and giving it and her his very soul. As his latent distress about his affair crescendos into vindictive rebellion in the last two lines, he defiantly asserts that he will add "some bravery" to his humility by burying some of his beloved after his death, since he succeeded in burying none of her before. He will overcome her spiritual domination, which is causing his death, through a final physical triumph. And his suppressed anger and frustration rise so sharply to the surface in these lines that he no longer speaks of his mistress in the third person, but adopts the second and speaks to her directly, as if he had summoned her before him in order to at last return scorn with scorn.

Twicknam Garden is yet another poem on this Petrarchan theme. In the other poems Donne has exploited the Petrarchan tradition by using it as a context, by borrowing and extending its images or themes, and sometimes by temporarily turning it on its head. But in this poem he is writing within the Petrarchan tradition almost completely. Its pattern of development is nearly identical to that of many of the early sonnets in the *Canzoniere*. The lover begins by recognizing his error in loving and wishes to escape, but his attempts to cure himself fail, for his passion is still too strong. And so he remains in misery, but now heightened misery; he is not only unhappy because his mistress will not return his love, but also because he recognizes his need for repentance and is unable to fulfill it. *Twicknam Garden* closely follows this Petrarchan theme of the strength of the ill directed will and the weakness of corrective reason. Or in other terms, it is a Petrarchan study in the stubborn strength of habitual sin.

Twicknam Garden

Blasted with sighs, and surrounded with teares,
    Hither I come to seeke the spring,
    And at mine eyes, and at mine eares,
Receive such balmes, as else cure every thing;
    But O, selfe traytor, I do bring
The spider love, which transubstantiates all,
    And can convert Manna to gall,
And that this place may thoroughly be thought
    True Paradise, I have the serpent brought.

'Twere wholsomer for mee, that winter did
    Benight the glory of this place,
    And that a grave frost did forbid
These trees to laugh, and mocke mee to my face;
    But that I may not this disgrace
Indure, nor yet leave loving, Love let mee
    Some senslesse peece of this place bee;
Make me a mandrake, so I may groane here,
    Or a stone fountaine weeping out my yeare.

Hither with christall vyals, lovers come,
    And take my teares, which are loves wine,
    And try your mistresse Teares at home,
For all are false, that tast not just like mine;
    Alas, hearts do not in eyes shine,
Nor can you more judge womans thoughts by teares,
    Then by her shadow, what she weares.

O perverse sexe, where none is true but shee,
  Who's therefore true, because her truth kills mee.

Twicknam Garden is the most iconological of Donne's profane love poems. Its heavy concentration of religious imagery in the first stanza sets up the standards of value upon which the remainder of the poem is based. Recognizing that he needs a cure which will bring renewal, the lover has come to a garden, which he identifies in the last line of the stanza with paradise, to seek the spring. It is the season of rebirth, and he wishes to share in it, to escape from the blasts and floods of sighs and tears. That it is spiritual renewal which he seeks is made clear in the third and fourth lines:

And at mine eyes, and at mine eares,
  Receive such balmes, as else cure every thing. . . .

The metaphor is that of extreme unction. The lover, aware that he is undergoing spiritual death, wishes that the oil of grace could be applied to his offending senses to cure him of his diseased love. But his search is hopeless, for he is a "selfe traytor" who brings within him a sinful love so tenacious that it will nullify or transubstantiate the corrective strength of divine love and its vehicles.

The imagery of this passage would resonate more richly for a Renaissance reader, however, because Donne has compressed together a formidable group of figures drawn from sixteenth-century religious commonplace: transubstantiation, manna, paradise, the spider love, and the serpent. Through these images Donne is working variations on the idea of transformation. What the "spider love" would have conveyed to Donne's audience, at least when yoked to the later reference to the serpent, is suggested by the comment of the *Glossa Ordinaria* on Luke 10:19, "I have given you power to triumph over serpents and scorpions":

Serpentes sunt mali homines vel daemones qui inchoandis virtutibus venena pravae persuasionis objiciunt.

146

Scorpiones, qui consummandas virtutes ad finem vitiare contendunt.[3]

Scorpion or spider love would be that kind of love which damages virtue, which transubstantiates what is good so that it becomes something corrupt; in the words of the poem, it converts manna to gall. The idea of transubstantiation is also extended by the manna-gall image since manna was conventionally considered to be an Old Testament foreshadowing of the bread of the sacrament, itself transubstantiated on the altar so that it conveyed to the recipient the saving grace of Christ Himself, the ability to triumph over serpents and scorpions. Augustine, for example, says of manna as he explicates texts:

This is the bread which cometh down from heaven. Manna signified this bread; God's altar signified this bread. Those were sacraments. In the signs they were diverse; in the thing which was signified they were alike. . . . "This, then, is the bread that cometh down from heaven, that if any man eat thereof, he shall not die." But this is what belongs to the virtue of the sacrament, not to the visible sacrament; he that eateth within, not without; who eateth in his heart, not who presses with his teeth.[4]

And Augustine adds the customary stern warning that the sacraments can be as poison, can convert manna to gall as it were, if taken in an evil condition:

How many do receive at the altar and die, and die indeed by receiving? Whence the apostle saith, "Eateth and drinketh judgment to himself." For it was not the mouthful given by the Lord that was poison to Judas.

[3] "Serpents are evil men or demons who, having taken the virtuous in hand, throw the poisons of perverse counsel in their way. Scorpions are those who strive to corrupt the virtuous completely and finally." *Patrologia Latina*, ed. J. P. Migne (Paris, 1852), cxiv, 285.

[4] St. Augustine, *Tractati on the Gospel of St. John*, trans. the Rev. John Gibb, in *A Select Library of the Nicene and Post-Nicene Fathers*, ed. Philip Schaff (New York, 1908), vii, 171-172.

And yet he took it; and when he took it, the enemy entered into him: not because he received an evil thing, but because he being evil received a good thing in an evil way. See ye then, brethren, that ye eat the heavenly bread in a spiritual sense; bring innocence to the altar. Though your sins be daily, at least let them not be deadly. (VII, 171)

To the Renaissance reader who approached the poem with such associations and beliefs, the resonance of the compressed imagery would be clear. The lover has come to the garden for renewal, but because he brings his sinful and deadly love with him, he cannot cure himself; instead, his very desire for repentance is transformed into bitterness, since the healing power of the sacraments are poison to him in his self-willed state of sin. He turns good into evil, hating it because he knows evil for evil, yet still willing it because he has become debilitated through his love. He is a man caught between two powerful standards of value: that of the corrupt *cupiditas* from which he suffers and that of *caritas* which he envisions and yet cannot achieve.

So he concludes the stanza with a bitterly ironic comment on himself and his situation:

And that this place may thoroughly be thought
True Paradise, I have the serpent brought.

"True Paradise" would normally be the Garden of Eden before the Fall, a place of innocence, grace, and joy. But as the lover admits, in this garden he is reenacting the pattern of the Fall, with the difference that he has brought his own poison within him and need not be tempted from without. The serpent which he has brought to complete the authenticity of the Garden would signify, to readers familiar with the *Glossa Ordinaria* or any other standard commentary, that same "malum luxuriae" which the serpent who tempted Adam and Eve signified.[5] Because of his destruc-

---

[5] *Patrologia Latina*, CXIII, 95; in *De Universo* (*Patrologia Latina*, CXI, 233), Rabanus Maurus makes a similar identification and says that Christ is the remedy for the serpent's venom.

tive love, "True Paradise" is for him the Garden of the Fall rather than the Garden of Bliss, although the implied polarity between the two Gardens continues to suggest the polarity of sin and grace between which he is still wavering.

Because he is still wavering, the next stanza begins with a note of hope and health, although like the first it ends with despair. Looking around the garden decorated with the green life of spring, he murmurs to himself:

> 'Twere wholsomer for mee, that winter did
> Benight the glory of this place. . . .

For spring, although the season of rebirth and renewal, is also the time when a young man's fancy is inspired, whereas winter traditionally dims the fires of concupiscence. And, the lover adds, winter also brings a grave frost which robs the trees of their leaves, whose joyous rustling seems a mockery to him in his present state of depression. Casting about for a remedy, he admits that he wants one which will not end his love. Grierson finds this passage, "But that I may not this disgrace/ Indure, nor yet leave loving. . . .," difficult to understand:

> It is strange to hear the Petrarchian lover (Donne is probably addressing the Countess of Bedford) speak of "leaving loving" as though it were in his power.
>
> (II, 26)

But that it *is* in his power is just the point. His tragedy is not the result of whimsical accident, but is caused by his own choice: he has brought his own serpent with him to Paradise. His sin is in his own will, which Donne's readers would believe him free to transform if he so chose. The pathos of the poem grows out of this very paradox. As he reveals by using religious imagery to describe his search for relief in the first stanza, the lover recognizes a higher love toward which he ought to strive, yet he wills to continue in his corrupt love rather than to strive. The tension of the poem is exactly the same as that which occurs and recurs in the *Canzoniere*, the struggle between the reason which recognizes sin and the rebellious will which has taken the bit in its teeth and runs unbridled to destruction.

At the conclusion of the stanza the lover proposes another remedy, one which is a diabolic parallel to the cure proposed at the beginning of the first stanza; he prays to the Blind God of Love that he may be turned into some insensible object in the garden, into a groaning mandrake or a weeping stone fountain.[6] Instead of receiving balms at his eyes and ears, he will now have his senses sealed off by being made inhuman. With this prayer, however, the lover has at last committed himself to the course he will take. Hitherto he has vacillated between two attitudes toward life and love, the divine and the diabolic, the one capable of bringing good out of evil, the other of bringing evil out of good. Once the choice has been made, however, it seems the only possible one and obscures his earlier vision of goodness and grace. In the setting of a garden, possessed of free choice, he has reenacted the pattern of the Fall. Like Milton's Adam and Eve after the Fall, his choice brings with it distrust and hatred. And now the poem takes a sudden shift. Abandoning his meditation on his love and its possible cure, the speaker turns with fierce invective and scorn on the woman who has refused his love and upon women in general. In contrast to the joyous confidence of the lover of *The good-morrow*, who announces that "true plaine hearts doe in the faces rest," he warns other lovers that "hearts do not in eyes shine," that they cannot discern their lady's thoughts even if she is weeping, although the truly sad tears which he will weep as a fountain may be used as a test of her truth or falsity. His own lady, presumably, has given him the traditional refusal of the Petrarchan mistress; weeping, she said that she must deny him in order to be true to someone else, but that her tears were

---

[6] Donne is referring to the conventional belief that a mandrake groans when uprooted. See Sir Thomas Browne, *Pseudo-doxia Epidemica*, ii, 6; Browne also adds that it was popularly believed that the uprooting was fatal to both the mandrake and the uprooter, a consideration perhaps relevant to the lover's ability to poison all that he touches.

proof that she felt a charitable pity for him. But the lover, made incapable of charity through the corruption of profane love, can only see her tears as lies, her fidelity as motivated by sadistic cruelty, and women in general as perverse creatures.

Again we encounter a harsh and vindictive response to scorn, Donne's most characteristic extension of this Petrarchan theme. But in *Twicknam Garden* he seems to have tried to imagine and dramatize this reaction with even greater psychological realism and with more tragic effect. Unlike *The Apparition* or *The Funerall*, *Twicknam Garden* has no lightness or wit to alleviate its sighs and tears, and its gravity is increased by its suggestion of the possibility of redemption in the early stanzas. But their imagery of poison and gall is prophetic, for in the end this blinded and bitter Petrarchan lover can see his beloved's truth and fidelity only as malice and perversion.

Twicknam Garden is a terrifyingly bitter poem, and one cannot help wondering why it is apparently named after the estate of the Countess of Bedford. Three different inferences are possible: (1) that Donne was in love with the Countess and secretly unlocked his heart in this poem; (2) that Donne was describing an actual unfortunate love affair which occurred at Twicknam and involved neither himself nor the Countess; and (3) that Donne wished to draw upon the traditional associations of gardens and spring in order to write a poem about the emotions of a profane lover, and he used Twicknam Garden as a setting for the hypothetical monologue because he knew it well or perhaps was there at the time of writing. The first inference, however, is the least likely, for Donne would hardly unlock his heart and then permit the poem to circulate in manuscript as he did, especially since the poem would not be likely to please or flatter the Countess. On the contrary, Donne would probably have permitted the poem to circulate with the title "Twicknam Garden" only if he were quite sure that the Countess would *not* interpret it as a personal address to her. Either of the other two possibilities could be correct, and a reasonably good case could be made for either. But for the moment the final answer to our puzzlement must rest with John Donne.

ii Mutability and Despair

In *A nocturnall upon S. Lucies day* Donne turns his attention to another theme of the Petrarchan tradition, the reaction of a lover who has loved a mortal woman inordinately, so inordinately that he is overwhelmed with grief and despair when her death reveals to him that she was only mortal. In the *Canzoniere*, however, the death of Laura led Petrarch to transform his love into *caritas*. The lover of *A nocturnall* reacts to the death of his beloved, not with *contemptus mundi* and a search for eternal and immutable values, but with empty misery and despair. The man who delivers this monologue grimly recognizes his love as destructive; like the lover of *Twicknam Garden*, he deplores it but cannot escape from it. His helpless despair is so vividly expressed that *A nocturnall* ranks as one of Donne's finest and most powerful poems. It is a poem which somehow captures the sensation of being at the bottom of a bottomless abyss.

A nocturnall upon S. Lucies day,
Being the shortest day.

Tis the yeares midnight, and it is the dayes,
Lucies, who scarce seaven houres herself unmaskes,
     The Sunne is spent, and now his flasks
     Send forth light squibs, no constant rayes;
         The worlds whole sap is sunke:
The generall balme th'hydroptique earth hath drunk,
Whither, as to the beds-feet, life is shrunke,
Dead and enterr'd; yet all these seeme to laugh,
Compar'd with mee, who am their Epitaph.

Study me then, you who shall lovers bee
At the next world, that is, at the next Spring:
     For I am every dead thing,

In whom love wrought new Alchimie.
　　For his art did expresse
A quintessence even from nothingnesse,
From dull privations, and leane emptinesse:
He ruin'd mee, and I am re-begot
Of absence, darknesse, death; things which are not.

All others, from all things, draw all that's good,
Life, soule, forme, spirit, whence they beeing have;
　　I, by loves limbecke, am the grave
　　Of all, that's nothing. Oft a flood
　　　Have wee two wept, and so
Drowned the whole world, us two; oft did we grow
To be two Chaosses, when we did show
Care to ought else; and often absences
Withdrew our soules, and made us carcasses.

But I am by her death, (which word wrongs her)
Of the first nothing, the Elixer grown;
　　Were I a man, that I were one,
　　I needs must know; I should preferre
　　　. If I were any beast,
Some ends, some means; Yea plants, yea stones detest,
And love; All, all some properties invest;
If I an ordinary nothing were,
As shadow, a light, and body must be here.

But I am None; nor will my Sunne renew.
You lovers, for whose sake, the lesser Sunne
　　At this time to the Goat is runne
　　To fetch new lust, and give it you,
　　　Enjoy your summer all;
Since she enjoys her long nights festivall,
Let me prepare towards her, and let mee call
This houre her Vigill, and her Eve, since this
Both the yeares, and the dayes deep midnight is.

We will probably never be able to recover the resonance
which this poem must have had for a Renaissance reader—
familiar with nocturnal vigils, living in a day before elec-

tricity and reliable heating when nights were blacker and winters damper and colder than most of us experience today. But nonetheless we cannot help feeling the tragic irony of this powerful description of death-in-life and hell-on-earth.

The tragic irony of the poem begins with the title. It is called a "nocturnal," obviously to suggest the nocturns or night offices of the Roman Catholic Church; these may be either set services or (as in the case of Donne's poem) simply night prayers in general and synonymous with *vigilae*. In the primitive church, evidence from the Church Fathers indicates, nocturns were held at midnight.[7] Further, it is a nocturnal in celebration of the festival of St. Lucy, beheaded as a virgin martyr during the persecution of Diocletian, patron saint of sight, and through her name traditionally associated with light (*luce*). But the condition and love of the man who speaks in this poem are far different from what the title suggests. His vigil is a black vigil, his condition far from holy, his love far from virgin, his eyes dark and blinded. His mood is not festive, but sardonic and melancholic.

Two stanzas from Donne's *A Hymne to Christ, at the Authors last going into Germany* also illuminate the irony of *A nocturnall*, for they contain much of the same imagery —night, darkness, winter, nocturnal prayer, visionary knowledge, death—but the state of mind which they convey is totally different:

> I sacrifice this Iland unto thee,
> And all whom I lov'd there, and who lov'd mee;
> When I have put our seas twixt them and mee,
> Put thou thy sea betwixt my sinnes and thee.
> As the trees sap doth seeke the root below
> In winter, in my winter now I goe,
>   Where none but thee, th'Eternall root
>   Of true Love I may know.

· · ·

[7] *The Catholic Encyclopedia*, ed. Charles G. Herberman, *et al.* (New York, 1911), XI, 87.

Seale then this bill of my Divorce to All,
On whom those fainter beames of love did fall;
Marry those loves, which in youth scattered bee
On Fame, Wit, Hopes (false mistresses) to thee.
Churches are best for Prayer, that have least light:
To see God only, I goe out of sight:
    And to scape stormy dayes, I chuse
    An Everlasting night.

The Hymne to Christ, through its negative imagery, expresses the religious Way of Negation, in which darkness becomes light and emptiness produces plenitude. The speaker wants to die to the world not because of misery but because of desire for what is not in the world except through a glass darkly. The *Hymne* is positive in its negativeness, so to speak, whereas *A nocturnall* is the quintessence of nothingness—death in the world, of the world, and for the world.

A nocturnall begins its drama with the setting of the cosmological and sublunary stage. The time is midnight—both of the year and of the day, for this St. Lucy's day occurs at the time of the winter solstice, on the shortest day of the year; after the day's midnight has passed, the year will begin to renew itself again as the sun begins to move northward from its lowest southern point. But that movement, although about to come, has not yet come. The moment is the very center of night. The sun has set, and there is no light except that given by the feeble twinkling of the stars, shining by light reflected from the invisible sun:[8]

    The Sunne is spent, and now his flasks
    Send forth light squibs, no constant rayes. . . .

A squib, was, of course, a common type of firework which produced a slight explosion. Thus the stars are powderflasks, producing an erratic fire and explosion when lighted

[8] The belief that the stars shine by light reflected from the sun apparently circulated during the Renaissance. See Sir Christopher Heydon, *An Astrological Discourse* (London, 1650) [written in 1608], 2.

by the sun, a process which makes them seem to twinkle inconstantly. But "squibs" is a pun, also meaning "a mocking remark"; even the dim light of the twinkling stars seems ridiculing to the lover in his present mood. The death of the year and of the day is also reflected in the earth itself, where not just the trees', but the world's whole sap is sunk; life has shrunk to the center of the sinful earth and rests there, dead and interred. But, like the faint stars, the soggy passive earth seems also to mock the lover, for his life has sunk yet deeper. As he says, in lines which capture in their rhythm the slow death march of his misery:

> . . . yet all these seem to laugh,
> Compar'd with mee, who am their Epitaph.

At the beginning of the second stanza, the lover warns others who plan to become lovers when the dead world is reborn at the next spring to study him, for in him they will discover the effects of love. (Although he believes that he should be a negative *exemplum*, he shows in the last stanza that he does not really expect others to learn from his experience.) In another poem, *Loves Alchymie*, the speaker has taunted love because it produces no elixir, because lovers imagine that they will gain a quintessence of happiness and pleasure, and in fact do not. The speaker of this poem asserts that love's alchemy *has* produced a quintessence, but it is a quintessence of nothingness. Love has taken a group of negatives which usually accompany love— dull privations, lean emptiness, absence, darkness, death— and artfully reduced them to their fifth or simple essence, producing an elixir that gives not life, but death.

Stanza three goes on to intensify the already intense depression and despair by contrast; the opposition is between the speaker's nothingness and the all of all others. All other people and things seem to be able to live happily and to extract the essence which gives them being (life, soul, form, spirit, or whatever) from all the things which surround them. But the lover himself is simply the grave of all: that is, nothing. And his love affair was the limbeck, or alchemi-

156

cal vessel, which transformed him into the quintessence of misery and nothingness. Although reciprocal, his affair was not joyful, for he and his beloved often wept and drowned themselves, who seemed so all-important as to be the whole world. His affair was jealous and possessive, for so involved were they with one another to the exclusion of all else that they became "two chausses" if they turned their attention elsewhere. And when they parted from one another, they became carcasses, since each was the soul of the other.

The first three stanzas thoroughly set the mood of death. If the poem ended here, it would be simply a powerful dramatization of the destructive effect of idolatrous love, of the way its alchemy transforms a lover into a spiritual nothing. But the first line of the next stanza adds a new fact which suddenly extends the overwhelming depression of the earlier part: the lover's mistress has died. The poem is actually a dramatization of two kinds of nothingness: the spiritual death which results from idolatrous love and the overwhelming despair which an idolator feels when he must confront the fact of mutability. Because the poem is presented as the dramatic monologue of a distracted man and follows his thought as it would proceed naturally, the central fact which is preoccupying him has not been stated until the poem is three-fifths over. Now he reveals that her death has made him an even more negative nothing; through her death he has been made the elixir of the *first* nothing, the nothing which existed before the world was created *ex nihilo*; she was his world, and now that she has been removed, he must move back in time to the period before the creation of the world in order to express his vacuity. He is not a man, not a beast or plant, not an inanimate object, not even an ordinary nothing such as a shadow, for all light is utterly gone from the world for him.

To his statement that his mistress is dead, however, he adds the parenthetical "which word wrongs her." Presumably this rather puzzling remark is the lover's futile attempt to grasp at a straw. Even in his total despair at the loss of his goddess, he is unable to admit that she is irrevocably

157

dead. And so he asserts that she, a divine being, has not died but instead, as he later says, is a saint who "enjoys her long nights festivall" in heaven. Even though his idolatry has reduced him to total nothingness, the lover cannot shed it; although the death of his mistress has proved her to be a mortal being, he will continue to worship her anyway, to turn her into the patron saint of death. Instead of redirecting his love toward a genuinely eternal object, he will deceive himself about her and continue his devotion to her, and thereby to sin, to spiritual death, and to nothingness. In imagining a response so complicated, Donne has created another of his complex and psychologically fascinating characters. Both tragic and pathetic, the lover confronts his own state of damnation with unflinching honesty, yet in order to escape from his sorrow at her death momentarily tries to fool himself about the state of his mistress. This paradox in his personality gives *A nocturnall* its peculiar power, making it both a grim and a touching poem.

In the last stanza the lover concludes by predicting that although the sun will climb up again from its southernmost point to light the world again and return it to life, *his* sun will not renew. The lover here contrasts two suns:

> . . . the lesser Sunne
> At this time to the Goat is runne
> To fetch new lust. . . .

This is clearly the real sun, now in the zodiacal sign of Capricorn. This sun is the one which other lovers will take as their patron at the next spring, having studied the lover who speaks and followed his example rather than his warning. The suggestions of lustful love, hinted at in the phrase "to fetch new lust," are also implicit in the image of the goat.[9] And the irony of "Enjoy your summer all" is heavy,

[9] See George Chapman's *The Amorous Zodiac*, where the poet makes himself the sun and his lady the zodiac through which he travels; of the sign of the goat he says:

> In fine, (still drawing to th'Anartick Pole)
> The Tropicke signe, Ile runne at for my Gole,
> Which I can scarce expresse with chastitie,

since it also implies "You will learn from your own experience that it cannot last." The other sun, which will not renew, is of course the dead mistress, the antecedent of "she" in "Since she enjoyes her long nights festivall." In the previous stanza, in which the lover states that he is less than a man, a beast, or a stone (that is, without rational control, incapable of choice of ends and means, incapable even of movement), he has shown himself totally lacking in both reason and will, both of them needed for escape from his state of despair. From his position at the bottom of the abyss, all he can do is make his beloved, who in life made him the quintessence of ordinary nothings and whose death made him the elixir of the first nothing, his Saint, just as he made her his God when she lived. As she enjoys her festival of night in eternity, he in his despair will declare the hour of midnight the time of her vigil and the eve of her saint's day, since it is the sum of all deaths.

This black mass said in honor of a patron saint of nothingness is a profane parody of the religious Way of Negation; Donne is imagining a dark night of the soul which leads only to emptiness. Although the poem itself forms a circle, beginning "Tis the years midnight, and it is the dayes," and concluding ". . . since this/ Both the yeares, and the dayes deep midnight is," and although much of its imagery is drawn from the cycle of death and rebirth, it evokes instead a broken circle, both ends of which are death. The lover insists that among all created things, only he is completely negative and only he is incapable of being reborn with the return of the sun and the spring: "But I am None; nor will my sun renew." His feeling toward the death

---

I know in heauen t'is called *Capricorne*
And with the suddaine thought, my case takes horne,
  So (heauen-like) *Capricorne* the name shall be.
This (wondrous fit) the wintry *Solstice* seaseth,
Where darknes greater growes and day decreseth,
  Where rather I would be in night then day. . . .

(*The Poems of George Chapman*, ed. Phyllis Brooks Bartlett [New York, 1941], 91). For other identifications of the goat with lechery, see *1 Hen. IV*, iv.i.103; *Hen. V*, iv.iv.20; *Lear*, i.ii.138.

of the year and the hibernation of life is the exact reverse of "If winter comes, can spring be far behind?" His condition is one of total hopelessness, total despair, total depression.

Behind this reaction to death is a refusal to believe in the possibility of renewal, an implied refusal to believe in the possibility of redemption and resurrection. This Petrarchan lover whom Donne has created will remain in the depths of night long after the night has passed. The difference between his total despair and the milder reaction to death which Donne dramatizes in other poems, such as *Holy Sonnet XVII*, is due to a difference in the kind of love from which each grows. The lovers of *A nocturnall* passionately worshiped one another as the total good and the total reality, and therefore the speaker cannot recover from his shock of discovery that his God has proved to be mortal. He prays to her as a saint, but as a saint of midnight, a saint whose festival falls at the hour of death, a saint who (as a sun) will not renew. In *A nocturnall* Donne has imagined a man who, having already incurred spiritual death when his beloved was alive, has somehow managed to become still more dead spiritually when faced with the fact of her death.

iii   Self-Deception

Petrarchan love can be a serious disease, and Donne's description of what it feels like to be an idolator is grim medicine. But Donne also had an irrespressible sense of humor, and he could not help applying it to idolatry too. Carrying his fine sense of irony over from his Ovidian poetry, he wrote two poems, *The Canonization* and *The Extasie*, in which he makes fun of idolatrous lovers who take themselves too seriously. The two characters he has created in these poems are Don Quixotes of love, but without the good Don's sweet and gentle (and genuine) nobility. Having misread too many volumes of Petrarchan love poetry, these two lovers announce to the world, with solemn vanity, that their love affairs fulfill every ideal, even that they offer other lovers an ideal on earth to follow. And indeed they do fulfill every ideal of profane love. But although Petrarchan, these lovers do not have the painful self-awareness and talent for self-analysis so characteristic of lovers in the Petrarchan tradition; instead, it is as if the prayer of the speaker to Blind Cupid in *Loves exchange* had been fulfilled:

> Give mee thy weaknesse, make mee blinde,
> Both wayes, as thou and thine, in eies and minde;
> Love, let me never know that this
> Is love, or, that love childish is. . . .

The lovers of *The Canonization* and *The Extasie* are blind in eyes and mind, eager to defend a love which most Petrarchan lovers would admit to be wrong.

The Canonization is sometimes said to be built upon an opposition between the Things of the World and the Things of the Spirit. The speaker in this monologue is replying to the criticism of a benightedly prudent friend who values the Things of the World and who has urged him to abandon love and seek wealth and power. In order to defend himself, the speaker suggests that he is made saint-like by his love, for he too has chosen to renounce the World so that he can devote his life to a higher good; and although worldlings may persecute or condemn him, subsequent generations will recognize his worth and canonize him. If we take him at his word, *The Canonization* becomes a melodrama in which the worldly listener acts the part of bourgeois villain and the impetuous and unworldly lover emerges as an heroic martyr.

But it is hard to take him at his word, since he has so obviously forgotten to renounce the Flesh along with the World. In the third stanza the lover shows through his fly, taper, and phoenix imagery that sex is an important part of his love. And although he says his affair offers a pattern for others to imitate, the Petrarchan sigh-and-tear imagery in the second stanza indicates that it is not a very happy pattern. So while he announces that he is a saint, devoting his

161

life to the Things of the Spirit by his complete surrender to profane love, iron wedges of contradiction drive the two halves of his metaphor apart. Like Donne's Ovidian poems in its techniques, *The Canonization* is a satiric comedy in which Donne dramatizes the polarity between sacred and profane love through the speaker's absurd and contradictory attempt to make them identities. In his literal-mindedness Donne's self-deceived and self-righteous lover is unable to recognize that metaphors are only metaphors.

The Canonization

For Godsake hold your tongue, and let me love,
   Or chide my palsie, or my gout,
My five gray haires, or ruin'd fortune flout,
    With wealth your state, your minde with Arts improve,
      Take you a course, get you a place,
      Observe his honour, or his grace,
   Or the Kings reall, or his stamped face
    Contemplate, what you will, approve,
    So you will let me love.

Alas, alas, who's injur'd by my love?
   What merchants ships have my sighs drown'd?
Who saies my teares have overflow'd his ground?
    When did my colds a forward spring remove?
      When did the heats which my veines fill
      Adde one more to the plaguie Bill?
Soldiers find warres, and Lawyers finde out still
    Litigious men, which quarrels move,
    Though she and I do love.

Call us what you will, wee are made such by love;
   Call her one, mee another flye,
We'are Tapers too, and at our owne cost die,
    And wee in us finde the'Eagle and the Dove.
      The Phoenix ridle hath more wit
      By us, we two being one, are it.

162

So to one neutrall thing both sexes fit,
   Wee dye and rise the same, and prove
   Mysterious by this love.

We can dye by it, if not live by love,
   And if unfit for tombes and hearse
Our legend bee, it will be fit for verse;
   And if no peece of Chronicle wee prove,
      We'll build in sonnets pretty roomes;
      As well a well wrought urne becomes
The greatest ashes, as halfe-acre tombes,
   And by these hymnes, all shall approve
   Us *Canoniz'd* for Love:

And thus invoke us; You whom reverend love
   Made one anothers hermitage;
You, to whom love was peace, that now is rage;
   Who did the whole worlds soule contract, and drove
      Into the glasses of your eyes
      (So made such mirrors, and such spies,
That they did all to you epitomize,)
   Countries, Townes, Courts: Beg from above
   A patterne of your love!

The Canonization is written on another set Petrarchan
theme, the answer of a lover to the criticism of a friend, and
Donne manages to let us know a great deal about the personality of his lover in the first stanza alone. In defensive and
self-assertive tones, he violently overreacts to the criticism:

For Godsake hold your tongue, and let me love. . . .

Or, he continues, if you wish to attack me, find fault with
something other than my love affair—such as my five gray
hairs, my palsy, my ruined fortune, or my gout. The de-
fensiveness of his response suggests that the friend's criticism must be at least partially warranted, and the physical
details indicate that he is a relatively young man whose
body is already approaching old age, but who is sufficiently
vain to have counted the precise number of his gray hairs.

Donne is dramatizing the stock comic situation of an extra-marital love affair between an aging man of the world and a youthful mistress, an affair which further injures the debilitated rake's already-ruined fortune. In spite of the lover's tough tone in the first line, his is not the strong masculinity of the clenched fist, but the *precieux* self-consciousness of the sweeping gesture made with trembling hands, expressed later in his desire to "build in sonnets pretty rooms."

The next stanzas reveal more about the nature of his love affair. And at this point at least, it seems hardly a satisfactory consolation for his failure in the World. He begins by asking:

> Alas, alas, who's injured by my love?

Donne has made his speaker give the usual reply to a criticism of a love affair: "Who am I hurting by it? Leave me alone." But the speaker also unwittingly gives the usual answer to his rhetorical question: "Yourself, you fool." For as he describes his affair's effects on himself and others—ostensibly to defend himself, but with the actual result that his description undercuts his argument—he reveals himself as a typical profane Petrarchan lover: his sighs are gales, although they overturn no ships; his tears are a flood, although they have drowned no crops; he is "ridlingly distempered, cold and hot," but his chills do not hold back the spring and his fever does not give men the plague; and his love does not make the world more harmonious, so soldiers and lawyers do not lack business. As he tries, by interpreting standard Petrarchan metaphors literally, to prove that his love does not injure anyone else, he shows it to be violent and grief-ridden and therefore injurious to himself.

But in spite of his use of Petrarchan imagery, his mistress has not answered his advances with disdain. The lover begins the next stanza by saying:

> Call us what you will, wee are made such by love. . . .

The lover seems to be saying this as a defense and justification—as if "love" is a sacred word whose incantatory chanting will banish the demons of condemnation. (He ends the first and last line of every stanza with this incantatory word.) But the following lines indicate that he really means:

Call us what you will, wee are made such by lust. . . .

The lover is attempting to import the honorific connotations of love as *caritas* to justify love as *cupiditas*, for his contemporaries would believe any act righteous, however bizarre, if it was genuinely motivated by the spirit of charity; thus he uses the intermediate term which is open to both interpretations. Donne, expecting us to recognize the irony, is playing one of his favorite word-games: using a word with a variety of meanings and shifting them iridescently as the poem moves along. The second and third lines are the clues to the irony:

Call her one, mee another flye
We'are Tapers too, and at our owne cost die. . . .

The fly was a common figure for lechery. The taper, when taken together with "and at our owne cost die," has phallic connotations and suggests that sexual indulgence is self-destructive. Through his choice of such images the speaker is admitting that their lust in action is an expense of spirit, although he does not think it a waste of shame.

Almost as if to get out of the difficulty, he adds another image to the catalogue; they are even more like the Phoenix, the immortal Arabian bird who consumes himself in fire and arises to new life from his own ashes. Again the lover is importing an atmosphere of religious incantation in order to make his love seem holy and mysterious, for the Phoenix was an allegorical type for Christ, Who also died and yet rose again after His death.[10] Because the Phoenix figures forth the mystery of the Resurrection, the lover concludes that since he and his beloved die sexually and

[10] See, e.g., T. H. White, *The Book of Beasts* (London, 1954), 126-127.

rise again from their death, they also "prove/ Mysterious by this love." And again the lover is taking metaphors literally, this time the metaphor of sexual "death." But in spite of the lover's serious attempts at self-justification, Donne has shown his readers that in renouncing the scramble for wealth or position, the lover has simply committed himself to another of the Things of the Flesh. He imports religious imagery not because his love affair is actually sacred, but in order to set up a false opposition between the Things of the World, and the Things of the Spirit. He believes his own argument, however, and in his self-deception he goes on to turn his defense into a glorification.

The fourth stanza begins on an ironically ambiguous note:

We can dye by it, if not live by love. . . .

The literal-minded lover is equating the metaphorical death of consummation ("Wee dye and rise the same") with literal death, as he reveals through his subsequent vision of himself as a martyr in the cause of love and as a canonized saint after his death. But for the poet's ironic purpose, the line reminds his readers of the destructiveness of lust, of its power to produce both physical and spiritual death, and makes the speaker's prediction of his canonization seem wildly incongruous. Equally comic is the lover's parody of the Renaissance belief that great poetry is itself a lasting monument. Admitting that their legend is not fit to be printed on a tomb and that their love affair is not likely to be immortalized in sober chronicle, he imagines his story outliving and surpassing other more gilded monuments not by being preserved in "powerful rhyme," but in "sonnets pretty roomes." Scorning worldly magnificence as ostentation, he goes instead to the other extreme of preciousness. Subsequent generations, he predicts, will hear these hymns commemorating his love affair and, recognizing his greatness, declare him a saint.

In the final stanza the misunderstood lover continues to forecast the future as he now imagines the invocation which he and his mistress will receive after their canonization.

Lovers of the future will admire the splendid isolation, the joy, and the intensity of his love. And yet the lover, pronouncing the imaginary invocation, inadvertently includes some more incongruous touches. Later lovers will, for example, believe that his "love was peace, that now is rage," that *he* miraculously managed to avoid the anxiety and sorrow inherent in profane love; but the sighs and tears and fevers and chills of stanza two have already shown the reader that he performed no such miracle at all, that his love too was rage. And without realizing it, the lover also suggests that his love ultimately resolves itself into self-love; he and his mistress contracted the whole world ("Countries, Townes, Courts") and the "whole worlds soule" so that they were contained in one another's eyes; but these eyes are also "glasses" or "mirrors," and when one lover looks into the other's eyes, he sees his own reflection, which epitomizes "all" to him.

Through his self-important glorification of his love as saintly and ideal, the lover thus only makes it seem worse. Further, his parody of sacred love suggests the ideal of *caritas* to which his *cupiditas* does not conform. The religious imagery is a reminder of the positive *exempla* of saintly love, quite different from the profane love of which the speaker and his mistress are negative *exempla*. Donne's readers would have been vividly aware that saints of *caritas* do not forsake the world in order to find it again in their own reflection, that they "die and rise the same, and prove/ Mysterious by this love" in quite another sense than the "canonized" lovers do.

All these incongruities between the ideal which the lover pretends to represent and the real ideal, of which his love would have seemed a profane mockery, reach their culmination in the last sentence of the imagined invocation:

> Beg from above
> A patterne of your love!

Although the speaker is predicting that future lovers will pray to him to intercede with God so that they may experience love according to the pattern he has set, the sentence also would have inevitably suggested that it is the speaker himself who needs to pray for help in finding a higher pattern of love. His love is one by which he can die, but not live; yet the tears and sighs, the heats and colds, the palsy and ruined fortune which he has endured all suggest that his love is hardly worth dying for. His love, by his own description, if not by his own statement, follows a pattern which most of his contemporaries would wish to avoid rather than imitate. His love, although it pretends to be unworldly and has ruined his worldly career, has proved to be quite as earthly in its inspiration as greed and ambition are. Thus, given the ironic contrast between sacred and profane love implicit throughout the poem, what the lover says in the conclusion means something quite different than he intends; that he himself needs to beg from above the pattern of *caritas* which he has failed to achieve.

Like *The Canonization*, *The Extasie* is also a satiric comedy which makes fun of lovers who deceive themselves into believing that their profane love is not profane. Both sets of lovers arouse a smile because of the ironic discrepancy between the claims they make for their love, in which they appeal to religious concepts for justification, and the real ideal of love which their appeal recalls. In *The Canonization* that real ideal is Christian sainthood; in *The Extasie* it is Christian Platonism. The lovers of *The Extasie* persuade themselves that their love is essentially spiritual, but as the poem works toward its conclusion, they show that their professions of spirituality are only special pleading, a hypocritical pretense which inadequately masks an essentially sensual attraction. As in *The Canonization*, it is their smug self-deception which Donne amuses himself with exposing. But that Donne dramatizes Platonic lovers who are sanctimonious hypocrites does not mean that he is attacking Platonism itself. On the contrary, poems like *A Valediction: forbidding Mourning* show that he took it very seriously indeed, seriously enough to satirize its perversion in *The Extasie*.

The Extasie

Where, like a pillow on a bed,
    A pregnant banke swel'd up, to rest
The violets reclining head,
    Sat we two, one anothers best.

Our hands were firmely cimented
    With a fast balme, which thence did spring,
Our eye-beames twisted, and did thred
    Our eyes, upon one double string;

So to'entergraft our hands, as yet
    Was all the meanes to make us one,
And pictures in our eyes to get
    Was all our propagation.

As 'twixt two equall Armies, Fate
    Suspends uncertaine victorie,
Our soules, (which to advance their state,
    Were gone out,) hung 'twixt her, and mee.

And whil'st our soules negotiate there,
    Wee like sepulchrall statues lay;
All day, the same our postures were,
    And wee said nothing, all the day.

If any, so by love refin'd,
    That he soules language understood,
And by good love were growen all minde,
    Within convenient distance stood,

He (though he knew not which soule spake,
    Because both meant, both spake the same)
Might thence a new concoction take,
    And part farre purer then he came.

This Extasie doth unperplex
    (We said) and tell us what we love,
Wee see by this, it was not sexe,
    We see, we saw not what did move:

But as all severall soules containe
    Mixture of things, they know not what,
Love, these mixt soules, doth mixe again,
    And makes both one, each this and that.

A single violet transplant,
    The strength, the colour, and the size,
(All which before was poore, and scant,)
    Redoubles still, and multiplies.

When love, with one another so
    Interinanimates two soules,
That abler soule, which thence doth flow,
    Defects of lonelinesse controules.

Wee then, who are this new soule, know,
    Of what we are compos'd, and made,
For, th'Atomies of which we grow,
    Are soules, whom no change can invade.

But o alas, so long, so farre
    Our bodies why doe wee forbeare?
They are ours, though they are not wee, Wee are
    The intelligences, they the spheare.

We owe them thankes, because they thus,
    Did us, to us, at first convay,
Yeelded their forces, sense, to us,
    Nor are drosse to us, but allay.

On man heavens influence workes not so,
    But that it first imprints the ayre,
Soe soule into the soule may flow,
    Though it to body first repaire.

As our blood labours to beget
    Spirits, as like soules as it can,
Because such fingers need to knit
    That subtile knot, which makes us man:

So must pure lovers soules descend
    T'affections, and to faculties.
Which sense may reach and apprehend,
    Else a great Prince in prison lies.

To'our bodies turne wee then, that so
    Weake men on love reveal'd may looke;
Loves mysteries in soules doe grow,
    But yet the body is his booke.

And if some lover, such as wee,
    Have heard this dialogue of one,
Let him still marke us, he shall see
    Small change, when we'are to bodies gone.[11]

The Extasie falls into two basic parts—the long introduction which describes the setting and the situation, and the longer "dialogue of one" which occurs during the "spiritual ecstasy" of the two lovers and concludes with their decision to consummate it with sexual ecstasy. And the dialogue of one itself breaks down into two parts; in the first the lovers analyze the nature of their love and the significance of their ecstatic union. In the second they reach the decision to return to their bodies, after a discussion of the nobility of the body and the importance of the senses in love.

As is so often the case with Donne's poetry, it is helpful to begin by imaginatively reconstructing the way this poem resonated for the sixteenth-century reader. Looking at its title, *The Extasie*, he would place it as religious and mystical, expecting a description of the going-out of the soul after contemplation of a sacred subject, of the temporary suspension of the senses, and perhaps of a flash of awareness of God or the Oneness of the universe. With these associations in mind, he would read the first line of the poem with something of a shock:

[11] I have departed from Grierson's text by dividing the poem into quatrains.

> Where, like a pillow on a bed,
> A pregnant banke swel'd up. . . .

And such sensual imagery continues for twelve lines; the word "soul" does not even appear until the fifteenth line.

As one reads on in the poem, the reason for the sensual imagery emerges. The poem is a monologue by a man who is either musing to himself or speaking to a silent listener; in either case, he is describing an event of the past, for he consistently uses the past tense until he reaches the moment when the two souls speak together, and then he shifts to the dramatic present. The experience which he recollects shades his language; his ecstasy, whatever it may have contained of the spiritual, ended in the physical; and thus he begins his description of his experience with sensual imagery. The two lovers sat in a pastoral setting, but in retrospect its fertility seems most memorable. The pregnant bank on which they sat swelled up and seemed like a pillow on a bed. The lovers themselves held hands and looked into one another's eyes, while their hands were cemented together with perspiration, a physiological reaction which would have suggested lustfulness to Donne's readers.[12] This "entergrafting" of their hands, the lover adds, was *as yet* their only means to make them one, just as begetting pictures on one another's eyes was their only propagation. At this point, all the connotations of the language would have suggested to Donne's audience that some kind of physical union beyond that of their eyes and hands was forthcoming.

As the lover goes on to tell what their souls were doing, however, the ecstasy of the title begins to emerge, although it seems somewhat incongruous with the imagery of the preceding twelve lines. The metaphor changes from sex to warfare as their souls meet somewhere between them, while their bodies lie still like two equal armies between whom victory is as yet uncertain. We later learn that both armies win this battle. But if the reader's suspicions were not aroused, this passage would seem an innocent description

---

[12] See, e.g., *Othello*, III.iv.38-43.

of the external appearance of ecstasy, of the impervious-
ness of the bodies of the ecstatics to outward sensations;
they are like sepulchral statues, stone beings who are temporarily hollow inside and insensible outside. But, although
their bodies do not move and do not speak, their souls communicate through a union so complete that "both meant,
both spake the same." And, the lover adds, if anyone
stood near them who "by good love were growen all
minde," and thus were able to understand the language of
souls, even he would be purified by hearing their dialogue
of one.

The two souls, joined in ecstatic union, now begin to
analyze their exemplary love; their analysis, presumably,
produces the "new concoction" which will inspire any nearby lover to imitate its perfection. With impeccable logic,
they say what their love is not before saying what it is. Although they were once confused about what attracted them
to one another, their ecstasy "unperplexes" them. They
now know that they were not moved to love one another for
physical reasons:

Wee see by this, it was not sexe . . .

The use of the verb "was" in the midst of a passage otherwise in the present tense, however, strongly suggests that
they once found one another sexually attractive and mistakenly believed that sex was the reason they loved one
another.

But now they know what really moved them to love—
their souls, not their bodies. Their ecstasy has taught them
the depth and power of their spiritual attraction, and in
their dialogue of one they explain its value. Their dialogue
is, of course, the speech of their two souls clasped together
in space; since they are spiritual substance and not corporeal, they do not simply join, but mix together, forming one
soul which speaks in the plural "we." The speech which
this soul makes is essentially an extended explanation of the
Platonic commonplace that lovers are both One and Two-
in-One. Souls, the united lovers say, are themselves mix-

tures,[13] and love mixes them again so that the two souls become one and each partakes of the qualities and immaterial substance of the other; each is both "this and that," both he and she. Turning to an analogy to express the value of this mixing, they say they are like a single violet, which upon transplanting becomes double and improves in strength, size, and color; their souls too improve through their spiritual transplanting, for when love "interinanimates" two souls, the single abler soul which is produced controls "defects of lonelinesse," since if broken down into two again, each single soul contains part of the other. And not only does their spiritual love free them from the anxieties of separation, but it also banishes the fear that they will sometimes stop loving one another; their love must be eternal, since it grows from their souls, "whom no change can invade."

Content with their view of themselves as a single abler soul, however, the lovers abruptly change their line of thought. After this lofty ethereality, the next lines might come as something of a shock:

> But O alas, so long, so farre
> Our bodies why doe wee forbeare?

But the reader who had noticed the clues already strewn about the countryside would probably smile. The lovers, having persuaded themselves that their love is really spiritual and eternal, now feel they can enjoy its corporeal and mutable aspects. They have had an ecstasy of souls and now will proceed to have an ecstasy of bodies. In his title Donne is punning again, for as the *OED* indicates, the word "ecstasy" was used technically to refer to the ex-stasis of the soul from the body and more loosely to refer to any intense feeling which drove reason out of the brain.

In preparation for their reincarnation, the lovers summon up another series of arguments and analogies. The

---

[13] Traditional theology, however, teaches that the soul is a simple, not a mixture of things; see, e.g., *Summa Theologica*, I.Q.75.Art.5-6.

thesis which they defend, in itself quite orthodox and pious, is that the body is *not* the prisonhouse of the soul:

> So must pure lovers soules descend
> T'affections, and to faculties,
> Which sense may reach and apprehend,
> Else a great Prince in prison lies.

Donne was naturally vividly aware that Platonism can tend easily to a Manichaean scorn for the physical universe and the human body and that Christian Platonism modified this tendency by stressing that God is immanent in His creation and that Christ sanctified the body through His incarnation. Although the lovers seem guilty of willful obscurantism in some of their arguments, Donne's contemporaries would believe their basic line of reasoning to be sound. But the lovers would still sound ridiculous and wrong-headed—not because of their philosophy but because of the tone in which they pronounce it and the use to which they put it. "Pure lovers" sounds unduly smug and "descend" too condescending, for example, when juxtaposed with the "Where, like a pillow on a bed" of the beginning and the "small change" which occurs in their union when they return to their bodies at the end. Their pretense that they are pure and exemplary thus seems incongruous. Donne is not imagining lovers who are making Platonism more Christian; rather, he is ironically dramatizing lovers who pervert Christian Platonism by arguing that it demands ("So *must* pure lovers soules descend . . .") sexual indulgence. These lovers are using the right reasons as an excuse for doing the wrong thing.

Their arguments drawn from Christian Platonism fill three stanzas. The theme of all three is the bond of love which holds the universe together, causing the higher orders to act upon and animate the lower and the lower to yearn toward and emulate the higher.[14] Sidney's Astrophil also uses this argument, with equal casuistry if with less elabo-

[14] See, e.g., Ficino, *op.cit.*, 169-172, 148-150, 125-129.

rateness, in his attempts to seduce Stella in the Eighth
Song:

> Love makes earth the water drink,
> Love to earth makes water sinke;
> And if dumbe things be so witty,
> Shall a heavenly grace want pitty?[15]

The first of these Platonic stanzas ("On man heavens influence workes not so . . .") refers to the way in which the
higher spiritual orders become immanent in the physical.
Donne seems to have had in mind a process by which the
mold or form of the soul was marked out (imprinted on the
air); this form can in one sense be called the soul, but it
more completely fulfills its Idea when soulful substance
flows into it, a process which is completed when the soul
becomes incarnate in the body. In this way human beings
are created by God and his mediaries, the angels and dae-
mons who inhabit the spheres and stars ("heavens influence"); it differs from the process which the lovers are
about to undergo ("On man heavens influence workes not
so . . .") because theirs is a second incarnation, wrought
by their own influence.[16] In the next stanza the lovers explain that just as God has decreed the interdependence of
body and soul by placing spiritual substance within the
physical, so man recognizes it and struggles to make the
physical spiritual; his blood "labours to beget spirits," the
intermediary between body and soul.[17] Reaching their conclusion in the third stanza, the lovers argue that according
to these two precedents, their souls must also descend to
their bodies, and more specifically, to the affections and
faculties of their bodies. The only alternative, they say,
would be for the soul to be like a great Prince detained in a
prison, ignoring the other choices on the continuum of love

[15] *The Poems of Sir Philip Sidney*, ed. William A. Ringler, Jr.
(Oxford, 1962), 219.

[16] A process something like this is described by Ficino; see 172, 186.

[17] Cf. Ficino, 186, 194-195, 221-225; in the latter passage Ficino
explains that that love which is a kind of madness or bewitchment is
communicated by the spirits begot by the blood.

between the extremes of sensual love and Manichaean asceticism.

But Donne has left other clues besides illogicality to show that he is treating the two lovers ironically. Most telling of all perhaps is the lovers' conviction that their love is not only acceptable but exemplary and the terms in which they state this conviction. Having already argued that God set the example for incarnation by placing the soul within a body and that they should therefore follow His example, they now import His motive as well as His method. Recalling the incarnation of Christ through the phrase "love reveal'd," they make the rather blasphemous suggestion that by returning to their bodies, they too will be able to reveal love to "weake men." Yet the "love reveal'd" through their evangelical crusade, as the last quatrain makes quite clear, will be sexual union.

It can be argued that the conclusion has nothing to do with sex and refers simply to the decision of the lovers to return to their bodies in order to describe their ecstatic experience in love to others. But this view seems to ignore the overtones of the beginning and to deny the organizational progress of the poem. The souls of the lovers have been united in ecstasy, and a lover who understood the language of souls could have heard them speak. Now they are about to return to their bodies, and a nearby lover will see small change in them after they have done so. Not only does it seem clear that they will unite physically from their assertion that there will be small change in their dialogue of one after their return, but it is also implicit in the contrast between the fact that the anonymous observer could hear the spiritual ecstasy and *see* the physical one.

That the lovers call upon an audience to witness their physical union at the end of the poem is perhaps shocking. But Donne is simply indulging in bawdy Elizabethan humor to demonstrate vividly the blindness to which their casuistry has led. The lovers are making an unhappy extension of the belief that to the pure all things are pure. Having first convinced themselves that their love is pure and spiritual, they conclude that its sexual expression will be pure too; and any observer who was able to follow their spiritual dialogue of one and take its "new concoction" will also find their physical dialogue pure. The flaw is not in the aphorism, nor is it in the poem. This conclusion is Donne's way of revealing the flaw in the lovers' loudly proclaimed purity.

In *The Canonization* and *The Extasie* Donne is extending the satire on the glorification of sex which was handled more narrowly and less psychologically in *Elegie XIX*. In general, Donne's Ovidian lovers know what they are doing; these two Petrarchan lovers differ from them as Malvolio does from Edmund, for they are hypocrites rather than villains. Although their love is worldly and lustful, they insist on convincing themselves that it is spiritual and ideal, even that they perform a pious service in loving so. In self-defense they summon up all the clichés about the nobility of spiritual love, blissfully unaware of the incongruity between the high claims they make for themselves and the lowly actuality of their affairs. Donne must have had a wonderful time inventing their literary and philosophical malapropisms and imagining them said with such glib self-confidence. In these poems he has dissolved the potential sorrow and tragedy of profane Petrarchan love in objective laughter.

iv *Remedia Idolatriae*

Unless he is as willfully self-deceived as the lovers of *The Canonization* or *The Extasie*, the idolatrous Petrarchan lover is normally in a state of pain and misery. He offers inordinate love to his mistress and is usually not repaid in kind. Even if his devotion is returned, then he must eventually discover that his mistress is not the divine creature that his imagination has made her; such a lover ultimately receives pain and disillusionment in return for a brief period of happiness. And just as Donne wrote Ovidian poems which dramatized lustful lovers who, in their disillusionment with sex, determined to remedy their excessive interest in it, so too he wrote poems which dramatize lovers

178

who are seeking remedies for idolatry in order to escape from their self-created misery.

Like the poems of self-deception in section iii, Donne's poems on the theme of *remedia idolatriae* are a blend of Ovidianism and Petrarchanism. These two traditions have analogous "plot lines," since either tradition the typical lover moves from involvement in love to *remedia amoris*. But the Ovidian lover usually remedies his love by denial, by refusing any longer to court a woman who refuses him, forgetting her by turning his attention to practical and worldly matters. The idolatrous Petrarchan lover rectifies his love by redirecting it toward the unchanging *imago Dei* within his beloved or by scorning the worldly and transient and turning to divine love. Donne has also written poems, discussed in Chapter v, which follow the Petrarchan plot line, poems which dramatize the state of grace in human love which results when a lover adores the unchanging spiritual qualities of his beloved and the state of grace in divine love which occurs when a lover frees himself from worldly involvement and turns his whole heart toward God.

But other poems provide an Ovidian remedy for a Petrarchan problem. In *Loves diet* and *The Blossome* Donne depicts lovers who idolize a mistress who in return only disdains their adoration. These lovers, instead of weeping and lamenting, simply decide to abandon the unwilling mistress. Arguing that physical love which is reciprocated, although more lowly, is better than unreciprocated spiritual love, they substitute lust for idolatry. Although they are only substituting bad for worse, a lesser error for a greater, they do conform to moral tradition in assuming that it is better to be a libertine than an idolator.

Loves diet is a simple and straightforward example of this kind of remedy for idolatry. In this poem Donne, borrowing his metaphor from Ovid, imagines the lover acting as his own physician. Assuming the role of love's doctor, the speaker sternly prescribes a diet for his love so that it will be reduced from its troublesome obesity to inconspicuous leanness, so that love can become a minor and unimportant aspect of his life.

Loves diet

To what a combersome unwieldinesse
And burdenous corpulence my love had growne,
    But that I did, to make it lesse,
    And keepe it in proportion,
Give it a diet, made it feed upon
That which love worst endures, *discretion*.

Above one sigh a day I'allow'd him not,
Of which my fortune, and my faults had part;
    And if sometimes by stealth he got
    A she sigh from my mistresse heart,
And thought to feast on that, I let him see
'Twas neither very sound, nor meant to mee.

If he wroung from mee'a teare, I brin'd it so
With scorne or shame, that him it nourish'd not;
    If he suck'd hers, I let him know
    'Twas not a teare, which hee had got,
His drinke was counterfeit, as was his meat;
For, eyes which rowle towards all, weepe not, but sweat.

What ever he would dictate, I writ that,
But burnt my letters; When she writ to me,
    And that that favour made him fat,
    I said, if any title bee
Convey'd by this, Ah, what doth it availe,
To be the fortieth name in an entaile?

Thus I reclaim'd my buzard love, to flye
At what, and when, and how, and where I chuse;
    Now negligent of sport I lye,
    And now as other Fawkners use,
I spring a mistress, sweare, write, sigh and weepe:
And the game kill'd, or lost, goe talke, and sleepe.

The basic medicine which the speaker prescribes to blunt

the appetite of his love is "discretion," since reason will dull its hunger by teaching it that its food is either dangerous or imaginary. His love badly needed this dietary medicine, he says, because it had grown excessive, acquiring a "burdenous corpulence" and "combersome unwieldiness." One aspect of the idolatry syndrome is, of course, that it can be almost pathologically ravenous and possessive, growing far out of proportion to what is normal and natural; and as its emotions become more and more violent and excessive, the beloved seems more important than anything else in the universe; she seems, in fact, to be the whole universe. Reason is, therefore, the most appropriate medicine for curing the lover's pathological passion.

In dictating the nourishment which will help to moderate his love, the speaker's discretion leads him to follow a strict principle of equality—insisting that the one sigh which he allows his love be shared with his fortune and his faults. If his mistress happened to produce another sigh, he refused to let his love have it, arguing that it was not healthful and was probably inspired by another lover. If he did happen to shed a tear, he added the salty sting of shame to it before giving it to his love. As for her tears, he told himself that they were as counterfeit as the lady herself, for they were not tears at all, but the perspiration which her eyes produced as they exercised themselves by flirting with her large retinue of lovers. If he received a letter from her, he again reminded himself that he was only one of many other lovers . . . and probably at the bottom of her list. Thus, he concludes with gaiety and relief, he freed his love from excessive devotion to a single mistress. He has not stopped loving altogether, but has changed to a leaner, tougher kind of love, one which costs him little time, few anxieties and tears, and no sleepless nights.

Like *Loves diet*, *The Blossome* is also built around a contrast between two kinds of love. In both poems the speakers reject as undesirable the love affairs in which they are currently involved, affairs which demand that they humbly submit themselves to the icy disdain of their "cruel fair," giving her spiritual adoration and receiving nothing in return. In order to combat this idolatrous kind of love, they regress to another kind, convincing themselves that women are not particularly divine after all and should be loved physically instead. *The Blossome*, however, develops this pattern more dramatically. A concrete situation is sketched in immediately: on a brief vacation in the country outside London, a man has been attracted to a woman and has watched his love for her blossom for "sixe or seaven dayes." But the love has been only one-sided, and his siege has been repelled. In spite of his failure, his heart still wants to stay and worship the lady silently, but the rest of the man, his body and his rational intellect, thinks the heart is jejune, naive, and foolish.

The Blossome

Little think'st thou, poore flower,
    Whom I have watch'd sixe or seaven dayes,
And seene thy birth, and seene what every houre
Gave to thy growth, thee to this height to raise,
And now dost laugh and triumph on this bough,
    Little think'st thou
That it will freeze anon, and that I shall
To morrow finde thee falne, or not at all.

Little think'st thou poore heart
    That labour'st yet to nestle thee,
And think'st by hovering here to get a part
In a forbidden or forbidding tree,
And hop'st her stiffenesse by long siege to bow:
    Little think'st thou,
That thou to morrow, ere that Sunne doth wake,
Must with this Sunne, and mee a journey take.

But thou which lov'st to bee
    Subtile to plague thy selfe, wilt say,
Alas, if you must goe, what's that to mee?
Here lyes my businesse, and here I will stay:

You goe to friends, whose love and meanes present
            Various content
To your eyes, eares, and tongue, and every part.
If then your body goe, what need you a heart?

     Well then, stay here; but know,
      When thou hast stayd and done thy most;
A naked thinking heart, that makes no show,
Is to a woman, but a kinde of Ghost;
How shall shee know my heart; or having none,
         Know thee for one?
Practise may make her know some other part,
But take my word, shee doth not know a Heart.

     Meet mee at London, then,
      Twenty dayes hence, and thou shalt see
Mee fresher, and more fat, by being with men,
Then if I had staid still with her and thee.
For Gods sake, if you can, be you so too:
        I would give you
There, to another friend, whom wee shall finde
As glad to have my body, as my minde.

As the poem begins, the mind of the speaker is already
outside the experience of love, observing it coolly and sci-
entifically as if it were a botanical specimen. The infatuation which has blossomed is, on the other hand, so impassioned and irrational that it is incapable of self-criticism.
As the speaker studies this enthusiastic little flower and
lectures to it, the poem becomes a Petrarchan debate between reason and emotion, but a debate in which reason retains full control. In the first two stanzas his coolly analyti-
cal mind threatens and warns his heart. Although it is now
happy and laughing, he will soon inflict a frost which will
make its blossom fall from its source of nourishment and
perhaps be destroyed altogether. Fruitlessly struggling to
besiege and bow the stiffness of a disdainful lady, the poor
heart, foolishly self-deceived, is striving to nestle in a "forbidden or forbidding tree." Through choosing the image of

the "forbidden tree," which recalls the outlawed tree of the Garden of Eden, the speaker is intentionally showing his heart that its love is sinful as well as futile. In order to remove his heart from this dangerous temptation, he intends to leave the country tomorrow and take his willful heart with him.

In the third stanza the heart is at last allowed to state its case briefly, although it is voiced by the mind and refuted by the mind as well. The speaker's reason, using the techniques of formal argumentation, is stating his opponent's objections only in order to refute them. The speaker prefaces his heart's case by saying that it loves to be subtle, and subtle in order to plague itself; his heart's passion, like sin itself, is ultimately masochistic. To the speaker's threats the heart will say: "Go ahead and leave, and take your body with you; I can get along very well without you. As for me, *my* business is here, and I intend to remain here without you. You can get along very well without me, since you will be among friends who will, in their various ways, please your eyes, ears, tongue, and other parts. If your body is thus made happy, why do you need a heart?"

After the heart pleads its case, the speaker gives it permission to remain, but he tempers his permissiveness with some coolly benevolent advice about the mistake which it is making and the frustration and failure it can expect, advice which should eventually help it to curb its enthusiasm. The heart's love is spiritual adoration, and the speaker tries to point out that women are unworthy of such adoration and do not enjoy receiving it. Although the speaker indulges in a rather cynical *contemptus feminae* in order to make his point, his cynicism is a wholesome corrective to the romantic idolatry of his heart. The speaker's thesis is among Donne's most oft-quoted lines:

> A naked thinking heart, that makes no show
> Is to a woman, but a kinde of Ghost.

Loving with a bare and silent worship, the heart is naked because it is beyond corporeality (the body is its clothing) and because its love is stark and intense; it is a thinking heart because it contemplates instead of speaking or acting. But women, the speaker maintains, do not appreciate such silent adoration; they are as realistic and heartless about love as he himself is. The heart's spiritual love seems like a ghost to women, because they cannot "know" its language or methods of procedure. But, continuing the sexual pun on "know" and echoing the pun on "part" in the previous stanza, the speaker advises the heart that there *are* kinds of love which women do understand and appreciate; practice may make them "know" some other "part" even if they cannot understand naked hearts.

Thus the speaker attempts to cure his benighted heart by telling it that women are purely physical beings, not goddesses who wish to be worshiped. He is sufficiently persuaded of this to dare to leave his heart behind him, to trust that the heart will try an experimental spiritual courtship and meet with total failure. So the speaker will leave and give his heart twenty days to run its experiment without him. He is convinced that he can do nothing but grow healthier in that time, since he will be in the company of men. And he urges his heart to try to cure itself successfully in that period of time too; for after it has shed its foolish infatuation, he would like to give it to another woman—a woman who will be as glad to have his body as his mind. In this conclusion the speaker indicates that the cynicism which he used to discourage his heart in the fourth stanza was not actually complete, that he does not really regard women as bodies without hearts or brains as the lovers of *Elegie XVIII* or *Loves Alchymie* do. The woman in London to whom he wishes to give his love, after his heart has cured itself, will be glad to have both body and mind, neither exclusively. She will return whole love for whole love.

This man has not "reclaimed his buzzard love," as the lover of *Loves diet* did, "to flye/ At what, and when, and how, and where" he chooses. But although he has not remedied idolatry with predatory promiscuity, he still speaks

185

with undertones of Ovidian libertinism. He too substitutes
lust for silent worship, harsh naturalism for hazy romanticism. At the other end of the continuum from these two
poems is *Elegie X, The Dreame*, a poem which dramatizes a second and worse kind of *remedium idolatriae*. In
this poem a man temporarily tries to escape from an idolatrous love affair, not by Ovidian cynicism, but by attempting a remedy which is worse than the affair itself, an escape
from hazy romanticism into the total unreality of wish-ful-
filling fantasy. At the conclusion, however, the lover recognizes that his remedy is worse than the disease, and so he
returns to idolatry and embraces it with relief. He has temporarily tried a *remedium idolatriae* which substitutes self-
love for self-abnegation, since self-love seemed a way to escape from the inevitable pain of idolatry. *The Dreame*
ranks as one of Donne's most powerful studies of the depths
of depravity to which involvement in sinful love can lead.

ELEGIE X

The Dreame

Image of her whom I love, more then she,
    Whose faire impression in my faithful heart,
Makes mee her *Medall*, and makes her love mee,
    As Kings do coynes, to which their stamps impart
The value: goe, and take my heart from hence,
    Which now is growne too great and good for mee:
Honours oppresse weake spirits, and our sense
    Strong objects dull; the more, the lesse wee see.

When you are gone, and *Reason* gone with you;
    Then *Fantasie* is Queene and Soule, and all;
She can present joyes meaner then you do;
    Convenient, and more proportionall.
So, if I dreame I have you, I have you,
    For, all our joyes are but fantasticall.
And so I scape the paine, for paine is true;
    And sleepe which locks up sense, doth lock out all.

After a such fruition I shall wake,
  And, but the waking, nothing shall repent;
And shall to love more thankfull Sonnets make,
  Then if more *honour, teares*, and *paines* were spent.
But dearest heart, and dearer image stay;
  Alas, true joyes at best are *dreame* enough;
Though you stay here you passe too fast away:
  For even at first lifes *Taper* is a snuffe.

Fill'd with her love, may I be rather grown
Mad with much *heart*, then *ideott* with none.[18]

In the beginning lines of the poem the lover sounds somewhat more like a Platonist than a profane Petrarchan, for he worships the image or idea of his mistress more than her physical qualities, and this image, engraved on his heart, improves him and gives him value. But later in the poem he shows that his love is idolatrous *eros*: first, when he is trying to escape from it and says, "And so I scape the paine," and later when he decides not to stop loving after all and returns to being "Mad with much heart." As he runs from his idolatrous worship in order to indulge in a sensual fantasy, he reveals himself as the archetypal Petrarchan lover, rejected and dissatisfied. Insofar as his love improves him, his lady may love him; but the image engraved on his heart makes him love spiritually, and he does not want this "strong object" to dull his senses.

So in the second stanza he banishes the image, and reason as well, so that he can dream an erotic fantasy. In this stanza it becomes clear that Donne, a master psychologist, is dramatizing a new kind of reaction to scorn, a morbid and neurotic one which is worse than profane love itself. The lover recognizes that profane love is transitory and painful, and yet he chooses another kind of love which is still more transitory, if less painful; he is rejecting love which involves some self-sacrifice and self-restraint for completely selfish love which yields pleasure without sacri-

---

[18] I have departed from Grierson's text by dividing the poem into three 8-line stanzas and a final couplet.

fice, although it demands that he close out the rest of the world. He does not worship even the creature. He worships only himself. So he withdraws into the illusory pleasures imagined by his fancy; the nature of his dream of pleasure is made clear when he says "So, if I dreame I have you, I have you. . . ." He is not strong enough to persist in spiritual worship of his mistress without sensual gratification; but instead of forsaking it for lust like the lovers in *The Blossome* or *Loves diet*, he abandons it for the unreal and sterile lust of erotic fantasy. This, he says with satanic pride, is perhaps a meaner joy, a more debasing joy, but it is more convenient and more proportional to his weakness.[19] And with satanic rationalization he adds that "all our joyes are but fantasticall" anyway.

Yet this is not his deepest point of degradation. After his fanciful orgy is over, he congratulates himself on his cleverness, for he has succeeded in obtaining pleasure without the pain which all those who live in reality know must sometimes accompany it. Religious tradition maintains that the burden of pain is one which mankind must bear; it is the curse of the Fall that human beings must earn bread by the sweat of their brow, feel the pangs of childbirth, and return to dust. To attempt to escape this curse is as bad as to seek it willfully in despair and self-contempt; for this reason, religious tradition stands firmly against both mercy killing and suicide. To run from suffering is bad enough, and to run while recognizing it as sin and cowardice is worse, but to revel in one's success in avoiding it is unpardonable. And yet the lover says:

And so I scape the paine, for paine is true;
And sleepe which locks up sense, doth lock out all.

Pain is true because it is part of the reality in which fallen

[19] There is, perhaps, a pun in "meaner," which would carry the meaning of "more moderate," as suggested by the use of the word "proportionall" in the next line; but the *OED* does not record any examples of the word "mean" ever being used in the comparative when used in this sense, whereas "mean" in the sense of debasing was frequently used in the comparative and superlative.

man must live. In trying to escape it, the lover embraces a shadow; he envisions a sensualist's Nirvana in which he alone exists, locking up all sense within himself and locking out all the pain which sense normally apprehends along with pleasure. If the profane love which sets up the mistress as God is evil, then this egocentric reordering of nature for personal gratification is still more evil, for the lover sets himself up as God. In running from the earthly reality of pain and suffering, the lover has chosen the road to insanity, to solipsistic isolation from the living and true, to a mad and irresponsible intoxication with personal pleasure.

The speaker begins the next stanza by continuing his self-congratulation, but in the process raises a consideration which saves him. As he imagines waking from his dream and writing love sonnets about his fantasy, he suddenly recognizes its illusory nature and begs his heart and the image not to leave him after all. He returns from his vision of an irresponsibly sweet and sordid madness to real life, with an acceptance of its painful realities and transitory joys. "Alas, true joyes at best are *dreame* enough" is an echo of an earlier line, "For, all our joyes are but fantasticall." But the latter is full of all the heavy irony of false rationalization, the former of the tremendous sorrow of true recognition. Now the lover affirms the sad transiencies of the profane love which he has tried to avoid. In choosing idolatrous love, which entails the pains of loss and frustrated desire, he may grow mad with much heart, but this is better than that madness which in annihilating suffering ultimately annihilates life, reason, and even the selfhood that it at first asserted. The final couplet asserts a firm decision to pick up a burden again:

> Fill'd with her love, may I be rather grown
> Mad with much *heart*, then *ideott* with none.

As any Renaissance reader with only the most elementary knowledge of Greek would have known, "idiot" is derived from "idios," meaning "private" or "own." The lover is choosing an involvement in life which brings sin and pain

189

instead of a retreat into selfishness so sinful and inhuman that it is without pain. After a descent into the unreal euphoria of erotic fantasy, the lover returns ready to accept real pain, which is a required part of his burden as a Petrarchan lover. And yet by choosing profane love of the transitory and earthly instead of the permanence of *caritas*, he still in a sense remains in the fantasy world of an earthly dream.

Probably none of the poems of *remedia idolatriae* discussed in this section is meant to represent a satisfactory remedy. By abandoning an unwilling mistress for a willing one, the idolatrous lover achieves only a temporary and partial cure; he moves from a painful and spiritually dangerous abuse of love to another less painful and dangerous. But he is still open to all the threats of infidelity, misery, and folly which beset the Ovidian lover. As Donne dramatizes in the poems of Chapter iii, Ovidian lust, which these idolatrous lovers use as their remedy, also catches lovers in the whirl of profane love's wheel of fortune. The true alternative to lust and idolatry, Donne believed, was to escape the flux which threatens human love by loving immutable and eternal things.

V · THE IDEAL ON EARTH

That our affections kill us not, nor dye . . .

Not all the lovers in Donne's gallery are rogues or melancholics, braggarts or fools. Donne was fascinated with varieties of amatory experience, and in his poetry we find, if not God's plenty, at least man's plenty. It is as if Donne wished to examine love by seeing it from every angle, both its good ones and its bad ones. And so he also imagined lovers who love wisely and well and made them deliver monologues in verse. His tragedies and his satirical comedies are complemented by these divine comedies, which provide a happy ending to his story of human love. Donne believed that human affections, when misused, could kill man physically and spiritually, but he did not believe that affections should therefore die.

The Ovidian and Petrarchan poems dramatize only the "thou shalt nots" of human love, revealing the dangers and follies of a distorted overemphasis on either the flesh or the spirit. By implication, they raise a series of questions about how human beings should love: how can a man and a woman achieve a love by which they can live rather than die, a love which is intense without being inordinate, a love which can exist in the world without the taint of worldly mutability, a love which can satisfy their thirst without being jealous and possessive? In writing the love songs which answer these questions with a genuine remedy for profane love, Donne creates some of his finest poetry.

The peculiar quality of these affirmative poems is that they seem both so old-fashioned and so new. When placed beside the Ovidian poems, which seem so slashingly iconoclastic and so brilliantly fast-moving, these poems seem to state only the most conventional clichés. Many of them express a relatively quiet security which could seem pallid next to the colorful emotional turbulence of many of the Petrarchan poems. And yet, if they are not sensationally daring or violent, these poems are still fresh and powerful.

That *The good-morrow, The Anniversarie,* and *A Valediction: forbidding mourning* are (together with *The Canonization*) the most frequently anthologized of Donne's poems is mute testimony to their greatness.

Some might say that they are greater because they are more sincere, because they grow out of Donne's relationship with his wife, and perhaps that is so. Perhaps Donne could write these poems because he discovered through the experience of his own life the truth of the old clichés about the blessedness of giving and the greatness of charity. To think so does no discredit to either John or Anne Donne, and Walton says Donne wrote *A Valediction: forbidding mourning* as a farewell to his wife before a journey to the continent; but Walton is notoriously inaccurate and often permits sentimental appropriateness to color his judgments. We simply do not know about the relationship between Donne's poetry and his biography. We do know that Donne had a powerful imagination and a dramatic flair and that he could therefore vividly convey situations and emotions which he had not experienced directly. And we can, by simply looking at the poems and the conventions on which they draw, see how Donne managed to write affirmative love poems which are simultaneously so traditional and so new. For Donne was, after all, a conservative revolutionary.

Donne began by being more or less conservative in form and revolutionary in content, but he ended by being revolutionary in form and conservative in content. At any rate, looking at the span and bulk of Donne's poetry from a distance, we can perceive two kinds of development: a progressive increase in technical originality and a progressive movement toward direct expression of the *consensus gentium* about love. Or to put the matter another way, Donne gradually grew less conventional as a poet while he simultaneously intensified his understanding of the need for love which drives man and began to express a rather derivative vision of the way that need could be fulfilled. One gets the impression that the Donne who wrote the Ovidian poems, although he was at heart rather old-fashioned in his beliefs about love, was hesitant to express views so ordinary and bourgeois unless he demonstrated his brightness and cleverness by putting on the mask of irony. Gradually he emerged from behind that protective armor and made his indirect statement direct, and by the time he ran the risk of seeming banal or sentimental, he was so polished a poet that he was beyond attack. As any young lawyer well knows, to ridicule weakness is always easier than to hold an affirmative position. Yet Donne eventually took the more difficult course.

Donne's Ovidian poems and his Horatian satires are very likely his earliest poetry. At least, if a poet's ability to assimilate and innovate within a tradition is any index of his poetic maturity, then we can say with some certainty that Donne wrote these classical poems before he wrote many others. For they are, as far as technique is concerned, his most conventional, although even in them he could hardly be called imitative. If he had not written other poetry, these poems would probably be admired for their originality; they seem derivative only by comparison with his later work. And among the Ovidian poems, those included in the *Songs and Sonets* are usually more original; in the *Elegies* he uses an Ovidian genre and verse form with few alterations. Donne does not invent his Ovidian themes, situations, or ironies, but he does, especially in the *Songs and Sonets*, play with the ironies of logical contradiction to an extent that Ovid never does. A poem like *Communitie* is, for example, already peculiarly Donnean, although its humorous treatment of logical casuistry draws on two Ovidian arguments, the doctrine of change and the doctrine of use. The movement from the casuistry of *Communitie*, with its Ovidian arguments in Donne's own syllogisms, to *The Flea*, the casuistry of which is based on Donne's own argument from analogy, suggests the way in which Donne's wit expanded within the framework of the Ovidian tradition. And in addition to adding to Ovidianism, Donne also subtracts; from the very outset he chose, for example, to leave out the mythological references prompted by Ovid's digres-

193

sive loquacity; the result is that Donne's Ovidian poems are more compressed, tight, and coherent than anything which Ovid wrote, and they are also much less coy and cute. Ovid belongs to the expansive leisure of the tapestry-hung boudoir, Donne to the dialectical limits of the Inns of Court and their nearby inns of pleasure.

But in his Petrarchan poems Donne uses conventions still more freely. Sometimes, it is true, Donne seems more original than he actually is simply because Donne imitated Petrarch himself when other Petrarchan poets were following Petrarch's imitators. The personality of Petrarch, as presented in the *Canzoniere*, is far from soft and sentimental. Donne doubtless learned much about psychological analysis and introspection from the *Canzoniere*, where Petrarch examines his mind and reproduces his reactions with startling honesty and realism. And sometimes Donne's wit, his yoking of opposites, is simply Petrarchan conflict and Petrarchan oxymoronism carried to its logical conclusion. But nevertheless Donne's Petrarchan poetry is much less derivative and much more unconventional than his Ovidian poetry. For in writing his Petrarchan poetry, Donne had his eye both on the *Canzoniere* and on the flood of sonnet sequences which imitated the *Canzoniere*. And his intent seems to have been to make his own Petrarchan poetry seem new rather than imitative.

As in his Ovidian poetry, Donne also compresses and toughens in his Petrarchan poetry. While his contemporaries were writing sequences which carried a frail plot-line through one hundred sugared sonnets, Donne told a complete story in a single dramatic monologue and invented many of his own stanza forms. When he borrows a Petrarchan theme such as the scorn of the disdainful mistress, he sometimes makes his lovers answer scorn with angry scorn, as in a poem like *The Apparition*. But this toughening up of the Petrarchan lover is not satire on Petrarchanism; Donne is being fresh, but not hostile. He is not so much attacking conventions as he is using them as a framework in which his own innovations stand out. Poems like *Loves*

Deitie or *The Funerall* typify Donne's relationship to the Petrarchan tradition; in them he takes a Petrarchan theme or situation and uses it as a point of departure, letting his own wit and inventiveness produce poems completely different from any others written on that theme.

Because these poems are original and hard-headed, Donne has been called anti-Petrarchan, but that term overstates the case. Perhaps, in recognition of Donne's desire to achieve freshness within a venerable convention, we should begin to call them "neo-Petrarchan" instead, for that name more accurately describes their blend of independence and deference. They are, in any case, less Petrarchan than his Ovidian poems are Ovidian; and they reflect his growing independence from poetic conventions. In neither group does he invent themes or philosophical assumptions about love. But in his Ovidian poetry he innovates by letting his wit play within the limits of convention, whereas in his Petrarchan poetry his wit begins to burst the limits and to create something which we may justly call new. There are precedents for most of the Ovidian poems, while there are only forerunners for many of the Petrarchan poems.

Thus the Ovidian and Petrarchan poems show a progressive increase in technical originality and a progressive liberation from conventional forms of expression. The farthest reaches of this technical originality are affirmative love poems like *The good-morrow* or *A Valediction: forbidding mourning*, which seem to have no clear precedents at all. In them Donne is also drawing on an established tradition, Christian Platonism, but the tradition has been so fully absorbed and submerged that it seems only a point of departure that has long since been left behind. These are love poems which happen to express Platonic love, not Platonic poems. We need only mentally to juxtapose them with Spenser's *Fowre Hymnes* or the *Amoretti* in order to see how Donne has revolutionized artificial conventions and become fully Donnean. Now Donne is writing of human love when there is no great poetic tradition intervening between the underlying philosophy and the experience dramatized in the poem. In Donne's affirmative love poems Christian Platonism is converted into poetic experience without the aid of intermediary traditions. If Donne often seems to have invented a new philosophy of love, it is because he manages to make Christian Platonism seem immediate and real—to express, with amazing originality and power, the way a man can love a woman in conformity to the rule of charity and to convey the intense joy and expansive liberation which such love gives.

But the vulnerability of the philosophy of love which these poems draw on is obvious. Prosaic defenses of idealistic love were so rampant during the Renaissance that it quickly became commonplace and shopworn, a fashionable garment which poets could put on without thinking. The Platonism of men like Ficino can also become ethereal and hazy, so unrelated to "real life" as to alienate this-worldly minds altogether and partially blight the enthusiasm of the most ardent idealist. It was only natural for Donne to make his cynical libertine say in *Loves Alchymie*:

> That loving wretch that sweares,
> 'Tis not the bodies marry, but the mindes,
> Which he in her Angelique findes,
> Would sweare as justly, that he heares,
> In that dayes rude hoarse minstralsey, the spheares.

Or in *Loves growth*:

> Love's not so pure, and abstract, as they use
> To say, which have no Mistresse but their Muse . . .

In Donne's time Shelley had not yet begun to beat his fragile wings in the void, but nonetheless Platonism, then as ever, faced the accusation that it was at best futile and unreal, at worst hypocritical. And Donne, aware of all its dangers and weaknesses, also presented the latter accusation in *The Extasie*.

And yet, if we accept such poems as *The Anniversarie* or *A Valediction: forbidding mourning* as evidence, Donne did not consider idealism in love to be either futile or unreal. Donne's affirmative love poems are almost always tinged with Christian Platonism; the lovers in these poems proclaim that the ideal can be realized on earth without dishonesty or sentimentality. Donne usually does not, however, draw upon the fancy, ethereal, and ingenious aspects of Platonism; they appear only in *The Extasie*, in which the lovers themselves are, if not ethereal, at least fancy and ingenious. The Platonic notions which underlie the idealistic love poems are simple bread-and-butter ones: although human beings may enjoy and love transient physical beauty, it alone will never satisfy, and so they must also love spiritual qualities and ultimately the eternal and unchanging *imago Dei* which shines within the beloved; when people do love the image of God, their love helps them climb toward God; such love is lasting, because it is founded on something not subject to change; and because such love is selfless, sympathetic, and charitable, it produces an unshakable spiritual union between the two partners.

What gives these poems their peculiarly convincing quality is a further extension of the tendency to toughen that we have already observed in the Ovidian and Petrarchan poems. The lovers, although they do swear that their love is a marriage of true minds, do not think that they are therefore disembodied spirits; they do not try to fool themselves about either human nature or the nature of the universe. And although they may admire the rosy lips and cheeks of their partners, these lovers choose instead to describe their relationship through those hard dry images which have made metaphysical poetry famous: before Donne, what lover dared compare his lady to the leg of a compass, let alone manage to flatter her by the comparison? If the philosophical foundation of these poems is obvious and conventional, their hard-headed tone and apt but incongruous images prevent them from seeming mere literary exercises upon a set theme. Again Donne's startling yoking of incongruities is functional, but now it provides an atmosphere of realism rather than irony. If Donne wished to show that a man can love a woman's mind more than her body without being foolish or effeminate, he could not have chosen better methods.

i Surprised by Joy

Donne's libertine lovers frequently present themselves as frank realists who refuse to be tricked by the false façade of amatory conventions. The man who is trying to engineer a seduction in *The Dampe* says that his beloved's disdain and sense of honor are like the giants and enchantresses which populate the Neverlands of chivalric romance:

> For I could muster up as well as you
> My Gyants, and my Witches too,
> Which are vast *Constancy*, and *Secretnesse*,
> But these I neyther looke for, nor professe;
> Kill mee as Woman, let mee die
> As a meere man . . .

Although the singer of "Goe, and catche a falling starre," is speaking instead to a masculine idealist, he also places fidelity and honor in the impossible realms of folklore and romance:

> Goe, and catche a falling starre,
> Get with child a mandrake roote,
> Tell me, where all past yeares are,
> Or who cleft the Divels foot,
> Teach me to heare Mermaides singing,
> Or to keep off envies stinging,
> And finde
> What winde
> Serves to advance an honest minde.
>
> If thou beest borne to strange sights,
> Things invisible to see,
> Ride ten thousand daies and nights,
> Till age snow white haires on thee,
> Thou, when thou retorn'st, wilt tell mee

All strange wonders that befell thee,
  And sweare
  No where
Lives a woman true, and faire.

But in two of his affirmative poems Donne creates cynics who are traitors to the cause of "realism." *The Relique* and *The undertaking* are monologues spoken by ex libertines. Initially skeptical about Platonic love, they have experimented in it anyway and are astonished to discover that it is not a romantic myth but that it actually works. Even if it is frequently commended by fools or hypocrites, they must grudgingly admit that there is something to it after all. It is this tone of grudging admission that makes these poems both convincing and delightful. These devil's advocates have been converted to a kind of love which they had thought ridiculous, and they find that instead of being miserable they have been surprised by joy. Each reacts a bit differently to this new situational irony.

The speaker of *The Relique* maintains the pose of a tough guy. Throughout the poem he makes cynical assertions with a continuous insistence which suggests that he is embarrassed to have done something noble and decent for once. His pilgrimage *has* led him to a woman who is true and fair, but he refuses to believe that such women are common; in fact, he still cannot help sniping at woman's inconstancy. The only way he can describe his relationship and the woman who inspired it is to say that they are miracles, things which deviated radically from the course of nature. And yet his pose of toughness is full of pathos, for, as we discover in the final line of the poem, his miraculous mistress is now dead. He has now only a lock of her hair as a relic by which he can recall their relationship.

The Relique

When my grave is broke up againe
Some second ghest to entertaine,

(For graves have learn'd that woman-head
To be to more than one a Bed)
   And he that digs it, spies
A bracelet of bright haire about the bone,
   Will he not let'us alone,
And thinke that there a loving couple lies,
Who thought that this device might be some way
To make their soules, at the last busie day,
Meet at this grave, and make a little stay?

   If this fall in a time, or land,
   Where mis-devotion doth command,
   Then, he that digges us up, will bring
   Us, to the Bishop, and the King,
      To make us Reliques; then
Thou shalt be a Mary Magdalen, and I
   A something else thereby;
All women shall adore us, and some men;
And since at such time, miracles are sought,
I would have that age by this paper taught
What miracles wee harmelesse lovers wrought.

   First, we lov'd well and faithfully,
   Yet knew not what wee lov'd, nor why,
   Difference of sex no more wee knew,
   Then our Guardian Angells doe;
      Comming and going, wee
Perchance might kisse, but not between those meales;
   Our hands ne'r toucht the seales,
Which nature, injur'd by late law, sets free:
These miracles wee did; but now alas,
All measure, and all language, I should passe,
Should I tell what a miracle shee was.

Like *The Extasie, The Relique* employs the shock technique of inverse development and juxtaposition of opposites, but with the opposite effect. We are led by the first
two stanzas to suspect that the relationship dramatized is
far from ideal, but in the last stanza we share the speaker's

surprise that it actually was. The first lines sound like the lover's conventional protest that he is being murdered by disdain. The next two place the speaker as a cynical libertine, and the reference to Mary Magdalen is ambiguously saintly and sexual, suggesting the possibility of seductive flattery. His assertion in the final stanza that their love was as asexual as the love of angels at first seems unbelievable, until the cumulative past tenses reveal that the poem is a death elegy as well as a love elegy. The famous "bracelet of bright hair about the bone" is almost an emblem of this poem, an emblem of the possibility of pure bright things in the midst of the death, decay, and disillusionment which pervade earthly life.

No subtle seducer addressing a reluctant mistress, the lover is soliloquizing on the theme of *memento mori*. He insists on being intermittently flippant, and yet in context his flippancy is more courageous than irreverent. The first line suggests how great is the danger of morbidity and despair:

> When my grave is broke up againe . . .

In one huge imaginative rush the speaker has already gone beyond the fact of death and reached the realization that there is no peace even in the grave. After a parenthetical pause to mock feminine inconstancy, the rush of loquacity and fancy moves on. (The entire stanza is a single sentence.) Whoever disinters him will find a bracelet of golden hair entwined about his bony arm, from which the flesh will have rotted away. And perhaps, the speaker hopes, the gravedigger will leave his corpse and the bracelet in peace, believing that there is already a couple in the grave who thought that by being buried together they might meet one another again at the day of judgment when their souls return to their graves to recover their bodies, two happy reunited souls dimly silhouetted against the red conflagration and confusion of that last busy day.

In the next stanza he imagines what will happen if he and his bracelet are disinterred in "a time, or land,/ Where misdevotion doth command. . . ." And he amuses himself with the prospect of their being made relics and he and his beloved being regarded as saints. He speculates that his beloved will be taken for a Mary Magdalen and he "a something else." The ambiguity is probably deliberate. That the speaker is mocking idolatry is obvious, for he calls it misdevotion; and by imagining that his beloved will be seen as a Mary Magdalen, he can ridicule two types of idolatry, Roman and amatory, at the same time. Roman idolators worship bits of wood or bone or hair, which they believe to be the relics of saints or of Christ Himself. But the saintly Mary Magdalen was also once a prostitute before she was redeemed, and the "something else" can also be the man who seeks out prostitutes; some people, the speaker satirically suggests, mistakenly idolize couples who love sinfully, although such love is at heart simply whoredom. And the same suspicion of sentimental excess also leads him to remark:

> All women shall adore us, and some men . . .

Again he is being cynical about the more pious and emotional sex, and he is also showing that *he* is no idolatrous lover, prone to a mistaken idealization of women. But since those foolish people who are prone to such nonsense will seek for miracles before they canonize himself and his beloved, he will tell them what miracles they did.

At this point one would expect to find in the last stanza something like the third stanza of *The Canonization*, something like its ironic treatment of the miracle of dying through intercourse and rising again the same. What we get instead is a description of a genuinely Platonic relationship, in this case a friendship between a man and a woman which is not based on sexual attraction. This, the skeptical speaker believes, is a miracle. They simply loved one another well and faithfully and, unlike the lovers of *The Extasie*, did not know what they loved in one another or why they loved at all. That righteous lovers cannot know what they love is a commonplace of Christian Platonism, based on the belief that the object of their love is the image of

God and they cannot know God face to face while on earth. Ficino explains it as follows:

> Hence it happens that the passion of a lover is not quenched by the mere touch or sight of a body, for it does not desire this or that body, but desires the splendor of the divine light shining through bodies, and is amazed and awed by it. For this reason lovers never know what it is they desire to seek, for they do not know God Himself, whose subtle incense has infused into His works a certain sweet aroma of Himself; by this aroma we are certainly every day aroused. We sense the aroma certainly, but we cannot distinguish its flavor, and so when we yearn for the indistinguishable flavor itself, being charmed by its sensible aroma, certainly we do not know what we desire. . . . (140)

So spiritual was their friendship that they were no more aware of a difference in sex than their guardian angels, who of course would not differ at all. Although they enjoyed a kiss of salutation or farewell when they met or departed from one another, they did not kiss at other times, for their affection was based on a metaphysical, not a physical, attraction, and its expression and rewards were beyond the physical.

For the speaker of the poem this is miraculous. His firm and irrepressible belief that the universe ordinarily does not operate in this way is capsulized in his wondering remark that

> Our hands ne'r toucht the seales,
> Which nature, injur'd by late law, sets free . . .

All his intellectual predilections are toward libertine naturalism, not Christian Platonism. He not only assumes that sexual love is natural, but also that limitations on sexual pleasure are an injury inflicted by stultifying and unnatural civil laws. And yet his own experience contradicts what his brain tells him. He has, in spite of himself, been involved in a love which was both satisfying and nonsexual. In the

203

final lines of the poem he speaks of the greatest miracle of all, the woman who aroused such a love in him and whose bracelet of hair he wears as a token of remembrance. The witty cynic is now at a loss for words, speaking with stunned and simple sincerity:

> ... but now alas,
> All measure, and all language, I should passe,
> Should I tell what a miracle shee was.

A tough and still somewhat defiant skeptic has been softened and conquered by the power of Platonic love.

Although *The Relique* contains much of the verbal paradox and trick organization which we associate with Donne, these are superseded in impact by the paradoxical personality of the man whom he has chosen to dramatize in the poem. The lover of *The Relique* is accustomed to being an iconoclast; in his relatively brief soliloquy he manages to ridicule women, Roman Catholics, idolatrous love, and sexual restraint; he is therefore rather defensive and embarrassed about his ability to love conventionally and virtuously, to worship an image while smashing images. He is man enough both to doubt widely held beliefs and to live them when his own experience tells him they are sound.

The undertaking dramatizes a similar paradox. Although its speaker is not so insistently a libertine, he too reacts to his enjoyment of nonsexual love with some amazement. Both lovers are paradoxical because their reactions to conventional beliefs about love are so complicated. The lover of *The undertaking* has also been converted to the Platonic friendship which his society decrees to be admirable. Ordinary mortals would be pleased with their ability to fulfill the expectations of society. Ordinary rebels would not try and would be pleased with their courage to resist majority opinion. But these two lovers are neither bourgeois snobs nor bohemian anti-snob snobs; they are rebels who find it takes courage to love conventionally. The lover of *The undertaking* speaks in self-congratulatory tones because he has had the courage to be ordinary, and yet he is still so skeptical about the likelihood that men actually may love Platonically that he considers his affair rare rather than ordinary. He is surprised both that Platonic love can be sustained and that he himself has been able to sustain it.

The undertaking

I have done one braver thing
    Then all the *Worthies* did,
And yet a braver thence doth spring,
    Which is, to keepe that hid.

It were but madnes now t'impart
    The skill of specular stone,
When he which can have learn'd the art
    To cut it, can finde none.

So, if I now should utter this,
    Others (because no more
Such stuffe to worke upon, there is,)
    Would love but as before.

But he who lovelinesse within
    Hath found, all outward loathes,
For he who colour loves, and skinne,
    Loves but their oldest clothes.

If, as I have, you also doe
    Vertue'attir'd in woman see,
And dare love that, and say so too,
    And forget the Hee and Shee;

And if this love, though placed so,
    From prophane men you hide,
Which will no faith on this bestow,
    Or, if they doe, deride:

Then you have done a braver thing
    Then all the *Worthies* did;
And a braver thence will spring,
    Which is, to keepe that hid.

Typically, the lover announces in the first line that he has done something incredibly worthy, but keeps us in suspense about its nature until the fourth stanza. There he tells us that he has discovered inward loveliness to be more lovable than mere outward beauty; he has learned from experience the truth of the Platonic doctrine that physical beauty, susceptible to change and decay, is but the old and fading clothing which hides a more real and more permanent beauty, that of the soul or spirit. This, he says, makes him worthier than the Worthies, and in the final three stanzas of the poem he challenges his listener to imitate his triumph.

But he also says there is yet a braver thing than loving Platonically, though it springs naturally from such love: "to keepe that hid." "Brave," it is clear, is used in a double sense; the comparison with the Worthies suggests the common Renaissance meaning of "worthy"; but when the lover says in the fifth stanza that

> If, as I have, you also doe
> Vertue'attir'd in woman see,
> And *dare* love that, and say so too . . .

he shows that he is also giving "brave" the secondary meaning of "daring" or "courageous." His reasons for thinking it "brave" in both senses to love Platonically are obvious; he has found it rewarding and therefore worthwhile, and he is also skeptical about idealistic love, as his remark that it is daring to tell a woman that you love her for her virtue ("and say so too") indicates. But if he is a converted libertine, why does he think it brave to keep love hid? If it takes audacity to give up cynicism about amatory idealism, it should take more to admit it to the world. He does not seem, at first glance, to have the courage of his newfound convictions.

The second and third stanzas suggest one reason why he has told no one about his love, although they do not explain why this makes it more worthy. There the lover, converted like the speaker of *The Relique* by a miraculous woman, says that it would not be possible for anyone to follow his example because "no more/ Such stuffe to worke upon, there is. . . ," that there are no more ladies who possess the same "lovelinesse within" which his beloved has. Like the skill required to cut the "specular stone," his ability to discover rewarding love is a lost art because there are no more raw materials. As Theodore Redpath explains in the notes to his edition of the *Songs and Sonets*, the specular stone is probably old selenite, a material which was once cut into thin sheets and used like glass, but was thought to be no longer available during the Renaissance.[1] But in addition to its connotations of rarity, Donne probably also intends it to connote the transparency by which "lovelinesse within" is revealed. Redpath quotes two other instances in which Donne refers to it. In a verse epistle to the Countess of Bedford he says:

> You teach (though wee learne not) a thing unknowne
> To our late times, the use of specular stone,
> Through which all things within without were shown.

And in a sermon:

> The heathens served their gods in temples,
> *sub dio*, without roofs or coverings, in a
> free openness; and where they could, in
> temples made of specular-stone, that was
> transparent as glass, or crystal, so as they
> which walked without in the streets, might
> see all that was done within.

The speaker's lady thus has the transparency of the specular stone; she is a temple through which her spiritual beauty shines—at least to the eyes of those who have learned the art of cutting through her outer layers. But since the last three stanzas are an exhortation to the reader or listener to follow the speaker's example, one must conclude that the metaphor of the specular stone is a compliment, touched with poetic hyperbole, to the beloved's rare virtue, but not

[1] *The Songs and Sonets of John Donne* (London, 1956), 9-10.

a flat statement that virtuous women are extinct. The speaker is not, therefore, keeping his love hid because no one else could follow his example.

In his exhortation the lover suggests two other motives, equally odd, for keeping Platonic love hid. He assumes that most of the world is populated with "profane men" who are so rooted in the earth that they will not believe such love possible and will think him a liar or a hypocrite. Or, if they do bestow faith on his statement that he loves spiritual beauty more than a handsome body, they will mock him for being a fool. He assumes, in short, that very few people actually take seriously the moral and religious laws to which most people pay lip service; most are, as he once was, cynics at heart though not aloud. But why then does he urge his listener to imitate him in loving spiritually and in keeping his love a secret? Why would it not be a braver thing to defy profane men, to love Platonically in spite of their skepticism or mockery, and even to hope that his example will enable them to see the light after a period of time has passed?

If we recall Donne's treatment of Platonic love in *The Extasie*, we may perhaps see why he has made the lover of *The undertaking* think it worthier to keep his love secret. The lovers in *The Extasie* are also self-congratulatory, but their smugness leads them to self-deception and hypocrisy. After persuading themselves that they really love one another spiritually, they use their supposed spirituality as a justification for recalling the "Hee and Shee" rather than forgetting it, and they offer their love as an example for mankind to follow. In them "Weake men on love reveal'd may looke," they say. Although he calls himself worthier than the Worthies, the lover of *The undertaking* is humble by comparison. He is surprised and pleased with his discovery of a state of grace in love, and so he cannot help speaking of it in hyperboles. But as if to avoid the danger of excessive pride, of overreaching himself as the lovers of *The Extasie* do, he insists that the desire to keep love hid springs naturally from genuine Platonic love. Since he refuses to appear as virtuous as he is, he becomes at worst an anti-hypocrite hypocrite. His motive is humility rather than vanity or timidity. Having no illusions about his ability to convert the rest of the world, he thinks it worthier not to try and more courageous to shut up about his worth. When we juxtapose these two Platonic poems, we get the impression that Donne believed that the genuine Platonic lover does not go around boasting about his nobility or purity while the false one does, that coins which ring too loudly do not ring true. Not a coward at all, the lover of *The undertaking* seems to agree with the advice of Yeats's *To a Friend Whose Work Has Come to Nothing*, which concludes:

> Be secret and exult,
> Because of all things known
> That is most difficult.

Virtue, both poems suggest, is an inner state, achieving its greatest intensity when it remains compressed within.

In *The Relique* and *The undertaking* Donne has written something quite unlike any of the Platonic poems of his predecessors. These are not versified philosophical discourses on the nature of True Love or thin-blooded hymns to a thin-blooded abstract Idea. Donne has created real human beings to speak in these poems, and by a stroke of genius he has made them cynical libertines who wear their newly-acquired idealism a bit uncomfortably. He has, in short, chosen an amusingly effective way of showing Platonic friendship as a thing which occurs in real life—with all the peculiar and contradictory rough contours of real life. Because these Platonic lovers have been converted from the opposition, they show that all things—even idealistic love—are possible on earth; and yet because they are hesitant and even embarrassed about their idealism, they are saved from sounding pure and abstract and unreal, as if they have had no mistress but their muse.

ii   Idealism Realized

Although they began as libertines, the lovers of *The*

Relique and *The undertaking* concluded by becoming Platonic lovers in the most conventional sense. These men loved women for their angelic minds alone. But Platonic lovers need not necessarily "forget the Hee and Shee" and ignore physical attractiveness or physical attraction. If lovers do not rest there permanently, Christian Platonism allows that they may instead enjoy the he-and-sheness of their relationship, using their pleasure in one another's mortal beauty as a complement to their enjoyment of spiritual beauty. In this more mundane form of idealism, two partners may adjust the ethereal spirituality of conventional Platonism to the hard dry demands of day-to-day life. And unlike most Renaissance poets, Donne usually makes this everyday Platonism the stuff of his affirmative love poetry. These poems synthesize earthly practicality with holy delight, and their effect is natural rather than synthetic.

Behind these poems seems to stand Donne's suspicion that human love runs too easily to extremes. It may place too much emphasis on physical gratification, as in the Ovidian poems; or it may assume that human nature is more divine than it actually is, as in the Petrarchan poems. When Donne imagines affirmative love between men and women, he sees it at its best when it takes both body and soul into account without placing a dangerously great stress on either. Although he assumes that love should be primarily spiritual, since the soul is immortal and governs the mortal body, he does not forget that human beings have bodies or that they live on earth. But for all its moderation, he does not dramatize this love as dull or joyless. Rather, he makes it answer the nervous and restless excess of Ovidianism and Petrarchanism with a tone of relaxed and easy grace.

In one of these affirmative poems, *Aire and Angels,* Donne has created a lover who muses to himself as he confronts and solves the problem of what two partners ought to love in one another. As the speaker reviews the various ways he has loved his beloved in the past, he rejects as unsatisfactory both the extreme of idealism with which he began and the extreme of sensuality to which he shifted. Be-

THE IDEAL ON EARTH

cause his love cannot inhere in either her body alone or her spirit alone, he concludes that it must inhere in *her love*, though why it is good that it should inhere *there* is at first not quite clear. Feminine love is, he says, less pure than men's; and since the poem takes the form of an address to the beloved, either direct or mental, the concluding comparison between men's love and women's could even be seen as a slap in her face, a bitter criticism which the disillusioned lover has deviously withheld until the end. In fact, however, the lover is saying that her love is an example of moderation which he should follow, superior to his love because it is better that love be less pure. The final lines are a high compliment.

Aire and Angels

Twice or thrice had loved thee,
Before I knew thy face or name;
So in a voice, so in a shapelesse flame,
Angells affect us oft, and worship'd bee;
    Still when, to where thou wert, I came,
Some lovely glorious nothing I did see.
    But since my soule, whose child love is,
Takes limmes of flesh, and else could nothing doe,
    More subtile then the parent is,
Love must not be, but take a body too,
    And therefore what thou wert, and who,
      I bid Love aske, and now
That it assume thy body, I allow
And fixe it selfe in thy lip, eye, and brow.

Whilst thus to ballast love, I thought,
And so more steddily to have gone,
With wares which would sinke admiration,
I saw, I had loves pinnace overfraught,
    Ev'ry thy haire for love to worke upon
Is much too much, some fitter must be sought;
    For, nor in nothing, nor in things

211

> Extreme, and scatt'ring bright, can love inhere;
>   Then as an Angell, face, and wings
> Of aire, not pure as it, yet pure doth weare,
>   So thy love may be my loves spheare;
>   Just such disparitie
> As is twixt Aire and Angells puritie,
> 'Twixt womens love, and mens will ever bee.

At first, the speaker says, he worshiped his beloved as if she were an angel, with a vague hazy love which existed even before he had seen her face or known her name; what he loved then was a spiritual Form or Idea of her. In an attempt to particularize the feeling, he says it was rather like our feeling toward angels when we think they are around us as disembodied voices or shapeless flames. But when he tried to go near where he thought she might be, he saw only "Some lovely glorious nothing. . . ." So he went on to argue with himself that since his spiritual love was the child of his soul, his love ought to assume a body, since his soul has done so; for love should not try to be more subtle than its parent, the soul. When he allowed his love to discover the physical object which embodied the Idea he had adored, it then fixed itself in his beloved's "lip, eye, and brow."

By investing his love in a corporeal object, he had thought to give it greater weight, to ballast it as one might a light ship so that it would move more steadily. But, as an extension of the metaphor suggests, the weight he used to ballast love was too great, for he used "wares which would sinke admiration." He quickly saw that he had over-freighted the little ship of his love, and knew he must seek yet another alternative. Even a single hair was too much for love to work upon. The next two lines summarize his two attempts before his final successful one:

> For, nor in nothing, nor in things
> Extreme, and scatt'ring bright, can love inhere . . .

He loved her first as if she were an angel (a lovely disembodied nothing); then he loved her physical beauty. But he found that neither of these extremes would satisfy.

The final six lines contain his solution of his problem, his discovery of the "object" in which love can inhere. In order to express it, he slips into another metaphor; but the lines are difficult because he has telescoped two related metaphors into one. (He did the same thing with the previous metaphor of the ship—first making corporeality something which love assumes and then making it a weight used to ballast the ship of love.) As Grierson first noted in his edition, Donne is drawing on Thomistic angelology, which maintained that angels, otherwise invisible to men, wear bodies of air so that they may manifest themselves to human beings (II, 21-22). And these lines, accordingly, may be paraphrased: As an angel puts on a body of air in order to manifest himself to men, so your *love* (which is, like air, a mean between nothing but body and total disembodiment) is the object in which my love can succeed in inhering. Thus he solves his problem of discovering a fit object for love to work upon by making it inhere not in the idea of his beloved nor in her physical beauty, but in her *love*. And the last three lines of the poem explain why this solution is satisfactory:

> Just such disparitie
> As is twixt Aire and Angells puritie,
> 'Twixt womens love, and mens will ever bee.

Men's love sometimes has the purity of an angel—that is, it tends to go toward the extreme of spirituality, which cannot become manifest; or sometimes, on the other hand, it goes completely to the other extreme of corporeality and tries to fix itself in "things/ Extreme, and scatt'ring bright," which is equally undesirable; in either case men's love is too "pure" (in the sense of "extreme") to be satisfactory, as the lover has found from experience; but women's love is more moderate—it too is pure, but with the purity of air; not pure as angels perhaps, but for that very reason corporeal enough to be manifest to human beings. Thus women's love is a proper kind of love for human beings, who are neither all soul nor all body.

But in these lines the figure of the angel also functions in another related way. When the speaker says, "So thy love may be my loves spheare," he is suggesting another function of angels and another sense in which the woman's love is a proper object in which his love can inhere; he is recalling the belief that angelic intelligence inhabits the planets and moves them in their proper course. Donne was fond of this metaphor and used it often for various purposes. In this case the lover is using it to reveal his recognition of the value of charitable love and his acceptance of the Renaissance ideal of love. He is saying to the lady: "It is not you who are like an angel, as I once thought, but myself; and my love, like an angel, must inhere in your love, which is like a sphere; my love can be to yours as the angelic intelligence is to the sphere which it moves. That is, after all, the divinely instituted order; men are meant to guide women, not to worship them or enjoy their bodies. Men's love and women's love are different, and that is as it should be; they are different, not in the sense that one is inferior to the other, but in the sense that each has its proper function, and in performing it each complements the other: men's love can inhere in the sphere of women's love, and women's love can be guided by it."

The lover's concluding discovery is actually far from cynical; it only seems so because it is paradoxical. He says quite frankly that women's *love* is the most fitting object for men's love to inhere in because it is *less* pure; but "less pure" is equivalent to *more* desirable. The moderation of his love adjusts it to the human world, saving it from either the extreme of worshiping his beloved's disembodied spirit or the extreme of rapt admiration of her physical beauty. That Donne was well aware of the dangers of such excess, particularly the danger of ethereality, appears in the last two lines of stanza XVI of *A Litanie*, where he prays:

> From thinking us all soule, neglecting thus
> Our mutuall duties, Lord deliver us.

It is moderated purity which makes possible the performance of "mutuall duties," and it is women's love which is of social necessity more concerned with performing these than men's love. Yet it is just the performance of these mutual duties that makes love most manifest. Thus the conclusion, complimentary rather than bitter, embodies the lover's realization that he must adjust his love to the human world and that he can learn something about love from the way in which women love. He has, in short, become aware of the importance of the practical charity which characterizes women's love and of his own practical duty to the woman he loves, an awareness embodied in the metaphor of the angelic intelligence and its sphere. He, and not his beloved, is like an angel. But even angels have their duties.

Donne also seems to have thought that *caritas*, although dutiful, is not therefore dull. The ethic behind the affirmative poems is hedonistic as well as pragmatic and liberating as well as moderated. As another poem, *The good-morrow*, shows, Platonic love seemed better than profane love to Donne because it was so much more enjoyable. In *The good-morrow* Donne has created a lover who, like those of *The undertaking* and *The Relique*, is a convert, but a convert to Platonic love rather than Platonic friendship. He too is surprised by joy, but he does not try to modulate his excited delight by dropping hints to show that he really is a tough guy after all. He is too busy being happy to be embarrassed.

Oddly enough, *The good-morrow* is an *aubade*, but one quite different from either *Breake of day* or *The Sunne Rising*. This poem dramatizes the dawn of a new day in a spiritual as well as a literal sense and, as the title emphasizes, it is a *good* morrow.

The good-morrow

I wonder by my troth, what thou, and I
Did, till we lov'd? were we not wean'd till then?
But suck'd on countrey pleasures, childishly?
Or snorted we in the seaven sleepers den?

T'was so; But this, all pleasures fancies bee.
If ever any beauty I did see,
Which I desir'd, and got, t'was but a dreame of thee.

And now good morrow to our waking soules,
Which watch not one another out of feare;
For love, all love of other sights controules,
And makes one little roome, an every where.
Let sea-discoverers to new worlds have gone,
Let Maps to other, worlds on worlds have showne,
Let us possesse one world, each hath one, and is one.

My face in thine eye, thine in mine appeares,
And true plaine hearts doe in the faces rest,
Where can we finde two better hemispheares
Without sharpe North, without declining West?
What ever dyes, was not mixt equally;
If our two loves be one, or thou and I
Love so alike, that none doe slacken, none can die.

In the initial stanza the lover can do little but express his astonishment at the intense satisfaction which his new-found love gives him and his wonder that he lived before without it. He feels as if he only slept through his earlier life and has now been suddenly awakened, as if he was a mere child when he sucked on the "countrey pleasures" of purely physical love. Sex seems juvenile compared to spiritual love. He can only describe the joy his new love brings by saying that it infinitely surpasses the "pleasures fancies" of inferior forms of love, that his earlier experience of love seems an empty and shallow figment of the imagination when compared to the powerful reality of the real thing.

What makes his new love so exciting, as the second stanza reveals, is that it can be both so intense and so relaxed. This lover's commitment is as complete as that of the lovers of *The Canonization*, but its basis and effect are quite different. The lovers of *The good-morrow* have achieved a devotion to one another by which they can live rather than die; their sensation of having undergone a death, from which they have been awakened on this good morrow, derives from the death of self which precedes charitable love, not the sexual death and resurrection of *The Canonization*. Having lost themselves in order to find themselves in one another, they no longer live in and for themselves, but in and for each other. Their experience of self-immolating charity is behind the sense of expansive liberation, of having won a new life and a new fearless love, which the lover expresses through his metaphor of sleep and waking.

The dogma which supports their experience is the familiar Platonic doctrine that charitable lovers are both one and one-in-two. Because they have overcome their own self-love, their two separate souls are so sympathetically united that they become one; and yet this one soul is divided between two people:

> . . . whenever two people are brought together in mutual affection, one lives in the other and the other in him. In this way they mutually exchange identities; each gives himself to the other in such a way that each receives the other in return . . . each has himself and has the other too. A has himself, but in B; and B also has himself, but in A. . . . In fact, there is only one death in mutual love, but there are two resurrections, for a lover dies within himself the moment he forgets about himself, but he returns to life in his loved one as soon as the loved one embraces him in loving contemplation. . . .[2]

Thus, as he and his beloved embrace one another in loving contemplation, the lover of *The good-morrow* says:

> My face in thine eye, thine in mine appeares. . . .

Only by losing himself in loving contemplation can he find himself in the other. And because their "waking soules" have returned to life from a death of self, when the two lovers look at one another they ". . . watch not one another out of feare. . . ." There is no jealousy or possessiveness in this

[2] Ficino, 144-145.

relationship. Because they have achieved a selflessly perfect love which casts out fear, they can trust one another completely and watch one another for the sheer delight of watching. And their love also liberates them from doubt and self-conscious hesitation, from the fear of loving one another too much; because it is selfless and charitable, it can never be excessive. Quite naturally, their feeling of grace and freedom produces contentment and delight. Their love, transforming their vision of the universe so that it seems filled with new significance and new brightness, ". . . makes one little roome, an every where."

Their discovery of Platonic *caritas* also liberates them from fear and brings them joyous self-confidence in another way, as the third stanza reveals. Because their two "waking souls" have returned to them after being "mixt equally," because their "two loves be one," the speaker believes that their love will be lasting in the future as well as rewarding in the present. Appealing to medical theory, he points out that things die when their elements are imbalanced, whereas he and his beloved have a perfect equilibrium in their love, an equal poise of their two wills which will prevent their love from dying. Having undergone a death of self, they have saved their love from death and made it supernatural, "Without sharpe North, without declining West."

Although this poem has as its situation the awakening of the souls of two lovers through a Christian and Platonic love, its Christian Platonism is not the aspect most immediately apparent. For *The good-morrow* does not assert dogmas about love, but expresses the experience of a love which dogma asserts to be good. The most obvious thing about the poem is its tone of delight, the speaker's exuberant gratitude that he should be so blessed in love. In *The good-morrow* Donne is recreating the enthusiastic thrill of discovery which a human being feels when he falls into a full and fulfilling love which is both "everyday" and "Sunday best." But to Donne, in spite of his speaker's tone of surprise, it would seem no accident that this love is both pragmatic and pleasant.

The Anniversarie is another testimony to the practicality
of idealistic love, especially to its security and endurance.
Here a lover celebrates the first anniversary of his love by
composing a poem addressed to his lady, and his anniversary
gift to her rejoices that although a year has passed by, the
love which they share has not been touched by time. His
poem is built upon contrasts between the mutable and the
permanent, the worldly and the otherworldly, the dynamic
and the static; in spite of the pervasive presence of decay,
fickleness, and change in the earthly world, he and his lady
have achieved a love which thrives in the world but is free of
earthly mutability.

The Anniversarie

All Kings, and all their favorites,
   All glory of honors, beauties, wits,
The Sun it selfe, which makes times, as they passe,
Is elder by a yeare, now, then it was
When thou and I first one another saw:
All other things, to their destruction draw,
   Only our love hath no decay;
This, no to morrow hath, nor yesterday,
Running it never runs from us away,
But truly keepes his first, last, everlasting day.

   Two graves must hide thine and my coarse,
   If one might, death were no divorce.
Alas, as well as other Princes, wee
(Who Prince enough in one another bee,)
Must leave at last in death, these eyes, and eares,
Oft fed with true oathes, and with sweet salt teares;
   But soules where nothing dwells but love
(All other thoughts being inmates) then shall prove
This, or a love increased there above,
When bodies to their graves, soules from their graves
     remove.

   And then wee shall be throughly blest,
   But wee no more, then all the rest;

Here upon earth, we'are Kings, and none but wee
Can be such Kings, nor of such subjects bee.
Who is so safe as wee? where none can doe
Treason to us, except one of us two.
    True and false feares let us refraine,
Let us love nobly, and live, and adde againe
Yeares and yeares unto yeares, till we attaine
To write threescore: this is the second of our raigne.

As the poem begins the lover looks around the universe, observing the transiency to which all things seem to be subject. As he lists them with slow stately periodicity, building to the statement that in changing all things are also drawing to their own destruction, he is recognizing the mortality of earthly delight, glory, and pleasure. The power of Kings and the privileges of their favorites will not last. Nor will more hard-won favors that man enjoys—"honors, beauties, wits." Even the source of time, the sun itself, is subject to its own self-created tyranny of transiency. Dynamic decay seems everywhere, but the lover turns from this *contemptus mundi* strain to the one thing which can escape time's tyranny, the love which he and his beloved share. Paradoxically, although their love is also elder by a year, it is somehow both in time and outside of time, in the world but not of the world, for "Running it never runs from us away."

In the next stanza the lover admits that, although their love is not subject to destruction, their bodies will certainly die, be buried, and decay like all other earthly things. Not only will they die, but they will lie in two separate graves. Although his warning of *memento mori* does not seem the most appropriate anniversary gift, the lover, having been created by Donne, turns its incongruity into a triumph: because their love lives in their souls rather than their bodies, their separation through death will increase their love rather than diminish it. He looks upon death with confidence, seeing it as a test of their love, the outcome of which is not in doubt. Theirs are souls where nothing dwells but love, and after death, when their souls arise from their graves and ascend to heaven to meet God face to face, this love will prove itself. To love such as theirs, loss of the physical world is no very painful loss, for their love is built on a spiritual base rather than a physical one and thus will achieve an even greater fulfillment when placed in its natural surroundings. In heaven, the lover says in the next stanza, they will be thoroughly blessed, more blessed than they were on earth. For in heaven they will enjoy the companionship of others who are no more blessed than they and who share their joy and fulfillment; his genuine devotion to *caritas* is clear, for he casually assumes that the highest happiness arises from seeing others who are equally happy; on earth, although they are kings, there are no others around them who have achieved the same calm delight. Because they have not committed themselves to the transient Things of the World, therefore, they need not fear their treason and inconstancy. They have only one another to fear, and nothing to fear in one another.

The lover does perhaps sound as if he feels there is cause for fear when he says "True and false feares let us refrain," especially in the light of the preceding lines. But he speaks of *true* and *false* fears; the fear that one of them will do treason to the other is a false fear, and the true fears are those of the first and second stanzas, of mutability and of separation through death. The lover is, in effect, saying "Since we have no reason to fear death, for heaven's sake let us avoid jealousy and suspicion while on earth." The poem is organized around the various temptations to fear which love must face: of decreasing with age and the passage of time, of loss of physical love through death, and of treason or dishonesty by one of the partners. Each is overcome. *The Anniversarie* expresses a state of grace in love, a love which brings faith and hope because it is built upon charity.

A paraphrase makes the sentiment of this poem sound more commonplace than it is. *The Anniversarie* does not strive for amazing wit or baroque complexity, and yet it is a compelling poem anyway. One source of its power is of course its metrical and verbal virtuosity, which shows that Donne could achieve sonority and liquidity when he chose to do so. In this poem, when he is expressing a sense of security and peace rather than confusion or brutality, his versification has a complementary tone of quiet joy, produced by such things as the alexandrines which conclude each stanza, the limitation of rhyme-words to a relatively small number, the repetition of vowel sounds and even of rhymes within the lines. In auditory quality it is as majestic as the recurring King-metaphor implies it should be.

But an even greater source of power is its combination of honest realism with equally honest but noble idealism. The lovers do not achieve their tone of confidence and otherworldliness by overlooking unpleasant facts, but by taking them into account and surmounting them. The creator of this anniversary gift is stating the case for their love, not overstating it; realistic idealism underlies such lines as:

> Two graves must hide thine and my coarse,
> If one might, death were no divorce.

> And then wee shall be throughly blest,
> But wee no more, then all the rest. . . .

The lover does not try to deny the fact of death, nor does he claim that he and his mistress are saints who will be glorified in heaven. Although this poem has much in common with *The Canonization*, both being justifications of an apparently otherworldly love, each conveys a different mood and a different love. In *The Anniversarie* the otherworldliness is genuine, and its glory is communicated convincingly because the lover is presented as a man who cannot lie even to himself, let alone to others; he does not pretend that his body will not decay, nor that the loss of eyes and ears and bodies is not a source of fear and sorrow, although a fear and sorrow which is ultimately overcome because their love dwells in their imperishable souls. And, finally, the poem does not end with a decision to die by love, since their love is spiritual anyway, but to live by love and to enjoy it, to "adde againe yeares and yeares unto yeares. . . ." Their love is otherworldly, but not so otherworldly that it is alien or impossible on earth. In *The Anniversarie* Donne has dramatized a love by which man can *live*, joyfully and peacefully.

iii   Idealism Proved

The lover of *The Anniversarie*, as he meditated on the threats which time and mortality offered to his love, concluded that his love was powerful to counteract them. He and his beloved would

> . . . prove
> This, or a love increased there above,
> When bodies to their graves, soules from their graves
> remove.

In *The Anniversarie*, however, death and separation were only possibilities; the lovers faced them in theory, but not in actuality. But in other poems Donne imagines the response of lovers when threats of separation or death do become actualities. Because their love is founded on a lasting spiritual base, because it is tempered by a recognition of the facts of the universe, it submits to tests and trials successfully. In poems such as *A Valediction: forbidding mourning* or *A Feaver*, realistic idealism proves itself when faced by temptations to fear or to despair, when faced with separation, sickness, and death.

Donne wrote a good many valedictions which show the response of a lover when he was about to leave his beloved. But the love expressed from one poem to another is quite different in quality. The song "Sweetest love, I do not goe," seems to be an *aubade* of the same bawdy type as *Breake of day*, although it is considerably more subtle. *A Valediction: of the booke* is liberally laced with flippancy and cynicism, and *A Valediction: of weeping* is a turbulent and violent poem in which the tears of the beloved are "Fruits of much griefe,/ Emblemes of more," although it develops into a valediction forbidding weeping at the conclusion.

The speaker of *A Valediction: of my name, in the window* is a typical jealous lover who engraves his name on his beloved's window in the suspicion that another lover's gold will thaw his mistress as well as her maid. Only *A Valediction: forbidding mourning* expresses a sustained mood of confidence and trust in a love relationship which cannot be damaged by separation.

A Valediction: forbidding mourning

As virtuous men passe mildly away,
  And whisper to their soules, to goe,
Whilst some of their sad friends doe say,
  The breath goes now, and some say, no:

So let us melt, and make no noise,
  No teare-floods, nor sigh-tempests move,
T'were prophanation of our joyes
  To tell the layetie our love.

Moving of th'earth brings harmes and feares,
  Men reckon what it did and meant,
But trepidation of the spheares,
  Though greater farre, is innocent.

Dull sublunary lovers love
  (Whose soule is sense) cannot admit
Absence, because it doth remove
  Those things which elemented it.

But we by a love, so much refin'd,
  That our selves know not what it is,
Inter-assured of the mind,
  Care lesse, eyes, lips and hands to misse.

Our two soules therefore, which are one,
  Though I must goe, endure not yet
A breach, but an expansion,
  Like gold to ayery thinnesse beate.

If they be two, they are two so
  As stiffe twin compasses are two,

224

Thy soule the fixt foot, makes no show
To move, but doth, if the'other doe.

And though it in the center sit,
   Yet when the other far doth rome,
It leanes and hearkens after it,
   And growes erect, as that comes home.

Such wilt thou be to mee, who must
   Like th'other foot, obliquely runne;
Thy firmnes makes my circle just,
   And makes me end, where I begunne.

It is apparent at the outset that this poem expresses the same idealistic kind of love as *The Anniversarie*. But both poems, while they ultimately assert that the physical companionship offered by the beloved is a minor part of love, do not totally deny either its importance or its value. Both poems have as their situation a lover's realization that physical companionship must eventually come to an end, either through death or through the temporary departure of one partner. The insistence of these lovers on the spiritual consolations of noble love grows out of a very real enjoyment of the companionship which the partners give to one another when they are together, and that is why they need consolation and stress that their love is spiritually enduring. They *will* miss each other, even though they are together in spirit, and because they will, the speaker must emphasize that their separation is only physical.

Among Donne's great secular love poems, however, *A Valediction: forbidding mourning* is perhaps the most consistently spiritual. This spirituality is evident even from the initial image of the poem, and the poem grows still more idealistic as it moves along. *A Valediction* begins with a simile drawn from a subject dear to the Renaissance heart, a religious death, the holy dying which was the happy culmination of holy living. The lover who delivers this farewell message is saying that the separation which he and his beloved must undergo is a kind of death; but the kind which

225

virtuous men die, a religious death, is the most appropriate to the love which they have lived and shared. So he asks that they part from one another as imperceptibly and painlessly and mildly as virtuous men part from their earthly lives. He explicitly dissociates their love from profane Petrarchanism, with its tear-floods and sigh-tempests; their parting will not be violent and grief-ridden because their love is not violent and grief-ridden. To indulge in showy emotionality to prove the intensity of their love would only profane it.

The third stanza shifts its imagery to cosmology and introduces the themes and concepts which will pervade the remainder of the poem. Using the earth and the spheres as examples, the lover contrasts erratic and irrational movement with ordered movement. When the earth moves without warning in an earthquake or other disturbance, he says, men become upset and afraid; they speculate about what evil significance its movement may have. But the trepidation of the spheres, although its movement may be much greater than that of the earth during an earthquake, has no evil significance and causes no fear in men. In choosing the word "trepidation" to describe the movement of the spheres, Donne is again punning. The *OED* indicates that this word meant an adjustment of astronomical calculations about the movement of the spheres in order to account more accurately for their ordered motion; in this sense it refers to a supposed oscillation of the eighth sphere with reference to the ninth. But in its general sense, it could also mean a tremor, agitation, or confusion, and in this sense the word looks back to the confused tremors to which the earth is subject. Thus the lover is saying that the spheres are subject to vibrations like the earth, but they vibrate according to an orderly divine plan which man's mind can discover, and he and his beloved are like the spheres—they too must move, but their movement is innocent and orderly, not a source of harm or fear.

Through his metaphor of the earth and the spheres the lover also implies another contrast, further extended in the following stanza. He is founding his farewell consolation on a series of distinctions between the heavenly and the earthly, the spiritual and the physical. Their love, like the spheres, is of the heavenly and spiritual order, quite different from that of "Dull sublunary lovers" who love according to the earthly and physical order. These sublunary lovers make sense the soul of their love, and thus they cannot bear to part from one another, since separation removes the physical object of their love. Rooted in the physical, their love dies when their bodies are separated.

In the fifth stanza, continuing his contrast between earthly love and their "love of the spheres," he shows that their love can bear separation. Although they may miss one another's eyes, lips, and hands, they care less about missing them. Their love is so refined, in fact, that they are not even certain what it is they love, although its object is secure enough to make them "Inter-assured of the mind." In this stanza Donne is again playing with the Platonic doctrine that righteous lovers cannot know what they love because they love the image of God in their partner, and they cannot know God directly while on earth. The speaker of the *Valediction*, because he does not know what he loves, can only reassure his beloved by telling her that separation will not matter because their love is refined and directed toward an eternal and spiritual object.

In the final four stanzas he extends, through a new series of images, his explanation of the way in which their Platonic love offers security even if they must undergo a temporary separation. The essence of his consolation is an assurance that they will remain spiritually united even when they are physically separated. Again, Platonic doctrine lies behind the lines. Now it is the familiar doctrine that in reciprocal love the souls of the lovers are united and they live their lives in each other, used by Donne ironically in *The Extasie* and directly in *The good-morrow*. The Platonic paradox that lovers are both two-in-one and one-in-two is behind the lover's statement in stanza six that their two souls are one and its apparent contradiction in stanza seven, which he begins, "If they be two. . . ." The two lovers are in one sense united identities, because they have given themselves completely to one another; but in another sense they have overcome self-love so completely that their private identities have died, been resurrected in their partners, and thus live again, producing two separate beings.

In order to explain their spiritual union, the lover uses a pair of astonishing metaphors which have made this poem so justly famous. First he describes how they are two-in-one through the metaphor of beaten gold. As well as being one of the most beautiful, precious, and cordial metals, gold is also one of the most cohesive, capable of being spread out even to the incredible thinness of gold leaf. Their souls cohere to one another like the atoms which compose gold; there can be no breach between them, no matter how far apart they are; instead, they stretch and expand, growing thinner perhaps, but broader too. Like gold, their love paradoxically combines delicate beauty with strength and endurance and purity. But the lovers are also one-in-two, and the speaker chooses another image to express this aspect of their love. They are two as "stiffe twin compasses are two," fulfilling different functions, but joined nevertheless and moving in harmony with one another. The beloved is the fixed foot at the center of the circle, and the lover moves around her when he must move, while she sympathetically describes an invisible circle at the center. These circles are the innocent trepidation of the spheres, the ordered movement of harmonious beings. The woman properly remains at home, acting as a stable anchor, and yet while at home she leans and hearkens after her lover; the man, forced to move because that is part of his masculine destiny, runs obliquely and, aided by her firmness at the center, returns to the place from which he began. Such, to the Renaissance mind, was the ideal relationship of man to woman.

Thus the lover concludes his farewell with an image which summarizes the perfection and security of their love, the circle, used for wedding rings because it symbolizes the eternal and ideal as well as because they must fit around fingers. The situation which inspires the poem is one which presupposes the necessity of movement and change in earthly life; and yet the lover stresses that it is still possible to experience unchanging love and to move according to eternal standards, to achieve the static immutability of the spiritual within the framework of the dynamic and earthly.

In *A Feaver* Donne imagines a lover faced with a threat perhaps more dangerous than physical separation. This poem is an exploration of the movement of a man's mind when, seated at the bedside of his beloved, he meditates on the burning fever which consumes her—and on the possibility that it may consume her completely. Like the lover of *A nocturnall* he is tested by sorrow, nothingness, and death. But his love is far more positive, and *A Feaver* is a far more positive poem. For this lover refuses to submit to the temptation of despair, which appears whenever the existence of a beloved but mortal thing is threatened, and he overcomes the temptation by turning away from introspection and self-pity and transforming his emotional energy into compassion for the beloved. Like the lover of *A Valediction*: *forbidding mourning*, he has achieved *caritas*, and his perfect love can cast out fear. But for all the tenderness and courage of its conclusion, the poem begins in the depths.

A Feaver

Oh doe not die, for I shall hate
 All women so, when thou art gone,
That thee I shall not celebrate,
 When I remember, thou wast one.

But yet thou canst not die, I know;
 To leave this world behinde, is death,
But when thou from this world wilt goe,
 The whole world vapors with thy breath.

Or if, when thou, the worlds soule, goest,
 It stay, tis but thy carkasse then,

229

The fairest woman, but thy ghost,
    But corrupt wormes, the worthyest men.

O wrangling schooles, that search what fire
    Shall burne this world, had none the wit
Unto this knowledge to aspire,
    That this her feaver might be it?

And yet she cannot wast by this,
    Nor long beare this torturing wrong,
For much corruption needfull is
    To fuell such a feaver long.

These burning fits but meteors bee,
    Whose matter in thee is soone spent.
Thy beauty,'and all parts, which are thee,
    Are unchangeable firmament.

Yet t'was of my minde, seising thee,
    Though it in thee cannot persever.
For I had rather owner bee
    Of thee one houre, then all else ever.

Initially the lover, faced with the agonizing thought that his beloved may die, attempts to escape it through aggressive hostility. His monologue begins paradoxically, for his helpless and impassioned appeal, "Oh doe not die," is followed by irrational violence. Her desertion of him through death will make him believe that all women eventually desert the men who love them, and he will retaliate by hating the entire class of things that hurt him, even hating her as a member of that class. In this first stanza the lover thinks only of himself: the word "I" is used three times in the first four lines, only twice more in the remaining twenty-four.

In the next three stanzas, however, the lover's thoughts shift to a somewhat fanciful forecast of the way her death will affect the world, as he tries to persuade himself that she cannot really die after all. But his metaphorical consolation is conspicuously weak. He is drawing on the elaborate Neoplatonic conceit which Donne also uses as a foundation for

230

the *First and Second Anniversaries*, that the lady is the World Soul. In Neoplatonic theorizing the World Soul resolves the apparent dichotomy between mind and matter: the realm of Ideas is by definition eternal and immutable, the order of matter by definition mutable and transient, and logically the two cannot meet or interact; but the *Anima Mundi* or World Soul links the two orders, animating the else inanimate matter of the earth.[3] By calling his beloved "the worlds soule" the lover is in effect equating her with the spirit which animates and governs the corporeal matter of the World and preserves it from corruption.

The lover tries to console himself in two ways by using this conceit. In the second stanza, arguing from a definition of death as "leaving the world behind," he maintains that she cannot die at all. Since her soul is the Soul of the World, the world will evaporate as she breathes out her soul in death, and so she cannot die because the world will die with her. This consolation is simply a word-game, and in the third stanza the lover plays another. If the world and its inhabitants do not vapor away completely with her death, then they will at least become inanimate carcasses without the animating soul which enables them to live. Thus the fairest woman will become but a ghost and the most distinguished man mere corrupt worms. Both these stanzas are peculiar because of their hollowness. Like the first, the second begins with a simple and impassioned statement: "But yet thou canst not die." And like the first it is followed by a complicated but empty argument. But Donne is portraying a lover's reaction realistically, showing how he gradually

---

[3] In *A Platonick Discourse upon Love* (trans. Thomas Stanley, ed. Edmund G. Gardner, Boston, 1914) Pico della Mirandola gives a relatively concise description of the nature and function of the World Soul: "After the pattern of that Minde [*i.e.*, the Angelick Mind, which contains the Ideas or Forms] they affirm this sensible World was made, and the exemplar being the most perfect of created things, it must follow that this image thereof be as perfect as its nature will bear. And since animate things are more perfect than the irrational, we must grant, this World hath a soul perfect above all others. This is the first rational soul, which, though incorporeal and immaterial, is destin'd to the function of governing and moving corporeal matter." (8)

works his way out of despair and self-pity. The hyperbole of his metaphor shows that for the moment the lover is grasping at straws; because his pain is great, he tries to defend himself by playing intellectual games. And at this moment his beloved doubtless seems the soul of the world, the animating principle of *his* world, whose destruction would annihilate it.

The fourth stanza contains a final outburst of anger and intellectuality before the gentleness and simplicity of the poem's conclusion. Now the lover metaphorically equates the burning fever which consumes his beloved with the conflagration which the schoolmen have said will consume the world at the time of the Last Judgment, although they could not agree about the nature of the fire. Again the lover is thinking of the beloved as the world, as his world. And the fever which consumes her will destroy his world with absolute finality. In his pain he is angry with even the schoolmen, who did not have the wit to see that *her* fever is the destructive fire about which they wrangled.

But the poem does not stop at this point. It goes on to produce a genuine consolation, as the lover turns his thoughts to the beloved herself. In the first three stanzas he seems to be speaking to her directly in what is to be imagined as a bedside scene. He addresses her as "thee" and "thou" rather than speaking of her in the third person. In the fourth and fifth stanzas, however, he temporarily turns aside and soliloquizes to himself, turning back to her again and addressing her directly in the final two stanzas of the poem. As he silently meditates on her death, in the fifth stanza his wit diminishes, and he thinks of his beloved simply as a suffering human being. His own pain now seems less important than hers, as she lies there flushed with fever and apparently dying. In turning his thoughts toward her, in trying to console her rather than himself, he triumphs over the bitterness and violence which he felt previously. He tells himself that she cannot live much longer, but that her suffering cannot last much longer either. The fever by which she is burned is a "torturing wrong," since her pain

232

is undeserved. But it is a torture which cannot last, since it feeds on corruption, of which she has little, either physical or spiritual.

Having reassured himself with the thought that her pain cannot last much longer, he turns back to the beloved to console her and encourage her. His mood is now quite different than it was at the beginning of the poem, when he pleaded "Oh doe not die, . . ." Now he gently tells her that the fever cannot last much longer, that whatever happens, her best parts are imperishable:

> These burning fits but meteors bee,
>> Whose matter in thee is soone spent.
> Thy beauty,'and all parts, which are thee,
>> Are unchangeable firmament.

In a submerged astronomical metaphor he compares her transient fever with the brief flashes painted on the horizon by falling meteors, consuming their matter in fire as they descend to earth. But her beauty (presumably spiritual because it is contrasted with matter) is like the eternally fixed and ordered stars, not subject to change except in accordance with the divine plan which governs their regular movement. The blend of consolation and compliment is superb, simple, and delicate. The lover has at last succeeded in separating what does not matter from what does, the mutable from the immutable, the earthly from the divine, his own sorrow from the need to ease his beloved's pain.

All this opens a way for a statement of his love for her in the final stanza. It is as if he has now realized that bodily decrepitude is wisdom, that his love for her is greater at this moment than it has ever been before, although it is adjusted to an awareness that immutability is blended with mutability in her. He says that the fever really comes from his own mind, which seizes her and consumes her during what seem to be the final moments of her life. And his fever of love consumes her in spite of the fact that he knows it cannot persevere, for it is directed toward a mortal woman who is subject to death. Yet he continues to love and to love deeply, even if it brings him the pain of watching his beloved suffer and the pain of loss. His love can conquer the pain it brings, for he has been able to stare down mortality, to recognize the presence of the immortal, and to fulfill himself in charity rather than self-love, in consolation of his beloved rather than in self-pity.

Holy Sonnet XVII ("Since she whome I lovd, hath payd her last debt") completes the progression of threats which love must face, for the separation which is foreseen in *A Valediction* and *A Feaver* has occurred with absolute finality. The beloved has died. This poem is usually assumed to describe Donne's relationship to his wife, and the fact that it did not circulate widely lends likelihood to the possibility that it is a purely private expression. But the poem contains much that is conventional. Before her death the lover felt a Platonic attraction to the image of God within his beloved and was led toward Him by his admiration for her. After her death, like Petrarch after Laura's death, his sense of loss is moderated by a thirst for divine love, and he feels contempt for the things of the world, setting his mind wholly on heavenly things.

Holy Sonnet XVII

Since she whome I lovd, hath payd her last debt
To Nature, and to hers, and my good is dead,
And her soule early into heaven ravished,
Wholy in heavenly things my mind is sett.
Here the admyring her my mind did whett
To seeke thee God; so streames do shew the head,
But though I have found thee, and thou my thirst
       hast fed,
A holy thirsty dropsy melts mee yett.
But why should I begg more love, when as thou
Dost wooe my soule, for hers offring all thine:
And dost not only feare least I allow
My love to saints and Angels, things divine,
But in thy tender jealousy dost doubt
Least the World, fleshe, yea Devill putt thee out.

In *Holy Sonnet XVII* the temptation to despair has been so fully overcome that if the poem is judged as a death elegy, it even seems cold and unfeeling. For the lover, facing his lady's death calmly and philosophically, turns his lament into a meditation on worldly and divine love, and worldly love is not enhanced by the juxtaposition. The octave of his sonnet is a mild expression of his indebtedness to her and his sense of loss, while the sestet answers his expostulation by turning her death into a divine blessing. The sonnet is an incomprehensible failure if the reader does not assume, while reading, a hierarchical set of values, for otherwise the speaker becomes an emotionally poverty-stricken Stoic and God a chillingly jealous lover.

After his conventional statement in the octave that his beloved whetted his thirst for God when she was alive, since His image was immanent in her and in loving her he was actually loving the head of the stream, the lover tries to console himself for his loss by seeing it as God's will. Although he feels a "holy thirsty dropsy" for more of the human love which has satisfied him so fully, he now asks, "But why should I begg more love?" For God, having removed her so that He Himself may be the speaker's beloved, now offers all His love in place of hers, and His love is both eternal and infinitely satisfying. Since the speaker is in danger of allowing too much spiritual love elsewhere ("to saints and Angels, things divine") and is also tempted to grant too much love to purely physical things ("the World, fleshe, yea Devill"), God's tender and attentive jealousy is warranted.

To the modern agnostic such "tender jealousy" might seem all the worse because it motivated a divine murderer to wipe out a being who stood in the way of His love. But the speaker in this poem is sincere rather than sardonic, and his tone of grateful thanksgiving would seem exemplary rather than psychopathic to his contemporaries. Human beings, they would all agree, ought to love God with all their hearts; that was the first and greatest commandment. The lover in this poem has been spared from going the way

of the lover of *A nocturnall*, from experiencing total nothingness and despair, because God's tender jealousy has in-
tervened. Human jealousy and divine are far different, for
the one festers and corrupts while the other saves and puri-
fies. God's solicitous desire that man love Him most seeks
only man's own good. The lover of the sonnet is completely
consoled for his cherished beloved's death because he is so
thoroughly convinced that this is true.

iv   The Total Pattern

Although *Holy Sonnet XVII* provides an apt and tidy
end, Donne did not consciously write his love poems to
"tell a story" in a sequence of lyrics as Spenser or Sidney
did. He wrote individual lyrics which dramatize a variety of
personality types responding to a variety of situations. But
his poetry falls into an ordered pattern anyway, for even if
he did not follow a plot-line, he did follow a systematic set
of beliefs about how and why people should love and por-
trayed the various ways people could fulfill or deviate from
it. If the affirmative poems of human love complete the circle of Donne's poetry by revealing the triumph of charity
over lust and idolatry, his poems of divine love remove its
circumference by revealing the superiority of divine love
to human. If righteous human love is liberating, these
poems say, God's love is infinitely liberating. Donne brilliantly expresses the miraculousness of human love in *The
good-morrow* or *A Valediction: forbidding mourning*, but
God's love is for him the grandest miracle; it is always
greater than human love, even when human love is at its
greatest.

In *The Holy Sonnets* too, Donne yokes opposites by
violence together; but when he describes divine love
through the images of the profane, he is neither being blasphemous nor is he attempting to bring the ineffable down to
earth. Behind his paradoxically profane imagery is a sense
of the total system of Christian love, a system which assumes divine love to be infinitely superior to human love;
thus many of the poems of divine love express an aware-

ness that God can love more than human beings ever can, and the profane images point up this distinction between human love and divine. Like the divine imagery in the profane love poems, they imply *discordia discors* rather than *discordia concors*.

Sometimes the distinction is between the limitations of human lust and God's lustful desire that human beings be saved by communion with His church or with the Holy Spirit. Donne concludes *Holy Sonnet XVIII*, for example, with this prayer to Christ:

> Betray kind husband thy spouse to our sights,
> And let myne amorous soule court thy mild Dove,
> Who is most trew, and pleasing to thee, then
> When she'is embrac'd and open to most men.

Donne is not being flippant. He is struggling to express the miracle of God's love by showing how different it is from man's. Unlike profane love, it knows no jealousy. The Church is a mistress who can receive all men without being inconstant or unfaithful. Human husbands and human mistresses cannot perform such miracles. But God can do what men can never do; His love is so complete and infinite that He can never give too much and human beings can never ask for too much. The same sense of wonder at the difference between human love and divine is beneath the paradoxical conclusion of *Holy Sonnet XIV*, in which the poet begs God to free him from the knot of sin by enthralling him:

> Divorce mee, 'untie, or breake that knot againe,
> Take mee to you, imprison mee, for I
> Except you'enthrall mee, never shall be free,
> Nor ever chaste, except you ravish mee.

Human love brings the danger of bondage to sin; God's love always and inevitably brings liberation from it. The more frequent a man's intercourse with God, the greater his spiritual chastity. The world and the flesh operate by far different rules.

But greatest of all is the miracle that human love, even in its highest form of charity, is infinitely surpassed by God's charitable love for man. Again and again in *The Holy Sonnets* and in his *Sermons*, Donne recalls with amazed comfort the doctrine of the atonement: man was lost and God sent His son to redeem him; after Christ donned man's flesh and died for him, he continued to sin, and God continues to reveal His love by granting him the grace which enables him to repent and liberate himself from bondage to sin. This strange selfless love, this infinite mercy, is something which human beings can only imitate imperfectly. In *Holy Sonnet XI*, as in many others, Donne meditates on this miracle of divine love:

> Oh let mee then, his strange love still admire:
> Kings pardon, but he bore our punishment.
> And Jacob came cloth'd in vile harsh attire
> But to supplant, and with gainful intent:
> God cloth'd himselfe in vile mans flesh, that so
> He might be weake enough to suffer woe.

At best human love can forgive, as when Kings grant pardons; but God both bore man's punishment and continues to forgive and bear as long as man continues to sin. Human love has no such infinity of mercy and patience.

Donne's total system assumes that love can be as good as it is powerful; when it conforms to the moral order of the universe, love can produce intense joy and satisfaction, whether it is directed toward another human being or toward God, although divine love, because it is divine, gives man an intenser joy than human love. But if love is a good thing, it can also be abused; and when it is abused, it produces sorrow and bondage to sin rather than joy and liberation. The Ovidian and Petrarchan poems dramatize lovers who abuse love; behind the comic satire or the pathos of these poems is the belief that human affection can and should be used for better purposes, a belief pointed up by the religious images through which this negative love is often expressed. The poems of profane love reverberate more authentically when they are heard within the framework of the Christian philosophy of love, when they are heard as a dull and distorted echo of the love expressed in the Platonic poems or *The Holy Sonnets*.

In his Ovidian and Petrarchan poems, Donne dramatizes a sinful and profane love which is dominated by change and rooted in self. The lovers in these poems place themselves upon love's wheel of fortune, for they focus their affections on objects which are not lasting and seek to gratify their desires through pleasures which are transient by nature. This improper love, whether lust or idolatry, brings misery upon lovers sooner or later, for it involves an excessively great commitment to the mortal and mutable. Things of the earth, so fickle and fragile, will not support the burden of devotion which profane lovers give them. Thus the lustful or idolatrous lover, having mistaken a lesser good for the greatest good, eventually faces disillusionment and despair.

What Donne sees in the things of the world, however, is not their inherent evilness. He sees, rather, the danger that men may overestimate their goodness and convert a potential source of happiness into a source of sin and misery. He sees, in short, that worldly goods may either lead men toward God or alienate them from God, depending on the way in which they are used. In his Ovidian and Petrarchan poems, he reveals the negative use of the things of the world; the lovers, overly committed to goods which are transient by nature, bring misery upon themselves because the joys of transient goods are transient joys; the lovers sin by making the things of the world an end rather than a means, and they punish themselves by choosing to love something which cannot fulfill their inordinate love. In his affirmative poems of human love Donne reveals the positive use of the things of the world. He dramatizes a state of grace in love, a love which thrives in the world and yet leads the lovers toward God, a love which surmounts the threats of worldly mutability. And whereas the sinful love which is tied to worldly goods is circumscribed and produces bondage, the state of grace in love is unlimited and liberating. Donne's sense of a total system, which presupposes that love is a good which can be turned to evil through abuse or misuse, is behind his implicit condemnation of profane love in the Ovidian and Petrarchan poems. Love, these poems suggest, should produce something better than misery and disillusionment. His affirmative poems answer the negative poems by revealing how and why love can produce something better. Their dramatization of a secure and joyful love is perhaps Donne's most final and devastating exposé of profane love.

BIBLIOGRAPHICAL NOTE

Donne is a controversial poet, and during this century scholars have debated about many aspects of the interpretation of his work. Quite naturally, many pages of this book were inspired (or provoked) by the work of my fellow Donne scholars. Because I wished to keep Donne within the context of his own era, most of the references in the footnotes are to primary sources, and these notes do not therefore adequately reflect either the extent of my indebtedness to my predecessors or the tenacity with which the issues discussed in this book have been debated. The following compilation of secondary works, although far from exhaustive, is intended as a supplement to the footnotes; it includes works which I have found useful and provocative or which concisely point up areas of disagreement about the interpretation of Donne's works.

The question of whether Donne is "medieval" or "modern" has long been a subject of debate. In *Les Doctrines Médiévales Chez Donne* (London, 1924), Mary Paton Ramsay defines the various ideas which Donne drew from the Middle Ages; on the other hand, Charles Monroe Coffin in *John Donne and the New Philosophy* (New York, 1937) and Michael Francis Moloney in *John Donne: His Flight from Medievalism* (Urbana, 1944) stress Donne's modernism; in "John Donne and the 'Via Media'" (*MLR*, XLIII, 305-314), H.J.C. Grierson rather sensibly suggests that Donne is a Renaissance man who belongs somewhere in the middle. Arnold Stein discusses problems of Donne's wit in *John Donne's Lyrics: The Eloquence of Action* (Minneapolis, 1962). In a complementary pair of articles in *Seventeenth Century Studies Presented to Sir Herbert Grierson* (Oxford, 1938), the particular question of whether Donne's attitude toward love is medievally ascetic or romantically modern is discussed, C. S. Lewis ("Donne and Love Poetry in the Seventeenth Century," 64-84) taking the former position and Joan Bennett ("The Love Poetry of John Donne: A Reply to Mr. C. S. Lewis," 85-

104) the latter. Several general studies of Elizabethan attitudes toward love have been made. Lu Emily Pearson presents a rather old-fashioned view of "courtly love" in *Elizabethan Love Conventions* (Berkeley, 1933); Ruth Kelso, in *Doctrine for the Lady of the Renaissance* (Urbana, 1956), covers many primary sources; in *Elizabethan Poetry: A Study in Conventions, Meaning, and Expression* (Cambridge, Mass., 1952), Hallett Smith has related love conventions to the various poetic conventions.

In " 'Thou, Nature, art my goddess': Edmund and Renaissance Scepticism" (*Joseph Quincy Adams Memorial Studies*, Washington, 1948), R. C. Bald discusses the background of the libertine point of view, and Louis I. Bredvold relates it to Donne in "Naturalism of Donne in Relation to Some Renaissance Traditions," *JEGP*, xxii, 471-501; however, Robert Ornstein to some extent disagrees with Bredvold in "Donne, Montaigne, and Natural Law," *JEGP*, lv, 213-229, and sees Donne as more conservative and Thomistic. Jean Seznec's *The Survival of the Pagan Gods* (trans. Barbara Sessions, New York, 1953) is a classic statement of the continuity of the allegorical approach to the classical tradition in the Renaissance. Specific studies of the influence of Ovid have been made by C. B. Cooper, *Some Elizabethan Opinions of the Poetry and Character of Ovid* (Menasha, Wis., 1914) and Edward Kennard Rand, *Ovid and His Influence* (Boston, 1925); L. P. Wilkinson's *Ovid Recalled* contains an excellent discussion of the love books. Finally, J. B. Leishman's *The Monarch of Wit* (London, 1951), interesting in other respects as well, contains the earliest discussion of Donne's indebtedness to Ovid.

For information about the Petrarchan sonnet in England, Sidney Lee's anthology of *Elizabethan Sonnets* (Westminster, 1904, 2 vols.) is still useful, as is its lengthy introduction; Lisle Cecil John, *The Elizabethan Sonnet Sequences* (New York, 1939) and J. W. Lever, *The Elizabethan Love Sonnet* (London, 1956) have also covered this ground more recently. Ernest Hatch Wilkins' *Studies in the Life and Works of Petrarch* (Cambridge, Mass., 1955) is useful for background information, and John M. Berdan has given a more stylistic treatment of Petrarchanism in "A Definition of Petrarchismo," *PMLA*, xxiv, 699-710. Paul N. Siegel has also discussed the connections between Platonism and Petrarchanism in "The Petrarchan Sonneteers and Neo-Platonic Love," *SP*, xlii, 165-182.

Nesca A. Robb's *Neoplatonism of the Italian Renaissance* (London, 1935) and Frances Yates' *The French Academies of the Sixteenth Century* discuss the ideas debated in the Florentine and French Academies. In *Renaissance Theory of Love* (New York, 1958), John Charles Nelson analyzes various love treatises and commentaries, chiefly Italian, in order to illuminate Bruno's *Eroici furori*; Paul Oskar Kristeller's *The Philosophy of Marsilio Ficino* (New York, 1943) treats the entire bulk of Ficino's work. Literary Platonism in sixteenth-century France has been well treated in Robert V. Merrill's *Platonism in French Renaissance Poetry* (New York, 1957, with Robert J. Clements). Although I find most of his conclusions unacceptable, it should be noted that Frank A. Doggett offers another discussion of "Donne's Platonism," *Sewanee Review*, xlii, 274-292.

In addition to these treatments of sixteenth-century literary traditions, several studies of Donne's intellectual background contain valuable information or insights. For the scientific background: Edgar Hill Duncan's "Donne's Alchemical Figures," *ELH*, ix, 257-285; Don Cameron Allen's "John Donne's Knowledge of Renaissance Medicine," *JEGP*, xlii, 322-342; W. A. Murray's "Donne and Paracelsus: An Essay in Interpretation," *RES*, xxv, 115-123. For logic and rhetoric: Elizabeth Lewis Wiggins, "Logic in the Poetry of John Donne," *SP*, xlii, 41-60; William Empson, "Donne and the Rhetorical Tradition," *Kenyon Review*, xi, 571-587; Thomas O. Sloan, "The Rhetoric in the Poetry of John Donne," *SEL*, iii, 31-44. Textual problems have been covered by George Williamson in "Textual Difficulties in the Interpretation of Donne's Poetry," *MP*, xxxviii, 37-72.

Brief general discussions of Donne's work are offered by Frank Kermode's *John Donne* (London, 1957, No. 86 in *Writers and Their Work*) and Merritt Y. Hughes' "Kidnapping Donne" in *Essays in Criticism*, Second Series, IV (Berkeley, 1932). Collections of essays have been edited by Helen Gardner (*John Donne: A Collection of Critical Essays*, Englewood Cliffs, N.J., 1962) and Theodore Spencer (*A Garland For John Donne*, Cambridge, Mass., 1931).

For the explication of individual poems, many sources are available; Pierre Legouis' *Donne the Craftsman* (Paris, 1928) is an early classic which suggests that Donne can be objective or satiric and which has provoked near warfare over the interpretation of *The Extasie* in particular. Some other points of view about this particular controversy are offered by Merritt Y. Hughes, "The Lineage of 'The Extasie,' " *MLR*, XXVII, 1-5, and "Some of Donne's 'Ecstasies,' " *PMLA*, LXXV, 509-518; George R. Potter, "Donne's *Extasie*, Contra Legouis," *PQ*, XV, 247-253; Helen Gardner, "The Argument about 'The Extasie'," *Elizabethan and Jacobean Studies Presented to F. P. Wilson* (Oxford, 1959), 279-306; and George Williamson, "The Convention of *The Extasie*," *Seventeenth Century Contexts* (London, 1960), 63-77. Cleanth Brooks' essay on *The Canonization* in *The Well-Wrought Urn* (New York, 1947) is a relatively early example of the rigorous application of the techniques of New Criticism to Donne's poetry, though his interpretation has been disputed by William J. Rooney in " 'The Canonization'—The Language of Paradox Reconsidered," *ELH*, XXIII, 36-47. Other useful studies which follow Brooks' precedent, though often sensibly modulating his principles by bringing in more matters of background, are Clay Hunt's *Donne's Poetry: Essays in Literary Analysis* (New Haven, 1954) and Doniphan Louthan's *The Poetry of John Donne: A Study in Explication*. Both of these, together with Leonard Unger's *Donne's Poetry and Modern Criticism* (Chicago, 1950), contain detailed explications of nearly all of Donne's major poems.

Finally, the introductory essays and editorial and textual notes in Herbert Grierson's *The Poems of John Donne* (Oxford, 1912) and Helen Gardner's *The Divine Poems* (Oxford, 1959) have been invaluable. From these two editions all quotations have been taken.

INDEX

Abrams, M. H., 8
aesthetic distance, 8-9, 133-34
aesthetic purpose, 6-8, 14-16
aesthetic theory, 14-16, 31-39
Aire and Angels, 210-15
The Anniversarie, 192, 196, 219-23, 225
The Apparition, 133, 139-42, 151, 194
Aquinas, St. Thomas, 28
Aristophanes, 31
Aristotle, *Poetics*, 5

Bembo, Cardinal, 69, 74-76
biographical interpretation, 9-11
Blake, William, 5
The Blossome, 133, 141, 179, 181-86, 188
Breake of day, 11, 117-18, 121, 215, 223
The Broken heart, 131
Browning, Robert, 11

The Canonization, 133, 134, 160-68, 178, 192, 216-17, 222
caritas, 23, 24, 28-30, 57, 105, 148, 165, 167, 215, 218, 229
Castiglione, Baldassare, 69
change, *see* mutability
Chaucer, Geoffrey, *Troilus and Criseyda*, 116
Christian attitudes toward love, 17, 23-31. *See also* Platonic love
Cicero, 69, 72
Coleridge, Samuel Taylor, 5
Communitie, 9, 11, 78, 89-94, 97, 115, 193
Confined Love, 85-89, 92, 94, 97, 98, 103
consensus gentium, 84, 89-93, 95, 97, 137-39. *See also* custom
contemptus mundi, 152, 220
Countess of Bedford, 10, 141, 149, 151
"courtly love," 27
Cupid, 6, 118, 119, 137-38, 161

cupiditas, 23, 30, 57, 105, 148, 165, 167
custom in love, 6-8, 137-39. *See also consensus gentium*

d'Amiens, Jacques, *L'Art d'Amors* and *Li Remedes D'Amors*, 38-39
The Dampe, 198
Devotions upon Emergent Occasions, 29
De Stael, Mme., 16
Diotima, 71, 74
Dipsas, 89
disdain, *see* scorn
Donne, John, attitude toward tradition, 14-17, 78-81; philosophy of love, 12, 19-20, 76-77, 78-79, 130-31, 190, 191-98, 208-10, 236-40
dramatic monologue, 11, 18-19

Ebreo, Leone, 69
Elegie III, 79, 100-06, 109, 114
Elegie VII, 105-09, 114-15
Elegie VIII, 134
Elegie X, 186-90
Elegie, XV, 84
Elegie XVII, 97
Elegie XVIII, 12-13, 78, 115, 118-21, 122, 185
Elegie XIX, 12, 78, 115, 120-21, 178
Elegie XX, 109-14
Erasmus, *Enchiridion*, 25
eros, 27, 187. *See also* idolatrous love
The Extasie, 8-9, 76, 133, 160-61, 168-78, 197, 200, 208, 227

Farewell to love, 24, 78, 115, 121, 124-29
A Feaver, 223, 229-34
The Flea, 193
Ficino, Marsilio, 69, 71-74, 175-76, 196, 202, 217
Florentine Academy, 19, 69-70
French Academy, 19, 69-70

247